ENCYCLOPEDIA OF
AUSTRALIAN MURDERS

200 Years Of Murder

T0359516

ENCYCLOPEDIA OF
AUSTRALIAN
MURDERS
200 Years Of Murder

Jim Main

Publishing

First printed 2005. Reprinted 2006 & 2009.

Published by:

Bas Publishing
ABN 30 106 181 542
F16/171 Collins Street
Melbourne Vic. 3000
Tel: (03) 9650 3200
Fax: (03) 9650 5077
Web: www.baspublishing.com.au
Email: mail@baspublishing.com.au

The National Library of Australia Cataloguing-in-Publication entry

Main, Jim, 1943- .
    Encyclopedia of Australian murders : 200 years of
    murder.

    Bibliography.
    ISBN 1 920910 66 2.

    1. Murder - Australia - Encyclopedias. I. Title.

364.152303

Design & Layout: Ben Graham

Contents

INTRODUCTION

Murder has been part of Australian society almost from the first settlement in 1788 and, over more than 200 years, there have been thousands of slayings, some sensationally famous, but most forgotten. There have been bodies found floating down rivers, others buried in the bush or even back yards and there have been mutilations almost beyond belief. Some murders have been committed in moments of rage, while others have been planned with meticulous care. There is no blueprint for murder and this makes them all the more fascinating.

In this book I have presented cases from all stages of Australia's development, from the early colonial years to the present day. Although the book is defined as something of an encyclopedia of murder, it would be impossible to present every Australian murder. Rather, this book is a sample encyclopedia of murder, presented in chronological order, with many famous cases and others barely rippling the surface of public consciousness. There are murders from every era, but not from every year. Yet there might be two or three murders from one year and this is the nature of this book as I have attempted to present the most interesting cases – the Pyjama Girl case, the Graeme Thorne kidnapping, the horrific Anita Cobby abduction and murder, along with tragic domestic murder-suicides, love triangles and acts of rage or revenge.

This encyclopedia of Australian murder will grow and grow and future editions will contain numerous more famous cases, some of which have yet to be committed. Future editions will present some of the famous cases which could not be covered in this edition and there will be other almost forgotten murders, as there is something gruesomely fascinating about murder. Some of the cases presented in this book were published in a different form in my previous casebook *Australian Murders* and most are here again, mainly in abbreviated form, along with more than 100 other cases.

My fascination with murder was sparked by one particular subject in a law degree course at the University of Melbourne – Criminal Law and Procedure. The subjects of Public International Law, Principles of Property, Equity and Mercantile Law bored me witless. However, I could not get my hands on enough murder reports. I started reading a wonderful series titled *Famous Criminal Trials* and other books on notorious British murders, as well as the biographies of criminal barrister Sir Edward Marshall Hall and the remarkable pathologist Sir Bernard Spilsbury. Murder grabbed me by the throat and I started reading as much as I could about famous Australian cases. This resulted in my first book on infamous killings, *Murder Australian Style*, followed by *Murder in the First Degree*.

This book, therefore, is the result of many years' work, not to mention an inexplicable fascination with the foulest of crimes. The killings in this book are chillingly real. This is a book about the killers who have been and are among us. Do not read alone at night.

JIM MAIN

THE CONVICT CANNIBAL

Two convicts escape from a Van Diemen's Land penal settlement, but are struck by hunger so severe that one convict kills his companion and eats parts of the body.

When convicts Alexander Pearce and Thomas Cox escaped from the Macquarie Harbour penal settlement, Van Diemen's Land, on November 13, 1823, they would have had no idea that they would become part of Australian folklore. The two men ran into the bush armed with an axe, but with no food. Several days later, they came across the King's River, but, because Cox would not swim, Pearce flew into a rage. He struck his companion several times with the axe and, as he was about to cross the river, Cox shouted to him: "Put me out my misery." Pearce turned back and again struck Cox over the head, killing him. Pearce, who was desperately hungry, saw his dead companion as a source of food and then committed the unthinkable. He cut a piece from Cox's thigh, roasted it and ate it before cutting off another slice for sustenance once he had crossed the river.

However, the remorse of turning cannibal saw him hailing a schooner and he then confessed to both murder and cannibalism. He said he was "willing to die" for his actions. A search party was sent to look for Cox's body and, when it was found, the head and arms were missing, along with parts of the thighs and calves. When asked about the head, Pearce said he had left it on the body. It was found several yards away, but the hands were never found. Pearce also said that after eating part of a thigh, because "no person can tell what he will do when driven by hunger", he threw the rest into the river. Pearce was found guilty of murder and sentenced to death. His execution on July 19, 1824, was watched by a large crowd, with a Rev. Conolly addressing those assembled before the drop. The minister told the crowd that Pearce, standing on the edge of eternity, wanted to acknowledge his guilt. Finally, he asked the crowd to offer their prayers and beg the Almighty to have mercy upon him.

THE BLACK NAPOLEAN

Aboriginal bushranger Musquito, known as "The Black Napoleon" because of his escapades, is the key figure in an horrific attack on stockmen in Van Diemen's Land.

A mainland Aboriginal, a man known as Musquito, was transported to Van Diemen's Land following the murder of his "lubra", or tribal wife. However, Musquito failed to settle in his new environment and, with a band of other disgruntled Aboriginals known as the 'Tame Mob', embarked on a brief reign of terror. The gang attacked homesteads and rustled cattle before killing several stockmen at Grindstone Bay in 1823. The colony's Lieutenant-Governor sent black trackers in pursuit of the gang and they were duly captured, but not before Musquito was shot in a thigh. He was hanged at Hobart on January 25, 1825, and was reputed to have said on the scaffold: "Hanging no good for black fella. All right for white fella, they used to it."

A FIERY DEATH

A sawyer working at a prison settlement outside Sydney is thrown onto a fire and dies several days later of burns.

Sawyer Thomas Brown was working with Irish convict John Donovan felling trees at the Emu Plains settlement on July 8, 1824, when he chastised the Irishman for not working hard enough. He told the convict he would report him and be punished for his laziness. Then, at four the next morning, Brown was thrown into a fire and suffered severe burns from feet to chest. He was taken by cart to a Dr West, a surgeon at Windsor, and temporarily treated. Brown then told Dr West the extraordinary story of Donovan and another man grabbing him and throwing him between two burning logs. Brown said he screamed and struggled, with Donovan and the unnamed man then running away.

The sawyer died of his burns four days later and, when Donovan was arrested, it was noted that his trousers had been singed and that he had marks on his face. Donovan insisted Brown had fallen onto the fire during the fight and also complained that the sawyer had called him "a Munster stork", a derogatory term suggesting a lazy attitude from that particular part of Ireland. He said Brown's death was an accident and that no third party was involved. The principal overseer of the settlement, Joseph Peters, said at Donovan's trial that he had examined the ashes and that they were pressed flat as if someone had been lying in a fire. Donovan was found guilty of murder and hanged on August 24, 1824.

'I RIPPED HIS BOWELS OPEN'

Two convicts escape from Macquarie Harbour, Van Diemen's Land, and, following an argument over eating a snake, one stabs the other to death.

Convicts William Allan and William Saul escaped from custody at Macquarie Harbour on August 25, 1824, with Allan returning by himself two weeks later. He claimed that he and Saul had been set upon by Aborigines and that his companion had been speared to death. As Allan was wearing some of Saul's clothing, this explained their torn condition. Then, while in the hospital at Macquarie Harbour, Allan confessed to another prisoner: "I am very uneasy in the mind; the devil terrifies me both night and day, so that I never have a moment's rest." He then told an extraordinary story of Saul catching a snake and offering him only a small part to eat. Then, when Saul refused him a bigger portion, Allan attacked him with a knife. He said: "Blood ran down his clothes and Saul cried out 'oh, Allan do not murder me – you may take all my clothes, but don't kill me'." The final part of Allan's chilling remark was: "I then struck my knife into his heart, and ripped his bowels open."

An examination of Saul's body revealed that not only had Saul been stabbed, but Allan had cut off his penis. The dispenser of medicine at the Macquarie Harbour hospital, George Eldridge, said at Allan's trial said that when Saul's body had been found, the stomach had been cut open and, indeed, the penis had been removed. Allan was found guilty of murder and executed on February 16, 1825.

KILLED OVER A FISH

Two convicts escape from a Van Diemen's Land penal settlement and one is killed in an argument over eating a fish without sharing it.

As in the previous case, two convicts – Francis Oats and James Williamson – escaped from Macquarie Harbour, Van Diemen's Land, on September 9, 1824. Like Allan and Saul, both men were wracked by hunger while on the run. When Williamson caught and ate a fish without giving Oats a share, there was a violent argument. Oats admitted when captured on September 13 that he hit his friend with a stick and, when he fell, "the back part of his skull was split by a stump".

Oats even led authorities to the corpse, but Macquarie Harbour hospital medical dispenser George Eldridge said Williamson's skull was fractured nine times, with pieces embedded in the skull. He insisted the wounds could not have been caused by a stick. Although Oates had claimed the two men had fought and that Williamson's death was an accident, there were no marks on him. Oats was found guilty of murder and executed on February 16, 1825, along with William Allan of the previous case and another convicted murderer, Thomas Hudson.

AXED AND ROASTED

In a drunken rage, Edmond Bates uses an axe to attack his wife and then burns her in a fire.

After sawyer Edmond Bates, his wife Julia and several others had been drinking heavily on Christmas Eve, 1824, an argument broke out the next day between husband and wife before Bates ran to a neighbour's home to say he had killed his wife and had "burnt her". The neighbour found Julia Bates' body near a fireplace and noted a strange remark by Bates, who said: "If I had killed her I would have put her where you could not have found her, no, not for six months." A surgeon examined the body and noted: "A contusion on the forehead, near the bridge of the nose; nearly all the ribs on the right side fractured and bent from their articulation with the spine, which could have been affected by an axe … a compound fracture near the ankle of the left leg and burns on the buttocks and right leg."

Bates was arrested and although he admitted he had killed his wife, added: "If I killed her I did it when I was drunk." Bates admitted that he threw a heavy kettle at his wife and inflicted other injuries, leading to her death. However, the neighbour told a jury that Bates was not drunk, but merely tipsy. It clearly was evident that Bates had killed his wife and, after the jury found him guilty, he was hanged on April 11, 1825.

THE BLOOD-THIRSTY MONSTER

A judge describes a confessed murderer as "a blood-thirsty monster" following the discovery of a body in a fire in Tasmania.

A man named Hugh McGinnis went in search of some missing bullocks in the Carlton district in Tasmania in mid-July, 1825, when he came across a huge, roaring fire on top of a hill. He found bones in the fire, which was extremely hot, and assumed someone had been burning dead cattle. However, he went to a local constable and told him of what he had seen. The constables and others found human bones and parts of clothing, including several buttons, in the fire. Pieces found included a clasp knife, a piece of skull, a lower jaw bone with one tooth, part of a spine and two human fingers.

The fragments of remains were those of an itinerant labourer named John Buckley, who was known locally as "Pretty Jack". An unsavoury character, Buckley was well-known by authorities and had warrants issued against him. The main suspect was another shifty character, Charles Routley, who had had some dealings with Buckley. However, there was no proof against Routley until he told several people in late 1828 that he had burned "Pretty Jack" alive and had even forced his victim to carry the wood for the fire. Routley was apprehended and eventually went on trial in Hobart in September, 1830.

A jury took just 15 minutes to find him guilty of Buckley's murder, but the sensational trial did not end there as the 48-year-old Routley confessed to six other murders. In sentencing Routley to death, Chief Justice Pedder told him: "You are one of the most horrid and blood-thirsty monsters that have yet degraded the history of humanity." When Routley was hanged, the Hobart Town *Courier* reported: "He had a florid aspect, and his hands and ankles which were uncovered had even a sort of swelled and livid appearance. He continued praying for the few remaining minutes that elapsed during the last awful ceremony, and when the fatal bolt was withdrawn he died almost instantly."

THE CROW ON THE CORPSE

In one of the first cases in which a white man is convicted of killing an Aborigine, Thomas Stanley escapes the gallows, but still pays a hefty penalty.

Thomas Stanley was a servant on a property at Port Stephens, New South Wales, on May 18, 1826, when he and others decided they would do some kangaroo hunting. Stanley and a man named Chips decided to get into a boat, along with a 12-year-old Aborigine known as Tommy. They planned to travel along the coast and meet up with others who had decided to walk through bushland. Stanley and Chips promised to take care of the Aboriginal boy but, when the two parties met up about an hour later, Tommy was missing. A witness, Joseph Pennington, told the NSW Supreme Court that Stanley had told Chips: "Don't tell them anything about it."

Pennington's suspicions were aroused, especially when the boy was found 10 days later, with a huge crow sitting on the corpse. Pennington immediately ordered the body to be buried, while Stanley suggested the boy had fallen from a tree and then drowned. Although no cause of death was given, a jury found Stanley guilty of murder at his trial on March 1, 1827. Stanley was sentenced to be hanged, but this was commuted and he eventually was sentenced to hard labour for life in chains on Norfolk Island.

THE BODY IN THE RIVER

Convict Charles Butler sets out for home by boat on the Hawkesbury River with Catherine Collins. However, her body is later found floating down the river.

Charles Butler, a convict assigned to work for his 17-year-old wife, travelled by boat with Catherine Collins (also known as Kitty Carman) down the Hawkesbury River in 1826 to visit a man named Summers. Butler returned alone and told everyone that he had dropped Collins off at Doyle's

Point. However, when her body was found floating down the Hawkesbury River, Butler immediately came under suspicion of murder, especially as the dead woman had a large gash on her cheek and was weighted down by two large stones.

Butler was tried for murder and found guilty. He was sentenced to death by hanging and contemporary reports suggested it was a botched execution. One report said: "His agonies appeared long and painful; and between seven and eight minutes had slowly expired, ere the body ceased to exhibit signs of animation." It was said that Butler's wife "exhibited symptoms of strong and unaffected grief".

SEATED ON THE GALLOWS

Two Aborigines, Jack and Dick, spear a stock-keeper to death and one of them has to be carried to the gallows and then seated while he is hanged.

Although the case of two aborigines, Jack and Dick, seemed straight forward, it sparked considerable debate in the colony of Van Diemen's Land. The two had speared stock-keeper Thomas Colley to death at Oyster Bay in 1826 and, after being found guilty, were sentenced to death. However, the *Colonial Times* of June 2, 1826, noted: "We are aware of the legal dogma, that all persons on English land become subjected to English law. Good. But as far as these poor wretches are concerned, it is not quite clear, that as relates to them it is English land." Jack and Dick, were set to be hanged on September 13, 1926, along with five others – William Smith, Thomas Dunnings and Edward Everett for murder, and John Taylor and George Waters for robbery.

The *Colonial Times* of September 15, 1826, reported that the Aborigine named Dick "received the Sacrament" on the morning of his execution but, because of "a loathsome cutaneous (skin) disease", had to be carried to the scaffold. He then was seated on a stool while the noose was placed around his neck and then "plunged into eternity". The other Aborigine, Jack, went to his death unmoved. The *Colonial Times* reported: "The old black (Dick) died very hard" before noting that the younger Aborigine, Jack, "bled profusely from the nose".

THE ESCAPE GONE WRONG

Nine prisoners plan their escape from the Macquarie Harbour prison settlement, Van Diemen's Land, but a constable is drowned during the breakout.

Nine prisoners – George Lacey, Samuel Measures, John Ward, John Williams, John McGuire, John McMillan, William Jenkins, James Kirk and James Reid – made a bold bid for freedom at Macquarie Harbour, Van Deimen's Land, on October 17, 1826. They planned to use a catamaran, made by Williams, for their escape and, during the breakout, took a constable, George Recks, as hostage. However, the catamaran later started sinking and Recks was drowned, with one witness saying that he heard "a gurgling sound as of water getting into a man's mouth".

The prisoners eventually were rounded up and all were charged with Recks' murder. A witness, James Cock, told the Supreme Court of Van Diemen's Land that he heard someone say: "Why didn't you keep the bastard down?" One of the arrested men, Lacey, also was reported as saying that he would rather hang than work in irons. A jury deliberated for only a few minutes before finding all nine prisoners guilty of murder. They were sentenced to death and, when the judge said "And may the Lord have mercy on your souls", one of them – believed to be Lacey – added "Amen".

'SMUTTY JACK'

A man known as "Smutty Jack" is shot dead in Launceston and his body is tied to a cart, along with a butchered calf.

Two men, William Thomas and John Warne, who was known as "Smutty Jack" were seen together leaving Launceston on April 14, 1829, when a shot rang out. Several men ran up to a place known as Magpie Hill and came across Thomas, who had blood on his coat pocket. They also came across a cart to which the body of Smutty Jack was tied, along with a butchered calf. A constable found silver and blood-stained money in Thomas' pocket and he was arrested for murder. However, Thomas said he and the dead man had been attacked by bushrangers and had had nothing to do with Smutty Jack's death.

Thomas also claimed at his trial that he had no motive to kill Warne as the dead man had promised to sell him all his property for 300 pounds. In his defence, Thomas also claimed that the blood on his pocket and money came from the dead calf. The jury refused to believe his story and took just 10-15 minutes to find him guilty of murder. Thomas was sentenced to be executed and his body then handed over to surgeons to be anatomised. He was hanged on June 30, 1830.

'I AM NOT ASHAMED'

A gentleman farmer is killed with a butcher's knife on his property at Lower Clyde, Tasmania.

At around midday on January 25, 1830, a man named Michael Best was seen on the property of gentleman farmer Richard Garner at Lower Clyde, Tasmania. One of Garner's servant's Samuel Lee approached Best and was struck on the face and told that he would "serve me as he had served my master". Lee and another man then entered their master's house and found Garner dead, with blood under his right ear.

When asked if he had anything to do with Garner's death, Best replied: "I am not ashamed of it." Garner had been stabbed three times in the neck and four times to the chest with a butcher's knife, with a surgeon later declaring that one of the slashes to the neck had proved fatal. Another servant, William Smith, told the court at Best's trial that he had seen Best, wearing only boots, at the back of a hut. Best ran about 100 yards away, but Smith told him if he didn't stop he would shoot him. Best returned and was apprehended with the help of two constables. He also told the court that Best's hands were wet, as if he had been washing himself.

Garner had accused Best of stealing sheep and this obviously was the motive for the frenzied attack on the 30-year-old gentleman farmer. Although evidence was given at Best's trial that he might have been insane, a jury took just 10 minutes to find him guilty of Garner's murder. Best was hanged at Hobart, on February 11, little more than a fortnight after he had killed Garner.

NOT A BLOODY WORD

When bushranger James Lockhard is asked to plead guilty or not guilty for the shooting murder of Murdoch Campbell, he replies: "I won't say a bloody word."

John Butcher, holder of a ticket-of-leave, was cleaning wheat at the Upper Minto property of Murdoch Campbell around dusk on January 15, 1833, when he heard a commotion and someone yell out "stop thief". He saw Campbell's servant hand him a blunderbuss and then watched as his boss confronted a man who was trespassing on his land.

When Campbell lowered his weapon, the man shot him dead. Butcher told the Supreme Court of New South Wales: "Mr Campbell never stirred after; he was wounded in the head just above the left eye; the blood flowed freely and he was quite dead." Butcher bravely confronted the trespasser, who pulled out two pistols before another of Campbell's workers fired two shots.

The killer fled, but Butcher spotted him two days later at Liverpool and constables arrested James Lockhard, who was wanted for bushranging. A witness, Thomas Eccles, told the court the man known as Lockhard had dropped a bundle after the slaying of Campbell; it contained two small loaves of bread, the skirts of a coat and a small amount of sugar. Lockhard, who earlier had robbed a man of one pound, nineteen shillings and sixpence, had nothing to say in defence of the murder of Campbell.

Meanwhile, Dr William Kenney told the court: "I was on the spot shortly after Mr Campbell was shot … he was quite dead, a large gunshot wound had been inflicted in the head, over the left eye, that was the cause of death. It was a wound of great depth; I think there must have been more than one shot, or the musket was of a large calibre. The wound had penetrated the brain and would cause instant death." Lockhard was found guilty of murder and was executed on February 5, 1833. The trial had been held on the Friday and the hanging took place the following Monday. This was customary at that time to give the condemned a Sabbath in preparation for death. Under the 1752 statute, An Act for Better Preventing the Horrid Crime of Murder, judges were empowered to order that a murderer's body be hanged in chains. Otherwise, the Act required that the body be dissected by surgeons before burial.

STONED TO DEATH

A country traveller's assistant pays the ultimate price when he informs a chief constable of the illegal sale of spirits. Andrew Gillies bashes Jon Kelly to death with stones near Yass, New South Wales, in April, 1835.

Andrew Gillies was part of a common profession in the early years of Australia. A travelling hawker, he roamed the countryside selling tea, sugar and other goods, plus the retailing of spirits – mainly rum – without a licence. His assistant, John Kelly, fell out with Gillies and informed Yass

Chief Constable James Dannagher of his boss' illegal activities. Dannagher therefore arranged for Kelly to summon the people he saw buying the illegal grog from Gillies. Kelly rode away, but that was the last time the chief constable saw him alive. A search was mounted for Kelly or his body and, a year later, stockman John Hoy stepped forward with information. He said he was with Gillies and Kelly when they went to a creek after discussing the reason for Kelly's visit.

Hoy told the Supreme Court of New South Wales: "Kelly and the prisoner (Gillies) went down to drink while I held the horses. Gillies first drank, then Kelly went, leaving his musket on the bank. When he (Kelly) stopped to drink, I saw Gillies pick up a stone of about two or three pounds weight and throw it sideways at Kelly. I know it struck Kelly, because he immediately fell on his mouth; Gillies then rushed down and, seizing him by the collar, struck him several blows to the back of a head with a stone which perhaps would weigh seven or eight pounds. I let go the horses and rushed towards him crying out, 'In the name of God, what in the hell are you doing?' He told me if I did not stand back he would shoot me … he tied his (Kelly's) legs and arms and fastened a stone to the body and rolled it into a water-hole." Hoy explained that he did not give information at the time because he feared for his own life. A jury in February, 1837, took just a few minutes to find Gillies guilty of Kelly's murder and the stone killer was sentenced to death.

KILLED FOR CLOTHES

Convict Patrick Kilmartin kills a man after a day at the races and steals his clothes, but insists they are his own.

James Hamilton kissed his wife goodbye as he left his home for a race meeting three miles out of Sydney on April 22, 1835; she never saw him alive again. Hamilton met up with convict Patrick Kilmartin at the races and the two were seen having drinks together. Hamilton's naked body was discovered two days later. There were strangulation marks around the neck, there was a long cut on the abdomen and a slash across the penis. Kilpatrick was arrested wearing what appeared to be Hamilton's clothing and, on the inside of a hat, the name J.S. Hamilton was written on the lining. Hamilton's wife Sarah also identified the clothing as her husband's and noted that they were a tight fit on Kilpatrick.

Surgeon James Stewart told the Supreme Court of New South Wales that when he examined Hamilton's body he noted an injury to the left side of the neck, wound to the abdomen and "an injury to the private member, apparently as if an attempt was made to sever it from the body". He said: "I am of the opinion that strangulation was the cause of death, and that the wounds were inflicted before vitality had ceased. I did not open the head to examine the brain as I consider the injury on the neck quite sufficient to cause strangulation. The pressure on the neck caused respiration to be intercepted; the knife produced (in court) would inflict such wounds as I saw on the deceased." Kilmartin, in his defence, claimed he had "the misfortune" to find the clothes and tied them up in a bundle before wearing them. He was found guilty of murder and hanged on May 11, 1835.

A RAZOR ACROSS THE THROAT

Bushman John Haydon is so severely slashed across the throat that his head is all but severed – all for the sake of a one-pound note.

A man named James O'Neale was delivering mail from Bungonia to Marulan, New South Wales, on September 22, 1835, when he came across what he thought was someone sleeping by the side of the road. However, when he took a close look, he was horrified. He had discovered the body of a man, John Haydon, whose throat had been slashed so that "his head fairly turned back". O'Neale immediately notified nearby sawyers who, in turn, notified authorities. Witnesses testified that the dead man had been seen in the company of a man named James Smith and that Haydon was seen trying to get change for a one-pound note from the Bungonia Bank. Another witness said that Smith had passed a one-pound note from the Bungonia Bank for his lodging at a Sutton Forest hostelry. Smith was arrested and indicted for the murder of Haydon.

Surgeon Francis Murphy told the Supreme Court of New South Wales he examined the body on the day of death and added: "The throat had been cut by a sharp instrument; all the vessels around the neck had been cut through to the bone; the vertebrae was partly cut; it was quite impossible that he minded for him to have done it himself. There was a wound below the left eye, which had broken the bone, another upon the left ear. These wounds were severe, but not quite sufficient to cause death. The body was then warm and the wounds fresh; a razor was lying across his breast with which I think the wound on the neck must have been inflicted." Smith pleaded his innocence, but was found guilty and sentenced to death and that his body then be delivered to surgeons for dissection.

The *Sydney Gazette* of November 15, 1836, reported on Smith's execution: "Yesterday the utmost penalty of the law was carried into effect upon William (James) Smith, convicted on Friday last of a wilful and atrocious murder. Smith was a native of the colony, about 30 years of age, of a very strong and muscular frame. He was attended in his last moments by the Rev. Mr. M'Encroe, being of a Catholic persuasion. He made no public statements as to his guilt, and every arrangement being completed, the drop fell, and he was launched into eternity. His struggles, before animation ceased, were long and violent."

BUTCHERED!

Butcher's assistant Michael Cagney goes berserk after a row with his master and, with a heavy paling, clouts another man to death.

A butcher named Wholaghan was slaughtering a beast behind his shop at Maitland on May 23, 1837, when assistant Michael Cagney chastised him over a minor matter. Then, when Wholaghan asked Cagney what right he had to question his master, the assistant picked up one of the slaughtered animal's feet and struck Wholaghan over the head with it. Although Wholaghan was dazed, he continued to butcher the slaughtered beast and, with the assistance of three other men, carted the beef to the shop. The 20-year-old Cagney was waiting for them and wanted to continue the argument with his master. Then, after a few minutes, he picked up a heavy paling and struck one of the men, Edward Hughes, across the head. Hughes was pole-axed and fell dead at the entrance to the shop.

Cagney ran away, but was arrested the following day and charged with murder. A surgeon testified in the Supreme Court of New South Wales that the cause of death was so obvious "it was quite unnecessary to open's the deceased's head". Mr Justice Burton explained to the jury the distinction of murder and manslaughter but, after just a few minutes' deliberation, Cagney was found guilty of murder. He was sentenced to death.

THE AXE
MURDERER

Dairyman Bryan Flannigan, paranoid over suggestions he would lose his small garden, goes berserk and uses an axe to hack three people to death.

Station overseer John Nagle, who was known as a troublemaker, would tease dairyman Bryan Flannigan that he would "have" his garden, ducks and fowls. Flannigan must have taken this to heart as, on the morning of February 5, 1838, he walked into a hut near Mudgee and told a man named John Sheering: "I have put an end to all three", at a hut across the Mudgee River. Flannigan then produced a pair of blood-stained trousers, so Sheering and a shepherd named Martin went to the hut across the river and came across the gruesome sight of three people who had been savaged by an axe. The dead were Nagle and his wife, and a man named Riley.

Flannigan seemed to rejoice in what had happened and said he "had put three bad members away". Surgeon Mr F. Hawthorn told the Supreme Court of New South Wales: "I saw the bodies of Nagle and his wife, and Riley. Nagle's body had five or six wounds on it; the top of the head was almost cut off; the left hand was severed at the wrist joint almost completely; there was a deep wound about five inches in length on the shoulder and a wound on the right side of the thigh near the knee; the wound on the head was sufficient to cause death; a large portion of the brain had fallen out; they (the wounds) must have been inflicted with a heavy sharp instrument. Nagle's wife and Riley had apparently been killed by the same means; the woman was pregnant, and there was a slight degree of warmth at the abdomen; I should think she had advanced to the seventh month of pregnancy. Riley had one very extensive would in the head, so large that I could put my hand in it; the skull was laid completely open; all the bodies were undressed as if they had been in bed."

Police could not find the murder weapon, despite a two-day search, including aborigines diving into the Mudgee River. Although Flannigan seemed pleased with himself when the bodies were discovered, he later denied all knowledge of the crime and pleaded not guilty. However, he was found guilty of the murder of Nagle and sentenced to death.

SPEARED TO DEATH

An aborigine is found guilty of murdering a fellow native in the first case of a native being tried by British laws for an offence committed against one of his own people.

The trial of aborigine We-war created enormous interest in Western Australia as there was considerable legal debate as to whether the Quarter Sessions had the right to try a native for killing one of his own people. The trial went ahead and the court was told that on July, 1840, that two members of the 51st Regiment, Privates Henry Maybee and Thomas Magee went to a homestead on the Canning River and were accompanied by an aborigine, known as Dy-ung. On the way, the party encountered We-war and it was agreed that he could accompany them on their journey, even though there was bad blood between the families of the two Aborigines.

However, no problems were anticipated as the two natives appeared to get on well with each other. They therefore agreed to spend the night in a hut 20 yards from a homestead the soldiers were visiting. However, Maybee told the court that he was awakened soon after midnight by a scream and later found Dy-ung running from the hut with a spear through the chest. We-war had driven the spear through him as his fellow native slept. Dy-ung died of his wound three hours later and although We-war fled the scene, he later was captured. After the court decided it did have the jurisdiction to hear the case, a jury found We-war guilty of murder. He was sentenced to death, but this later was commuted to transportation for life on Rottnest Island.

A BURNING RAGE

Convict Catherine Phillips dies almost a fortnight after another women, Catherine Wapshaw, pushes her into a fire in a domestic dispute.

A drinking session on the evening of April 5, 1840, resulted in tragedy over what seemed to be a relatively trivial incident. Convict Catherine Phillips, her husband and

Catherine Wapshaw were drinking in front of a fire at Patrick's Plains when Phillips struck one of Wapshaw's three children. Phillips flew into a rage and struck Wapshaw, who, in turn, pushed her attacker into a fire. Phillips' dress caught fire but, when she tried to escape the flames, Wapshaw pushed her back into the fire. Phillips eventually was able to make it to a tub of water and plunged into it to douse the flames. However, she suffered terrible burns and died on April 18.

The Supreme Court of New South Wales was told that the dead woman's torso was "one burned mass", while she also had burns on the face, arms, chest, back and shoulders. Wapshaw's defence counsel claimed that because she was drunk at the time, she was not responsible for her actions and that she had merely pushed Phillips away. Wapshaw, in fact, claimed Phillips had fallen into the fire and her death was an accident. The jury retired for just 10 minutes before returning a verdict of guilty. She was sentenced to three years of hard labour at what was known as "the female factory" at Parramatta, an institution for women prisoners.

Chief Justice James Dowling told Wapshaw: "The bare mention of such a death when arising merely from accident, fills the mind with anguish; but when it is the result of criminal design, the heart sickens with horror. It may be you possess the form and feature of woman – but no more! The soul that dictated such an act could never have been intended for so chosen a vessel. Nothing but the Temper of Hell could prompt your mind to such an enormity."

'GOODBYE CHUMMY'

A Malay sailor kills one of his shipmates on the high seas off the Australian coast, but there does not seem to be a motive.

The ship *Susan* was on the high seas near Jarvis Bay on March 22, 1840, when Malay sailor Gregory Tabee went below to the berth of his friend Peter Anderson and, as he said "goodbye chummy", stabbed him in the stomach. Anderson died of his wound 17 hours later, but Tabee denied any knowledge of the murder of his shipmate. Instead, he claimed, he was acting in a dream. Tabee even joked about the incident, even though some on board the *Susan* wanted to throw him overboard.

Tabee eventually was tried in the Supreme Court of New South Wales because the crime had been committed on a British ship and the victim was a British subject. The only real problem for the prosecution was that there did not seem to be any motive for the killing. Witnesses also gave evidence at Tabee's trial that he was awake for at least five minutes before plunging the knife into Anderson's stomach and therefore could not have killed "in a dream". The jury, without even leaving the box, found Tabee guilty of murder and he was sentenced to death.

THE OLD GOATHERD

A convict is hanged for the brutal pick-handle slaying of an old goatherd in Van Diemen's Land.

Convict Samuel Williams absconded from the penal settlement at Port Arthur on November 18, 1842, and, after a search was mounted for him, the body of goatherd James Harkness was found in scrubland. He had been bashed around the head and there were signs of struggle. Soon after, the searchers found Williams, who still had irons on his legs. His shirt and trousers were splattered wth blood and he therefore immediately became the prime suspect in the murder of the old goatherd. Later, in a prison cell, Williams admitted he was "uneasy" in his mind as he had killed Harkness after trying to take a goat from the old man.

At Williams' trial in the Supreme Court of Van Diemen's Land, a Dr Browbill told the jury that the man had taken 10 blows to the head and face, with one severe blow across the chin. He said: "The death of the deceased had been caused through a violent concussion of the brain; the injuries had evidently been inflicted by means of a blunt instrument, such as the pick-handle produced (in court). The court was also told that Williams, when escaping into the bush, was determined to kill the first person he came across as he was "tired of life". Williams was found guilty and sentenced to be hanged and dissected. According to one report, he created a scene on the gallows when he tried to remove his death cap.

THE REBEL CONVICT

William Westwood, known as "Jackey Jackey", is hanged on Norfolk Island after leading a convict rebellion.

William Westwood, born in Kent in 1821, was convicted in England of forgery at just 16 years of age and was transported to New South Wales, where he endured rough treatment at the hands of a violent overseer. The youngster escaped and embarked on a life of crime and deceit, although he sometimes was regarded as a "romantic villain" as he gatecrashed parties and sometimes distributed his ill-gotten gains to the needy.

However, he was arrested at Berrima in 1841 and sentenced to prison on Van Diemen's Land, only to be further brutalised. Westwood escaped and then was sent to Norfolk Island, where he eventually led a prison riot in which, armed with an axe, he personally killed two guards. Troops with fixed bayonets ended the riot and Westwood eventually was sentenced to death. He was hanged in October, 1846, and wrote in a letter to the prison chaplain: "No tyrant will disturb my repose."

SHIVERS AT THE GRAVE

Blood stains on a shirt and trousers condemn a man to the gallows after a brutally battered body is found in Gippsland.

It is doubtful if any man in Australian legal history was found guilty of murder and executed on such flimsy evidence as Irishman John Healey, who was hanged at the Melbourne Gaol on November 30, 1847, after police noted he had shivered when standing on the grave of the man he was supposed to have killed.

The body of a man named James Ritchie was found in Gippsland earlier that year. He had been brutally battered around the head and police constables were able to establish that the dead man had been drinking with Healey, a woman named Hannah Wilson and two men named Savage and Francis. Suspicion fell on Healey because he had blood stains on his shirt and trousers. Police also found a bloodstained axe in a shed attached to a house where he Healey had spent the night with Hannah Wilson, who claimed the axe had been used to decapitate a goose.

Police seemed determined to charge Healey with Ritchie's murder as they had heard that the two men often had quarrelled and, in fact, Healey had once threatened to kill Ritchie. Police did not seem interested in Hannah Wilson's information that Healey had once rescued the drunken Ritchie when he fell off his horse. The police therefore took Healey to a cemetery one moonlit night and made him stand directly over Ritchie's grave. They noted that Healey appeared to shiver and took this as a sign of guilt.

However, the police needed further "proof" and decided to accept the offer of an anonymous volunteer who suggested that he could get a confession from Healey. The volunteer was locked in a cell with the Irishman at the Melbourne Gaol and struck up a conversation. He told Healey: "If you did that murder and don't confess it and die like a man, the sight of God you will never have." Healey allegedly replied: "Well, I did it, and I'm willing to die for it." That comment was enough for the police, and Healey was charged with Ritchie's murder and sent to trial. He was found guilty and, when sentenced to death, protested his innocence. He was marched to the gallows still protesting his innocence.

A BUMP IN THE NIGHT

A man is knifed to death at a Melbourne boarding house after he accidentally bumps a visitor.

James Barlow and a friend visited a boarding house in Flinders Street, Melbourne, on the night of January 19, 1852, and was sitting on a stool in the kitchen when he decided to move into a passageway. At the same time, boarder Williams Jones also decided to move. Although there did not seem to be any bad blood between the two, they bumped into each other in the passageway and jostled. Barlow, obviously upset, pulled a knife and made a thrust at Jones' stomach with a knife.

Jones fell to the floor with a severe wound and Barlow was arrested by police before he could leave the premises. He was charged with wounding Jones, but this was changed to a charge of murder when Jones died of his wound two days later. Barlow's only defence was that he had been drinking before he stabbed Jones and therefore pleaded temporary insanity. The jury rejected this plea and Barlow was found guilty. He was hanged at the Melbourne Gaol on May 22, 1852.

THE BODY ON DISPLAY

Three bushrangers are executed for the killing of a dray driver during a bullion robbery and, later, one of the executed men's body is put on display in a Melbourne shop window.

It was too good an opportunity for Victoria's most notorious bushrangers to miss. On July 20, 1853, a Melbourne Gold Escort Company dray, driven by Thomas Fookes and escorted by an armed guard, left McIvor carrying more than 200 ounces of gold and 700 pounds in notes. It was a king's ransom and the huge delivery to Melbourne was honey to the likes of bushrangers George Melville, Williams Atkins, George Wilson and others.

The dray and escort had travelled just 20 miles when the path was blocked by a large log pushed across the road. Shots rang out and, after Fookes was shot dead, the escort fled. The bushrangers might have been able to plunder the gold and bank notes, but they soon were hunted down. Melville, Atkins and Wilson were arrested and charged with the murder of Fookes.

All three were found guilty and sentenced to death. They were executed in Melbourne on October, 3, 1858, and the bodies handed over to their respective relatives. However, Melville's wife placed his body in a coffin and put it on display in a shop window in busy Bourke Street. It remained there for several days before authorities insisted on a burial.

JUST ONE REGRET

John "Rocky" Whelan wins himself a reputation as one of Australia's most heartless bushrangers and kills most of his victims.

When John "Rocky" Whelan was transported to Australia from Ireland, he packed his hate along with his worldly possessions. Whelan's original crime was to incite a revolt against the British, but he fell foul of the law when caught sheep stealing after being given a conditional pardon. He hardened considerably after terms on Norfolk Island and on Van Diemen's Land and, on return to the mainland, embarked on a bloodthirsty career as a bushranger. He had a simple philosophy of killing all his victims; after all, dead men told no tales. However, he finally took pity on one of his victims, who promised not to tell the authorities of being waylaid.

The victim broke his promise and Whelan was captured in 1855. Another of Whelan's idiosyncrasies was to wear his victim's clothes and, when taken prisoner after a short gunfight, it was noted he was wearing the custom-made boots of police magistrate James Dunn, who had been shot through the heart. Whelan's last words before he was hanged were: "My only regret is that I didn't put a bullet through his head."

TOO YOUNG TO HANG

Elizabeth Scott becomes the first — and youngest — woman executed in Victoria after being found guilty of murdering her husband.

Elizabeth Scott, an Englishwoman who had migrated to Australia with her family after a year in New Zealand, was just 14 years of age when, in 1854, she married 36-year-old Robert Scott, a hard-drinking gold prospector. She bore him four children before she was 20 years of age, but only two survived. They lived in a shack near Mansfield, north-east Victoria, and Elizabeth despaired as her husband turned increasingly to drink. He ran a grog shop from his shanty, but seemed to drink more than all his customers combined. Meanwhile, Elizabeth became entangled romantically with young farm labourer David Gedge. To complicate matters, Malay labourer Julian Cross was infatuated with Elizabeth.

Matters came to a head on the night of April 11, 1863, when Robert Scott was shot in the head while in a drunken stupor. Elizabeth claimed it was suicide, but she, Gedge and Cross were charged with murder. At the trial at Beechworth the following October, Cross told the jury that Elizabeth had given himself and Gedge a shot of brandy each while they prepared to get rid of the drunken Robert Scott. All three were found guilty and hanged together at the Melbourne Gaol on November 11, 1863. Elizabeth Scott, who believed she would be given a last-minute reprieve because of her sex and age, was just 23 years of age when executed.

THE ROAD TO DEATH

Two business partners fall out and, in a busy Melbourne office, one shoots the other dead.

Christopher Harrison and James Marsh were business partners determined to flourish in the colony of Victoria. They held road contracts, but fell out over monies owed and arranged to meet at the Road Department office to settle the dispute. When Harrison requested Marsh to sign documents, his partner refused. Harrison then produced a pistol and shot Marsh dead.

There seemed to be an open and shut case of murder against Harrison as two witnesses had seen him shoot Marsh dead. As expected, Harrison was found guilty and sentenced to death. Although he felt he eventually would win a reprieve, Harrison was hanged at the Melbourne Gaol on the morning of August 3, 1864, along with two other men. William Carver and Samuel Woods were executed for armed robbery and wounding. Two bank officials had suffered minor wounds in a bank robbery gone wrong in Collingwood.

TWO INNOCENT CHILDREN

Two children spot William Griffiths stealing from their home near Glenorchy, Tasmania, while their parents are away and, to cover his tracks, he kills the little siblings with hammer blows to the head.

George Johnson left his home near Glenorchy, Tasmania, on the morning of September 12, 1865, to cart materials. Later, wife Emily, left the family home with daughter Mary to cut firewood on the opposite side of a stream. Two smaller children, Sarah (six) and George (eight), were left on their own to play outside. However, Mrs Johnson had not gone long when a man named William Griffiths started searching the home for goods he could see to raise money for alcohol. Sarah and George spotted him and ran off to signal an alarm. However, Griffiths caught up with them and bashed them violently with a hammer. Sarah died instantly from wounds to the head, while George lingered until he died late at night.

Griffiths fled to Hobart, but was captured in the Kings Arms hotel the day of the murders. Griffiths, naturally, denied all knowledge of the murders and even swore he would get even with the police for handcuffing him. The itinerant worker was charged with the wilful murder of the two children and claimed: "I am quite innocent of the crime brought against me. I would not take life away for anything. I haven't the heart to do it. That is known in the neighbourhood well." However, numerous witnesses gave incriminating evidence against Griffiths in the Tasmanian Criminal Court.

Before sentence, Chief Justice Sir Valentine Fleming told the prisoner: "You must look for a more enduring mercy in another world. For you who have mercilessly deprived two innocent children of their lives, it would be a mockery to suppose that any mercy could be extended to you … it is now my duty at the mouthpiece of the law to pronounce upon you the sentence which it provides for your crime, and which is that you be taken from the place from whence you came, and then to a place of execution, and that you there be hanged by the neck until your body be dead, and may the Lord God have mercy upon your soul." Griffiths was hanged on the morning of December 2, 1865, and was reported to have cried bitterly on his way to the gallows.

DEATH OF A TROOPER

A prisoner in South Australia stabs a police trooper and subsequently is executed.

William Nugent was an incorrigible rogue who had worked on the construction of rail lines but had turned to making a living any way he could, including the selling of liquor to Aborigines. Nugent was arrested for this offence at Kingston on May 18, 1881, and became entangled in a scuffle with the arresting officer, Police Trooper Harry Pearce. He stabbed the police trooper, who later died from his injury.

Nugent was charged with murder and stood trial at the Naracoorte Circuit Sessions in October, 1881. Although the Irish-born Nugent tried to have the charge downgraded to one of manslaughter and pleaded not guilty to a change of murder, a jury took just 15 minutes to find him guilty of murder. Nugent was hanged at Mount Gambier on the morning of November 18, 1881.

MURDER, BUT NO DEATH

A Victorian man shoots at a police detective and, despite merely wounding him, is found guilty of murder and executed.

As Charles Bushby walked along a road near Ballarat on December 12, 1884, he had no idea he would become the central figure in one of Victoria's most bizarre legal cases. As Bushby walked along the lonely road, he was asked to stop by three police officers who were investigating the theft of wool from a farm. However, it appears Bushby not only refused the police request, but turned and fired a shot which felled a

Detective Hyland. Bushby was overpowered by the other police officers and charged with murder, even though Hyland was still alive.

There was considerable debate at Bushby's trial over whether he should have a charge of murder as Hyland, in fact, made a full recovery. The charge was upheld and, despite appeals, the conviction stood. Whether it was murder or attempted murder, it was a capital offence and Bushby was hanged at the Ballarat Gaol on September 3, 1885. As Bushby went to his death, he proclaimed his innocence, of murder and, indeed, even of attempted murder.

CAUGHT BY HIS OWN WORDS

William Barnes might have been able to get away with murder if he had not told about suffocating a friend in South Melbourne.

When the body of John Slack was found in his bed with his throat cut in South Melbourne in September, 1884, it seemed an open and shut case of suicide and that was how the authorities reacted. There was not even a hint of murder – until one of Slack's friends, William Barnes, was arrested on a minor offence and told fellow prisoners that he had committed murder.

Police decided to exhume Slack's body and it finally was determined that he had been strangled or asphyxiated as a bone in his throat had been crushed. It was also learned that although Slack had a razor in his left hand when his body was found, he was right-handed and it was most unlikely he would slash his own throat with his non-preferred hand.

Barnes eventually confessed to police that he had robbed Slack of some jewellery and then killed his friend. Barnes was sentenced to death and was hanged at the Melbourne Gaol on May 15, 1885.

THE RICHMOND BORGIA

A woman poisons five members of her own family to collect on insurance policies.

Martha Needle, an extremely attractive young woman, was "unfortunate" enough to lose her entire family through "serious illnesses". She won enormous sympathy from friends and neighbours who could not believe that one delightful, frail, intelligent young woman could have so much bad luck. What the friends and neighbours did not know, until years later, was that Martha Needle was a mass poisoner. In fact, she was so adept at poisoning with arsenic that she was dubbed the "Richmond Borgia".

Pretty Martha Needle was raised in Adelaide, but moved to Victoria soon after her marriage to carpenter Henry Needle in 1881, Martha was just 17 and Henry Needle was regarded as an extremely fortunate man. It seemed an ideal marriage and the couple was blessed with the birth of daughter Mabel. However, Martha dreamed of running a boarding house, but where could she get the capital? That problem was solved by the death of Mabel, who was just three years of age when poisoned by her mother in 1885. Martha had laced her daughter's food with a preparation called Rough on Rats.

Naturally, no one suspected the attractive young mother of killing her own daughter – a death certificate was issued and Martha collected 200 pounds from little Mabel's insurance policy. Martha Needle's trail of death was just starting, with her husband next on the list. Martha, who have given birth to two more daughters – Elsie and May – spiced her husband's food with the same brand of rat poison and watched him die in agony. His death was certified as having been caused by "inflammation of the stomach" and Martha again collected 200 pounds from an insurance policy.

Next to die were little Elsie and May, both of whom were insured. Elsie, just four years of age, died of a "wasting disease" and Martha this time collected 100 pounds. Little May, just three years of age, died in October, 1891, the insurance this time netting just 66 pounds. Widow Martha Needle, free of her daughters, then renewed an old friendship with the Juncken brothers, Otto and Louis, in Adelaide. Louis took ill and died, while Otto planned to marry Martha. Another brother, Herman, objected to this planned marriage and took ill after drinking a cup of tea. He recovered but, after visiting the widow and drinking more tea, he became ill again. He saw a doctor and, at long last, arsenic poisoning was suspected and a trap was set for Martha Needle.

Herman again visited Mrs Needle and, when offered a cup of tea, called in police and handed them the drink. An analysis revealed poison and the bodies of Mrs Needle's husband and daughters showed signs of arsenic poisoning when exhumed. Louis Juncken's body also was exhumed and this again revealed arsenic poisoning. Martha Needle, who killed five people, was hanged in Melbourne on October 22, 1894. She refused help on her way to the gallows and told the hangman that she wanted to die quickly and with dignity.

THE POISONOUS WIFE

Louisa Collins, who used poison as a means of ending unhappy marriages, is the last woman hanged in New South Wales.

Louisa and Charles Andrews lived with their seven children on Botany Bay at a desolate place named Fog Hollow. Louisa, 20 years younger than her husband, was a regular at the local pub and eventually had an affair with young labourer Michael Collins. Louisa Andrews fell in love with the younger man and wanted to marry him. She therefore set a plan into action, insuring her husband's life and collecting 200 pounds on the policy soon after he died of "acute gastritis" on January 28, 1887. Just three months later she married Collins and, seven months after the wedding, she bore him a son. However, the baby died at five months of age, with Collins to die in agony soon after.

This time there was suspicion and, after a glass containing elements of arsenic was found in her kitchen, Louisa was arrested. Her first husband's body was exhumed, along with that of her dead infant, and traces of arsenic were found in both bodies. Louis Collins faced trial, not once, but four times for murder. The first three juries could not reach a verdict, but the fourth found her guilty. Louisa Collins was hanged at Darlinghurst jail in January, 1889, and went to her death "as if she were performing an everyday function". The media of the day has focused enormous attention in the Collins case, but there was little sympathy for the poisonous wife.

THE BODY UNDER THE HEARTH

Police in Melbourne unearth the body of a woman, sparking outrage on both sides of the world.

When the owner of a house in Andrew Street, Windsor (an inner Melbourne suburb) checked on a strong and offensive odour reported by a would-be tenant, he called in the police. A hearthstone was removed and, underneath, was the decomposing body of a woman. Police immediately launched an investigation and a post mortem revealed that the woman's throat had been cut. The previous tenant, a Mr Druin, had paid a month's rent in advance, but then disappeared.

However, police soon were led to believe that Druin really was a man named Albert Williams, who had arrived in Australia from England with his wife in 1891.

The body under the hearth was believed to be that of his wife, Emily Williams and, soon after her funeral, police in Western Australia arrested the man known as Williams. Meanwhile, police had learned that his real name was Frederick Bayley Deeming and that he and his family had lived at Rainhill, near Liverpool, England. Police from Liverpool went to Deeming's old address at Rainhill and discovered five bodies — of a woman and four children. A nine-year-old girl had been strangled, but the others had had their throats cut. The bodies were identified as those of Deeming's first wife, Marie, and their children.

There was outrage, both in Australia and England, with calls to "lynch the bastard". Deeming was extradited by ship from Perth to Melbourne where an inquest was held into the death of the woman now known as Emily Mather, who had "married" Deeming in England on September 22, 1891. Deeming was sent for trial at the Victorian Supreme Court and his defence lawyers, including future Australian Prime Minister Alfred Deakin, raised the question of insanity. However, the jury returned a verdict of "guilty" of the murder of Emily Mather and Deeming was executed at Melbourne Gaol on the morning of May 23, 1892.

THE MURDEROUS MAKINS

In one of the most sensational cases in Australian criminal history, husband and wife baby farmers John and Sarah Makin are found guilty of murder.

Workman James Mahoney was laying pipes in the Sydney suburb of Macdonaldtown in March, 1892, when he uncovered the remains of two infant children in the backyard of 25 Burren Street. Police immediately were notified and soon discovered the bodies of five more infants. They had uncovered an horrific scene of death, the result of what was known as baby farming – taking in infant children from distraught young women and, instead of looking after them as promised, killing and burying them. Police tracked former occupants John and Sarah Makin to the nearby suburb of Chippendale and dug up more bodies.

They tracked down earlier Makin residences and discovered even more bodies at a home in Redfern, taking the total to 12. The entire Makin family, including daughters Florence (17), Clarice (16), Blanche (14) and Daisy (11), was arrested, although only Florence and Blanche faced charges of "guilty knowledge". At a NSW Supreme Court trial at Darlinghurst, Mr Justice Stephen heard evidence from women who had given their illegitimate babies to the Makins for care. One woman identified clothing found on one of the dead babies, causing enormous public outrage. Both John and Sarah Makin were found guilty of murder, while both Florence and Blanche were discharged.

The judge told John and Sarah Makin: "You deceived her (one of the mothers) as to your address and you endeavoured to make it utterly fruitless for any search should be made and finally, in order to make detection impossible, as you thought, having bereft it of life, you buried this child in your yard as you would the carcase of a dog … three yards of houses in which you lived testify, with that ghastly evidence of those bodies, that you were carrying on this nefarious, this hellish business, destroying the lives of these infants for the sake of gain." John Makin was hanged, but his wife Sarah was reprieved and spent 18 years in jail.

THE BABY FARMER

Melbourne is horrified when Frances Knorr is convicted of killing three babies left in her care.

Frances Knorr preyed on unmarried mothers late in the Victorian era, running a home for unwanted children. Promising to look after the babies of unmarried mothers, Knorr quickly realised that it was possible to pocket the money without any expenses in feeding and clothing the unfortunate little victims. But, to ply this ghastly trade, she had to stay one step ahead of the law. She moved from her home in Moreland Road, Brunswick, but a new tenant started gardening and discovered the body of a baby which had been battered to death. The bodies of two other babies were discovered and Knorr was arrested in Sydney and sent to trial for murder.

Knorr, 26 and the mother of two children, insisted she knew nothing of the deaths of the three little innocents, but was found guilty and sentenced to death. She was hanged at the Old Melbourne Gaol on January 15, 1894, but not before confessing to killing the three babies. In admitting she had suffocated two and strangled the other. Knorr said she hoped her confession would be a "deterrent to those who perhaps are carrying on the same practice".

THE GATTON MURDERS

A brother and two sisters are killed in one of the most mysterious cases in Australian criminal history.

The Christmas period in Queensland in 1898 was one of the hottest on record. The inland area west of Brisbane was baked mercilessly under a flaming orange sun and drought ravaged even the best crop and grazing districts. The area around the tiny town of Gatton (population 450), 30 or so miles east Toowoomba, resembled a dustbowl and only the truly hardy ventured into the midday sun. However, Christmas was Christmas, drought or no drought, and the large Murphy family celebrated as if the drought was about to break and there soon would be prosperity for all. Daniel and Mary Murphy, as Irish as the shamrock, had 10 children – six sons and four daughters – with only one of them, Polly, married. Daniel and Mary Murphy had been married in Ireland, but had established themselves at Blackfellow's Creek, where they became relatively prosperous and well known in the Gatton district.

Michael Murphy, a 29-year-old police sergeant, and his sisters Norah, 27, and Ellen 18, had been to Mt Sylvia races on Boxing Day and had decided to attend a dance at Gatton that night. They returned home for a meal before Michael hitched family horse Tom to a sulky and drove his sisters to the dance at the Provisional Board's Hall in Gatton. The three Murphys passed their brother Patrick, who was on horseback, at about 8.15pm and arrived at the hall just after 9pm. However, there was no sign of activity and the dance eventually was cancelled because there were not enough women. The Murphys turned around to go home and again ran into brother Patrick, who chatted with his brother and sisters for several minutes. The four met only about a mile from an area known as Moran's Paddock and Patrick Murphy never saw his brother or two sisters alive again. It had been a brilliantly bright evening, but three of the Murphy clan met gruesome deaths under starlight.

The alarm was raised early the next morning when there was no sign of Michael, Norah or Ellen at the Murphy farm. Mrs Murphy sensed something was wrong and William McNeil, married to Polly and staying with the Murphys over the Christmas period, saddled a horse and rode to Gatton. He was shocked when told the three missing Murphys had headed towards home before 10 o'clock the previous night.

McNeil decided to retrace their route to Gatton, an easy task as the Murphy sulky had a wobbly wheel which left a distinctive mark on the dust road out of tiny Gatton. He followed the wheel marks to a sliprail at Moran's Paddock, a couple of miles out of Gatton, and decided to investigate.

McNeil at first believed the track would lead to a farmhouse. He was also convinced that the sulky or horse had broken down and that his three in-laws had decided to stay there overnight. He certainly was not prepared for what he found just one minute's ride into the paddock, where he discovered the bodies of the three Murphys; the horse also had been killed, shot through the head.

The bodies of Michael and Ellen were back to back, with the dead horse nearby. Norah's body was about eight yards away behind a large gum tree. McNeil, at a Magisterial Inquiry in January, 1899, said in evidence that he noticed ants crawling over Norah's face. He said: "Her jacket was pulled up at the back." It was obvious that both the Murphy girls had been sexually violated. Their hands were tied behind them and their heads had been battered with extreme savagery. Norah Murphy had a leather strap from the sulky tied around her throat and Michael Murphy, it later was proven, had been shot in the head.

McNeil rushed to the police and the officer in charge, Sergeant William Arrell, telegrammed more senior officers about the gruesome discovery before the bodies were removed to the Boru Hotel in Gatton, where government medical officer Dr William von Lossberg conducted post mortems. He noted that Ellen's face and body were smeared with blood and that the brain protruded from the right side of the head. There were fingernail marks on the body and abrasions on both hands. The skull had been severely fractured and the doctor concluded that the girl had been bashed several times over the head with a heavy, blunt instrument. The girl also had been sexually assaulted as there were traces of semen in her vagina.

Norah Murphy had been savagely beaten about the face and the strap around her neck was so tight that it had stopped circulation to the brain. In fact, it was so tight that it cut into her flesh and could barely be seen. There was a cut (made by a knife) near the right eye and there were fingernail marks on her breasts, arms and hands. Dr von Lossberg also determined that there were fingernail marks on the dead woman's vagina and anus and that she also had been raped. The doctor examined a piece of wood retrieved from the murder scene and said that he found traces of blood, hair and brain on it. It undoubtedly was the murder weapon. Dr von Lossberg suggested that both women had been hit when they were in a standing position and had been raped before they had had their heads bashed by the heavy piece of timber.

The post-mortem examination of Michael Murphy's body was not so straightforward. Dr von Lossberg noted that there was a bloody wound behind the right ear and, after washing the blood away, was convinced he would find a bullet in the dead man's skull. The doctor probed with his fingers, but stopped to wash his hands in disinfectant after pricking a finger on a sharp piece of bone. On resumption of his probing, he felt his hand go numb and realised he had been poisoned. He asked a local chemist to continue the probe, but no bullet was found. Dr von Lossberg's blood poisoning caused him more than three months of illness and a considerable amount of anguish.

However, he finally determined that Michael Murphy had also been bashed around the head by the heavy piece of timber, but said that this was after death. He originally believed that Murphy had been shot in the head, but as he was unable to find the bullet, he therefore assumed the wound had been made by a stick. Then, in a second post-mortem conducted on January 4, 1899, government medical officer Charles Wray, from Brisbane, found a bullet in the skull.

So who killed the Murphys? Police, of course, had their suspects, including a known criminal who had been in the Gatton area at the time of the killings. In fact, police concentrated their efforts on this suspect, who recently had been released from jail after serving a sentence for a sexual offence. The suspect, Richard Burgess, was even remanded for eight days, but was able to provide an alibi. Burgess, who died many years later in Western Australia boasted about killing the Murphys, but the evidence suggested otherwise. The other suspect was a young man named Thomas Day, who was working in the Gatton area at the time of the killings. Day, an army deserter, was seen with bloodstained clothes soon after the tragedy and had been seen near Moran's Paddock at least twice before that fateful night of December 26, 1898.

Police were unable to solve the Gatton murders and a Police Inquiry Commission noted in November, 1899: "We feel constrained to acknowledge that great mystery surrounds the Gatton murders, and it does not follow that if the police had been in the highest state of efficiency that the murderer or murderers would have been discovered. That there was inertness and dilatoriness at the outset cannot be gainsaid, but after the matter was fairly taken in hand the officers and men acted individually with zeal."

Police were never able to solve the Gatton mystery and, in New South Wales in 1973, a 95-year-old man made a death-bed confession to two elderly sisters that he was the killer. Then, after the old man's death, the sisters went to Murwillumbah police and said he had confessed. He even had told the sisters where he had hidden the revolver used to shoot Michael Murphy. The sisters, Mrs Margaret Rutherford and Mrs Violet Russell, insisted the old man had given them extremely detailed information and were convinced he was telling the truth. However, policed found numerous discrepancies in his story and assumed he could not have been the Gatton killer. The mystery therefore remains.

THE INDIAN AXE-MAN

An Indian hawker kills his business partner with an axe over an alleged theft from their van at Streaky Bay, South Australia.

Men like Indian hawkers Lollie Kaiser Singh and Sunda Singh were part of the Australian bush scene in the nineteenth and early twentieth centuries, travelling dusty roads to sell all sorts of goods from the back of a van or dray. The two Indians stopped near their store at Streaky Bay, South Australia, on October 31, 1899, to restock and, the following day, Kaiser Singh accused his compatriot of stealing something from the van. An argument developed and Kaiser Singh struck Sunda Singh to the head with an axe, killing him almost instantly.

Several witnesses had seen the axe attack and this made Kaiser Singh's defence an almost impossible task. However, he claimed he was under the effects of opium at the time and did not know what he was doing. A jury took just 18 minutes to find him guilty of murder and he was sentenced to death. The Indian hawker was hanged at the Adelaide Gaol on January 17, 1900.

THE CHURCH-GOER
WHO KILLED

Charles Beckman, a regular at Salvation Army services, pays the ultimate price after being found guilty of killing his best friend.

Charles Beckman, a 35-year-old with a passion for fossicking around the Bowen district in Queensland, asked his best friend Alfred Anderson to accompany him on a trip in search of gold. The two set off on November 12, 1900, and, after spending a night at Gypsy Creek, Beckman arrived at the Ida Creek Hotel five days later on his own. He then moved on to visit friends at the Upper Euri Creek and stayed almost two weeks, and with each passing day, the Anderson family fretted more and more, especially as Beckman was seen with Anderson's horse and various goods. Finally, brother Henry set off in search of Alfred, with police later joining in the search for the missing man.

Beckman was arrested on February 1, 1901 and was driven into the bush in a search for Anderson's body. A police officer noted that at one stage Beckman started staring at a particular rock. Suspicious, the police officer lifted the rock and discovered Anderson's body. His skull had been smashed to pieces and Beckman was charged with his friend's murder. The trial opened on February 12 and it did not take long for Beckman to be found guilty of murder and subsequently sentenced to death. Beckman was hanged at Brisbane's Boggo Road Gaol on May 13, 1901. A newspaper report suggested: "Charles Beckman met his death with unflinching courage, and made a last statement affirming he was innocent. Beckman to his final minute insisted Anderson had fallen to his death."

THE 'LAST BUSHRANGERS'

Brothers Patrick and James Kenniff, described probably incorrectly as Australia's "last bushrangers", kill police officer George Doyle and station manager Albert Dahlke.

It would seem brothers Patrick and James "Jimmy" Kenniff were born to a life of crime and were in trouble with the police from a very early age. Raised in New South Wales, they moved to Queensland, apparently to turn over a new life and earn an honest living on the land. However, the brothers were unable to stay out of trouble and in 1895 were jailed for horse stealing. After serving time on St Helena Island, in Moreton Bay, they took up grazing on a property in Queensland's Carnarvon district. Then, after being suspected on stealing cattle from a neighbouring property, they roamed the district stealing cattle and horses.

Police took out a warrant against the brothers over the theft of a pony and, in March, 1902, Police Constable George Doyle, station manager Albert Dahlke and aboriginal tracker Sam Johnson went in search of the Kenniffs. Jimmy Kenniff was apprended at Lethbridge's Pocket and, while the police officer went in search of Patrick Kenniff, the backtracker was left to retrieve the party's packhorse. When Johnson returned, neither Doyle nor Dahlke were to be seen. Then, when the Kenniffs rode towards Johnson, the blacktracker fled to seek help. A search party found evidence of a gun-fight and the *Sydney Morning Herald* of April 2 reported: "It appears that Mr Dalke (sic) was out with Constable Doyle when they overtook a man whom they believed to be one of the bushrangers. They attempted to arrest him, and they were in the act of doing so, when the blacktracker, who had been ordered to return with the police packhorse, left them. He had not gone far when he heard shots fired. The black tracker became frightened and made off as fast as his horse could go for eight miles. Then he met a fencer and returned with him to the spot where he had left the three men. No one was seen, but the manager's horse and saddle were found. The saddle had blood marks on it."

The newspaper reported a few days later that there had been a "ghastly discovery". The report read: "The police had a heavy day in deep stony gorges without success until a little before five o'clock, when they followed up the creek on the bank of which the tragedy occurred. They came on a large rock in the bed of the creek with all the signs of the awful sequel to the tragedy. This was a mile and a quarter from the scene of the shooting, and less than half a mile from the men's camp. A large basalt rock about eight feet in diameter and slightly hollowed in the centre, had been utilised to burn the bodies. It is supposed that the bodies were taken across the creek by a large log about 20 yards from where the shooting occurred, and had probably been cut up there, rolled in blankets and then conveyed to the rock referred to, where the ghoulish work was resumed. After being burned, all the bones were broken into small pieces with two hardwood sticks and a large round stone like a cannon ball ... the rock had scaled off in large flakes and under these were blood and other terrible emanations from the burning bodies. The scene was terrible."

Police mounted a massive manhunt for the Kenniffs, but the brothers escaped capture for three months before they were arrested, without a fight, at a camp on the Maranoa River. They were sent for trial in the Supreme Court at Brisbane and although the blacktracker's evidence was vital, the defence tried to discredit him because his evidence was not given on oath. However, both brothers were found guilty of murder and sentenced to death. At the request of the defence, the case went to the Full Court over matters of law and although Patrick Kenniff's sentence was upheld, his brother's sentence was commuted to life imprisonment. Patrick was hanged at Boggo Road Gaol on January 13, 1903, while Jimmy served 16 years jail; he died in 1940.

THE 'DEMENTED' FATHER

Travelling salesman John Peadon goes berserk at his Hurstville home and, in a frenzied attack on his family, kills two daughters before shooting himself through the mouth.

The *Age* newspaper of September 16, 1902, reported "a terrible domestic tragedy", probably sparked by heavy gambling at the races. Country traveller John Joseph Peadon was not his usual self on the Sunday night before the *Age* report and could not settle at his Gloucester Road weatherboard home. When his wife asked him if there was any problem, he merely replied that he had a cold. Mrs Peadon eventually dozed off, but was awakened by a blow to the head. Her husband continued to attack her with an iron bed key, but she finally managed to ward him off. Son Lancelot, hearing the commotion, rushed in to see what was happening and also was hit about the head.

Lancelot Peadon said his father looked like a "wild animal" as he left the bedroom in search of other members of the family. He slashed seven-year-old Nancy so savagely across the throat that he almost severed her head and killed 18-month-old Beatrice with a slash across the throat. Three-year-old Morton also was slashed but survived, along with three-year-old Alexander who was battered around the head. Peadon, 45, later put a gun in his mouth and a bullet through his head. Mrs Peadon, Lancelot, Morton and

Alexander survived their wounds and the only member of the family who was not attacked was eldest daughter Rokeby.

MERCY FOR ONE

German migrant August Tisler is executed for the murder of his lover's husband and although Selina Sangal is also found guilty, she escapes the ultimate penalty.

Soon after August Tisler arrived in the colony of Victoria early in 1900, he settled down to a life of routine and hard work. He was engaged to be married, but then met married woman Selina Sangal and started an affair with the wife of Keysborough market gardener Edward Christopher Sangal. The affair continued for 12 months before Tisler finally confronted the husband. According to Tisler's trial evidence, Mrs Sangal pestered him to kill her husband. Then, on the night of August 8, 1902, she placed a stick in his hand and again suggested Tisler commit murder. Tisler said he hit Sangal with the stick, but the husband hit back and a fight ensued. It was then that Tisler pulled a knife on his adversary and stabbed him to death.

However, Mrs Sangal told an entirely different story, of how she loved her husband and had nothing to do with his murder. She claimed she went to bed with her husband that fateful night and was awakened by Tisler entering the bedroom and rushed to another room. The jury took just two hours to find both accused guilty of murder, although it strongly recommended mercy for Mrs Sangal. Tisler, who was executed at Melbourne Gaol on October 20, 1902, said: "I only want to say that for anything I have done in this world I am prepared to suffer." Although Mrs Sangal also was sentenced death, this was commuted to imprisonment.

THE POLICE KILLER

Notorious criminal George Shaw commits suicide after killing a police constable in the Melbourne suburb of St Kilda, just three months after the killing of a police officer in Sydney.

Police Constable Richard Johnson was shot in broad daylight in Milton Street, St Kilda, on the morning of October 12, 1902. The police officer was just about to arrest a man wanted for the murder of a police officer in the Sydney suburb of Redfern the previous July. In the Sydney killing, on the night of July 19, Constable Denis Guilfoyle and another policeman had followed two men who had been passing counterfeit coins. Guilfoyle, in attempting to make an arrest, placed a hand on the shoulder of the man nearest to him and said: "What's your name?" The man replied that it was "Wilson" and, at the same time, fired two shots into the policeman's body. Sadly, the Melbourne slaying of a police officer echoed what had happened in Sydney. However, this time the killer turned the gun on himself and committed suicide.

The killer's body eventually was identified as that of George Shaw, who went under such aliases as Yates and Raingill. The deputy governor of Darlinghurst Gaol, Sydney, a Mr McKenzie, travelled to Melbourne specifically to identify Shaw's body. Mr McKenzie asked for the body be placed in a sitting position for easier identification and, after examining the dead man's face from several angles, said there was not the slightest doubt it was that of George Shaw, whom he had discharged from the Maitland Goal just a few months earlier. "There is not the slightest doubt in my mind that it is his body," McKenzie declared.

THE MAD SQUATTER

Queensland squatter Leopold Tuckerman goes berserk and bashes his wife to death with a crowbar.

When, in 1903, 41-year-old squatter Leopold Ernst Tuckerman went on a "bender" at his property Blairgowrie, about 100 kilometres from the Queensland town of Jericho, he ended up beating his wife Frances with a crowbar. Tuckerman left the property and it was assumed he travelled to Barcaldine to purchase sheep. Then, when his wife's badly battered body was discovered at Tuckerman's property, a massive search was launched. Tuckerman eventually was found in the bush, naked and ranting incoherently. It took six men to hold him before he was taken into custody.

One contemporary newspaper noted: "The family was greatly respected in the district and much sorrow has been occasioned by the lamentable tragedy." The squatter was charged with the murder of his wife, but a Queensland Supreme Court jury found him incapable of mounting a defence because of insanity. Tuckerman therefore was ordered to be detained at the Governor's pleasure.

THE LOCK-UP AXINGS

A Kanaka labourer, Sow Too Low, goes berserk and kills two men with an axe in the Mackay lockup yard while awaiting trial for the murder of a little girl.

The *Sydney Morning Herald* of March 30, 1903, reported what it described as "a horrible double murder" in the lock-up yard at Mackay jail. Kanaka labourer Sow Too Low, who was awaiting trial for the murder of Alice Gunning, was exercising with several prisoners when he went berserk with an axe. Prisoner John Martin was hanging washing on a line when Sow Too Low struck him in the head with the axe. Martin died instantly, but Sow Too Low's rampage was far from finished. Another prisoner ran to get help and when a warder named Johnson rushed to see what had happened, Sow Too Low smashed him over the head with the axe, also killing him instantly. The kanaka rushed to a cell, only to be shot in the thigh by a warder who had climbed a mango tree overlooking the yard. Other prison officers rushed Sow Too Low, who was captured after a fierce struggle.

Sow Too Low was hanged at Brisbane jail on June 22, 1903. The Melbourne *Age* of June 23 reported that the condemned man ate a last meal of fruit and then was attended by an Anglican clergyman. The *Age* report said: "When he walked onto the drop he scarcely appeared to realise his position, and looked around him in a somewhat dazed manner. Death was apparently almost instantaneous."

ARSENIC AND BULLETS

Lovelorn John Baker swallows arsenic and then shoots himself after he shoots Chinese dealer Tim Ah Doo in the head and chest.

Butcher John Baker was in love with a woman named Nellie Smith, who went to live with Chinese trader Tim Ah Doo at Cootamundra, NSW. Baker, on September 12, 1903, went to a chemist's shop and bought sixpence worth of arsenic "to poison cats and dogs". The following night he went to Ah Doo's house and shot his enemy in love, once through the head and once through the heart. Ah Doo died almost instantly, but Baker then went into the house and fired at Smith, hitting her in the hand.

Baker then told her: "I will do for you as I have done for the other." Then, after being wounded in the hand, she begged Baker to spare her life. The lovelorn butcher then told her: "No, I have only put three (bullets) into it (the revolver)." Baker then jumped over a house fence and, as he left, he told Smith: "I suppose I will swing for this." He later was found with bullet wounds to the head and neck and died in hospital several hours later. He also had taken some of the arsenic he had purchased the night before. An inquest jury returned a verdict of wilful murder against Baker.

A FINAL TREMOR

Burglars Henry Jones and Digby Grand are involved in the shooting death of a police officer during a break-in gone wrong.

Publican Theodore Trautwein, who ran the Royal Hotel in the Sydney suburb of Auburn, was awakened on the night of January 19, 1903, by what he thought was a revolver shot. He rushed to the bar room and heard someone jump on and over the bar counter before heading for the front door. When Trautwein eventually reached the bar room he found a police officer lying on his side in a pool of blood. Constable Samuel Long, about 35 years of age, had been shot while investigating noises and never regained consciousness. Trautwein ran across the road to the local police station and Long died just as colleagues reached him. Police spotted marks by hob-nail boots on the bar and a black tracker showed how footmarks had led to a horse and sulky which had been tied to a tree in a paddock opposite the hotel. Police six days later arrested a man who was trying to get away with boots in his hand; he also left a loaded revolver on a dressing table.

Two tearaways named Henry Jones and Digby Grand were eventually charged with murder and faced trial in the Criminal Court. The trial was a sensation and crowds waited outside the court while the jury deliberated on May 20. Finally, after five and a half hours, the jury announced it had found both men guilty of murder, with a recommendation of mercy. When Judge Rogers asked why they had added this rider, the jury foreman replied that they were not sure which one had pulled the trigger and, besides, they thought a third man might have been involved. Then, when asked if he had anything to say, Grand replied to the judge: "I have to tell Your Honour to your face that you have conducted the case more like a Crown prosecutor than a judge … I will meet you before our God, and then you will see whether I am innocent or guilty." Jones told the judge: "You have been prejudiced from the first."

When Grand and Jones were sentenced to death and the judge said "may the Lord have mercy on your soul", Grand replied: "Same to you." The two convicted police killers were executed at Darlinghurst Gaol on July 7. The *Age* reported that Jones died instantly, but Grand "was less fortunate". The newspaper noted: "For over three minutes he (Grand) struggled convulsively, and life was then apparently extinct. But a minute later his arms and shoulders could be seen working. These struggles continued for only a few seconds, however. 'He's gone,' said a warder to the newspaper reporters as the final tremor passed through the hanging body, and apparently that was the end."

THE FRENCH GUNMAN

Frenchman Fredrick Maillat and seven compatriots, including two women, get involved in a row with a West Australian vintner and Maillat shoots him dead.

A group of French men and women descended on a vineyard at Guilford, Western Australia, on February 4, 1903, and at least one of them used a revolver for target practice before approaching Charles Lauffer about the purchase of some wine. Lauffer refused and an argument broke out, with the French party breaking through a fence and attacking the vintner. They used sticks and stones in the attack but one of the men, Fredrick Maillat, told them the stones they were throwing we not big enough. He then went up to Lauffer and shot him dead. Lauffer fell dead and his body rolled down a hill. The killing seemed senseless, as there were at least two witnesses other than members of the French party. Tricenne Lauffer said she saw Maillat shoot her husband, as did vineyard labourer Francseco Rocchiccioli.

Maillat was charged with murder, was found guilty and executed at Fremantle Gaol on April 21, 1903. Maillat, 24, landed in Australia in 1898 as a deserter from a French barque and worked as a fisherman and general hand. While awaiting trial, he tried to marry Frenchwoman Marie Renaud, but permission was refused. However, Renaud was given her lover's body after he had been executed and organised his funeral. Before his death, Maillat gave Renaud some small items of jewellery and instructions not to tell his mother in France of the circumstances of his death.

A PRESENT OF BULLETS

A young man, Thomas Horton, shoots his wife dead in Rundle Street, Adelaide, after she declines to go into an alleyway with him. Horton promises her a "present", but she tells him it is "a present of bullets".

To use a common euphemism of the nineteenth century, Florrie Eugenia Horton had "a peculiar disease of long standing". His wife being infected with a venereal disease angered 24-year-old Thomas Horton as, apart from anything else, he was unable to "fulfil his duties". The two had separated, but Mrs Horton was worried that the man known as "Cranky Tom" or "Silly Tom" might do her some harm and therefore wrote a letter to a friend stating she was convinced her husband would kill her. Mrs Horton was walking down Rundle Street, Adelaide, on the evening of February 27, 1904, when she bumped into her husband, who invited her into an alleyway to give her a present. She replied: "Yes, I know, a present of bullets."

Horton followed her and the other women and shot his wife three times in the back, killing her almost instantly. Two of the bullets pierced the right lung and the other passed through the heart. Horton fled from the scene, but was arrested the following day by a mounted constable between Bridgewater and Ambleside in the Lofty Ranges. He had been walking along a railway line and, when confronted, said: "All right, sir, I have been driven to it." Horton had a loaded revolver and a number of cartridges when arrested.

Facing trial in the Criminal Court the following April, Horton pleaded not guilty on the basis of insanity. Evidence was given that his father had died in an asylum and that the young man himself suffered from convulsions and once had fallen on his head from a height of 13 feet. However, a Dr Ramsay Smith gave evidence that he believed Horton was sane and was shamming loss of memory. The jury returned a guilty verdict and Horton was sentenced to death.

THE BOLTING HORSE

A horse bolting in North Adelaide leads to a bizarre case in which a women's body is discovered in two parts in the Torrens River.

Two youths who stopped a horse bolting with a cart behind it in North Adelaide on the night of August 13, 1906, inadvertently turned the spotlight on one of the city's most sensational murders. One of the youths noted blood stains in the back of the cart and therefore notified a police officer, who believed the horse and cart belonged to Natalla Habibulla.

When he went to Habibulla's house, the police officer noted a large pool of blood in the backyard.

Habibulla, an Afghan, was not at home at the time, but later turned up at the local police station and explained that a blood-stained shirt found in the back of his cart was caused by a nose bleed. He also was at pains to explain that the horse had bolted after being frightened by a new-fangled motor vehicle and that he was at the station because he had heard police had taken control of the horse and cart. However, police were concerned about the amount of blood found in Habibulla's backyard and questioned him at length about this. Meanwhile, police made further investigations at the house and discovered that there were human fragments among the blood.

Police launched a massive search for Habibulla's wife, even using black trackers. Then, after scouring the Torrens River, they found a hessian bag which contained the lower part of a human corpse. The other half was found some time later and Habibulla was charged with murder after the body was identified as that of Edith Ellen Mary Habibulla, who had married the accused just a few months earlier. It was not a happy marriage and at one stage Habibulla threatened to stab his wife. Instead, according to medical evidence given at his trial, he strangled his wife and took her into his backyard where she was chopped in half, the pieces placed in hessian bags and driven by horse and cart to the Torrens River and dumped like a dead cat.

The jury at Habibulla's trial took less than an hour to consider its verdict – guilty. Although there was a strong recommendation of mercy, he was sentenced to death. He was hanged at the Adelaide Gaol on November 16, 1906.

THE ACID WOMAN

Martha Rendell becomes the last woman hanged in Western Australia after being found guilty of murdering step-son Arthur by swabbing his throat with hydrochloric acid.

When Martha Rendell moved in to live with Thomas Morris in 1906, she inherited a young family. However, the presence of step-children Anne, Olive, Arthur and George sparked feelings of jealousy as her new husband showered his children with affection. Anne, Olive and Arthur Morris died in suspicious circumstances, but Rendell was charged only with the death of Arthur. It was alleged she had swabbed his throat with hydrochloric acid after he had complained of a sore throat. Morris also was charged with the boy's murder, but was found not guilty.

Rendell was found guilty in the Supreme Court of Western Australia and this sparked enormous controversy as many wanted her to hang while others argued it would be wrong to hang a woman. Besides, there were serious doubts about her guilt and there were moves to have the heavily-set Rendell's sentence commuted to one of imprisonment. However, these arguments fell on deaf ears and Rendell was hanged at Fremantle Gaol on the morning of October 6, 1909.

MAD OR BAD?

A butcher shoots his sister-in-law dead and argues at his trial that insanity ran in his family.

For some inexplicable reason, 32-year-old butcher Joseph Victor Pfeiffer went to his sister-in-law's home in the Melbourne bayside suburb of Albert Park one night in November, 1911, and shot her dead. Pfeiffer admitted he was infatuated with Florence Whiteley, 23, but told police when he was apprehended that there was no reason for killing her and there had been no quarrel between them. The police thought otherwise and reasoned that Whiteley had rejected Pfeiffer's advances, prompting him to kill her.

Pfeiffer was charged with murder and, at his trial, said he could not remember shooting Miss Whiteley and that insanity ran on both sides of his family. He told of a brother who also had memory problems and of two other family members who had committed suicide. Incredibly, Pfeiffer did not call on expert testimony to back his claims of insanity and he was found guilty of murder. He was executed at the Melbourne Gaol on February 29, 1912.

THE BATTLE OF BROKEN HILL

Four people are killed and seven wounded in the Battle of Broken Hill when two Turks fire on a rail carriage in 1915.

Technically, Australia already was at war with Turkey when New Year's Day dawned in the Outback in 1915, but no shots had been fired in anger — until camel driver Mulla Abdulla and ice-cream vendor Gool Mahomed that day launched a private guerrilla war just outside the New South Wales mining town of Broken Hill. Picnicking families were travelling to nearby Silverton in open-air ore trucks when they noticed an ice-cream van by the side of the tracks. From it fluttered the red and white Turkish flag. Almost immediately, they had to duck for cover as shots rang out from a nearby trench. Police and soldiers rushed to the scene, where they surrounded the two gunmen. Finally, after several hours, the siege was ended when Abdulla was shot dead and Mahomed mortally wounded. They had killed Elma Cowie, Albert Millar, William Shaw and James Greig and the wounded included a police constable, Robert Mills. Abdulla had been armed with a Snider rifle, while Mahomed had been firing a Martini Henry rifle.

The *Barrier Miner* reported that the murderers had been "riddled with bullets". It is believed that after Abdulla had been convicted for slaughtering sheep illegally, the older Mahomed had convinced him neither had a future in Australia and it would be better to die as Muslim patriots. Although Abdulla was from north-west India (now Pakistan) and Mahomed an Afghan, they had sworn allegiance to the Sultan of Turkey as the leader of their faith. Their ambush sparked outrage in Broken Hill and a mob, believing the German community was behind the outrage, set alight the German Club before marching towards a camel drivers' camp. Police stopped them, but tension in Broken Hill was high for many weeks.

SINGLE PAY FOR TWO EXECUTIONS

An executioner tries to claim a double payment for the execution of two men in Sydney after they are found guilty of shooting a police officer.

Police constable George Duncan was sitting in his office at the Tottenham (about 100 kilometres east of Dubbo, New South Wales), police station on September 26, 1916, when he was shot through a window. Two brothers, Roland and Herbert Kennedy and their friend Frank Franz were arrested and charged with murder, with Franz turning king's evidence. He claimed that he was present when the shot was fired, but did not fire the bullet that killed Duncan. The three were members of the Industrial Workers of the World movement and the prosecution argued that the motive for the killing was tied up with international anarchy.

Herbert Kennedy was found not guilty, but his 20-year-old brother and Franz were found guilty and sentenced to death. There was considerable public animosity towards the elder Kennedy and Franz as 1916 was the mid-point of the Great War and Franz also had the misfortune of having a German father. They were executed at Bathurst jail on December 20, 1916, but not before the hangman requested double payment for his services. In normal circumstances he was paid five guineas for a hanging but, as he had to execute two men at the same time, asked for double payment "in view of the disagreeable nature of the duties involved". The NSW government refused on the basis that "when two or more criminals are hanged on the same day they are executed simultaneously" and, therefore, "they stand on the platform together and fall at the same time". The hangman had to do with a single payment, while it is believed Franz, 28 years of age, was the first man hanged after giving king's evidence.

THE VICTORIA MARKET MURDER

An Italian immigrant shoots a compatriot dead at Melbourne's Victoria Market and later is executed.

The execution of Antonio Picconi (sometimes spelt as Piccone or Piconi) at the Melbourne Gaol on September 18, 1916, hardly caused a ripple and, in fact, rated just two paragraphs on an inside page of the *Age* newspaper the following day. Naturally, the Great War hogged all public interest and the *Age* merely reported that Picone (as it referred to the executed man) was attended by a priest, the Rev. Father O'Donovan, as he was led to the scaffold and that death was instantaneous.

Piccone, an Italian immigrant, was hanged for the murder of another Italian, Joseph Lauricella, at Melbourne's Victoria Market on the morning of July 25, 1916. Lauricella was playing cards with another man when Piccone walked up behind him and shot him twice. Then, when Lauricella fell, Piccone pumped another bullet into him.

Piccone fled from the scene, but was caught by a witness and then handed to the police. When asked why he had killed Lauricella, Piccone said the dead man had caused his family financial grief through business transactions gone wrong. Piccone was examined for any possible mental illness, but was passed fit to stand trial. The *Age,* in its brief report of Piccone's death, said: "His request that a small photo in his possession and a lock of hair should be buried with him was granted." Asked if he had any last words, Piccone mumbled a few inaudible words.

THE MAN-WOMAN

Italian-born Eugenia Falleni is born a woman, but lives as a man and even marries. However, her "wife" discovers her true gender and is bashed to death.

Eugenia Falleni was born in Florence in 1875, but migrated to New Zealand with her parents as a small girl. At around 16 years of age, Falleni started dressing as a boy and, after running away to sea, she worked as a deck hand on ships plying the Pacific islands. Despite her obvious sexual leanings, she gave birth to a daughter, Josephine, in Newcastle in 1899. Falleni, who adopted the name Henry Crawford, took the baby to a childless couple in Sydney's Double Bay and told them that because the mother had died they could raise the little girl. Falleni often visited her daughter and continued to live and dress as a man, working at various jobs in and around Sydney.

Then, in 1914, she "married" widow Annie Birkett after a two-year courtship. Birkett believed Falleni was a man and, incredibly, did not discover her "husband's" real gender for three years. This was in September, 1917, and, on discovery, Falleni suggested she and Birkett discuss the problem during a stroll to a lonely bush spot in the Lane Cove River park. Falleni bashed his "wife" to death and then burned her body in a bonfire. The man-woman told everyone that "his" wife had left him and although Falleni at first appeared to have escaped detection, the charred remains of Birkett were found by two boys playing in scrubland. Although police at first could not identity the body, a dentist later confirmed it as Birkett.

Falleni disappeared but eventually was tracked down to a house at Canterbury where she was living after "marrying" a woman named Lizzie Allison. She was arrested for the murder of Birkett, found guilty after the jury deliberated for just two hours and sentenced to death. However, that sentence was commuted to life imprisonment following a plea to the New South Wales Executive Council and, after serving 11 years at Long Bay Gaol, she was released in 1931 under the strict condition she live as a woman. Falleni was killed when struck by a motor vehicle in 1938, living under the name of Jean Ford.

TWO LUCKY DIGGERS

Two Australian Diggers are found guilty of bashing a Canadian soldier to death in London and are fortunate to escape the gallows.

Although hundreds of British and Commonwealth servicemen were executed for desertion, cowardice or other military offences during World War I, only one Australian paid the ultimate penalty. Yet Private John King was an Australian serving in a New Zealand uniform, with the Canterbury Infantry Regiment. King, who was found guilty, not of desertion, but of being absent without leave, was executed on August 19, 1917. King's sentence of death was confirmed by General Sir Douglas Haig, who had made strong representations that Australian soldiers also should be subject to the extreme penalty. However, the Australian government decreed that none of its servicemen would be executed, regardless of the circumstances, mainly because all its soldiers were volunteers.

Yet two Diggers could have considered themselves fortunate to have escaped the hangman's noose in wartime England. Privates Ernie Sharp and Tom Maguire were absent without leave on the evening of August 21, 1917, when they went drinking at the Rising Sun Hotel off Waterloo Road in south-east London. Ironically, this watering hole now is just a few hundred metres from the Imperial War Museum. Sharp and Maguire started drinking with a petty English crook named Joe Jones and, late in the night, the three of them followed two cashed-up Canadian soldiers, Oliver Imley and John McKinley, into the dark, narrow Valentine Place.

The Canadians, to use an Australian expression, were "rolled". McKinley recovered from the injuries he received in the bashing and robbery, but Imley died four days later. Jones, Sharp and Maguire faced possible murder charges. Sharp, who recognised the gravity of his situation, turned King's evidence and, for stepping forward had a murder charge against him dropped and, instead, was handed a seven-year penal sentence. Sharp also insisted that it was English civilian Jones, who had been discharged from the army after twice being wounded on the Western Front, who was responsible for bashing the two Canadians and therefore killing Imley.

Both Sharp and Maguire claimed that Imley had laid into the two Canadians with a police truncheon. Jones denied he had a truncheon and even claimed that the Australians had done all the bashing, but other witnesses said they had seen him with a weapon earlier in the night. Jones' fate was sealed and he was sentenced to death. Maguire, for his part in the robbery that led to Imley's death, was sentenced to eight years' jail.

Jones' execution was set for dawn on February 20, 1918, and as executioner John Ellis slipped the noose over his head, he mumbled: "God forgive them." It is presumed that Jones was referring either to the jury that had found him guilty or to the execution party, including hangman Ellis. Or could he have been referring to the two Australian Diggers, Sharp and Maguire, his partners in crime, if not in murder, that night near Waterloo Road?

THE GUN ALLEY MURDER

A wine merchant is hanged after the body of a 12-year-old girl is discovered in the heart of Melbourne.

At about five o'clock on the morning of December 31, 1921, a bottle collector stumbled across the naked body of a young girl. The body lay across a grate in tiny Gun Alley, Melbourne. Gun Alley, a lane running off Little Collins Street, at that time was an unsavoury part of the city and the site later was occupied by the Southern Cross Hotel. The dead girl was 12-year-old Alma Tirtschke, who had been reported missing the previous afternoon after running a message for her aunt to a butcher shop in Swanston Street.

Alma had been wearing a navy blue box-pleated tunic, a white blouse with blue spots and a school hat bearing the badge of Hawthorn West High School. Alma had left the butcher shop at about 1pm and then "disappeared", although witnesses later gave various accounts of seeing her in the neighbourhood. Significantly, Alma's body was naked when discovered and, even more significantly, the body had been washed down before being dumped in Gun Alley. Alma had been raped and strangled and the New Year's Eve murder captured the imagination and horror of the whole of Melbourne.

A post mortem performed by government pathologist Dr Crawford Mollison revealed an abrasion on the left side of the jaw, another on the left side of the neck, a small abrasion on the outer side of the right eye, a small abrasion on the upper lip and a slight graze on the elbow. There was bruising on the right side of the neck and haemorrhages on the scalp and the surface of the eyes. Dr Mollison's expert view was that the girl had died of strangulation by throttling.

Several witnesses helped police in their investigations and the trail eventually led to Colin Ross, who operated the Australian Wine Bar in the Eastern Arcade. Ross, 26, had bought the wine shop business for 400 pounds but, ironically, the licence on the saloon was due to expire on December 31, the very day that Alma's body was discovered. Police interviewed Ross several times and, at the first interview, told police he had seen a girl answering Alma's description, but knew nothing of her death. Then, on January 5, 1922, he was interviewed for eight hours and made a lengthy statement in which he referred to a suspicious shop opposite his and later described it as a brothel. Then, on January 10, 20-year-old prostitute Olive Maddox was overheard saying she had seen Ross with the 12-year-old. Maddox made this remark to a woman named Ivy Matthews, who gave evidence at Alma's inquest on January 26 that she saw a girl in Ross' saloon at about 3pm on December 30 and that the girl "resembled" Alma Tirtschke.

Police went to Ross' home in the western suburb of Footscray and discovered 27 hairs on two blankets and these were identified as being from the dead girl. Ross had an alibi, supported by numerous witnesses, but circumstantial evidence saw him found guilty of Alma's murder. When Justice Schutt asked him if he wanted to say anything before sentence was passed, Ross replied: "Yes, I still maintain that I am an innocent man, and that my evidence is correct. My life has been sworn away by desperate people." The judge then sentenced Ross to death.

Appeals to the State Full Court and the High Court of Australia failed and Ross was due to hang on April 24. State Cabinet turned down a request for an appeal to the Privy Council and Ross was hanged as scheduled, spending his last hours with two ministers of religion. As he waited for the noose to be pulled tight around his neck, he said: "I am now face to face with my Maker. I swear by almighty God that I am an innocent man. I never saw the child. I never committed the crime and I don't know who did it. I never confessed to anyone. I ask God to forgive those who swore my life away, and I pray God to have mercy on my poor, darling mother and my family." Ross also wrote to his mother protesting his innocence.

Ross' counsel, Mr T.C. Brennan (later Dr Brennan) was so convinced of his client's innocence that he wrote a book about the case and its inconsistencies. Significantly, it was titled *The Gun Alley Tragedy*, Brennan leaving no doubt that he believed Ross to be as tragic a figure as poor Alma Tirtschke. In that book, there is an incredible index, telling of a letter Ross received while waiting for death. The letter read:

Colin C. Ross, Melbourne Gaol,

You have been condemned for a crime which you have never committed and are to suffer for another's fault. Since your conviction you have, no doubt, wondered what manner of man the real murderer is who could not only encompass the girl's death, but allow you to suffer in his stead.

My dear Ross, if it is any satisfaction for you to know it, believe me that you die but once, but he will continue to die for the rest of his life. Honoured and fawned upon by those who know him, the smile upon his lips but hides the canker eating into his soul. Day and night his life is a hell without the hope of retrieve. Gladly would he take your place on Monday (the day of execution) next if he had himself alone to consider. His reason, then, briefly stated, is this: A devoted and loving mother is ill and a shock would be fatal. Three loving married sisters, whose whole life would be wrecked, to say nothing of brothers who have been accustomed to take him as a pattern. He cannot sacrifice these. Himself he will be sacrifice when his mother passes away. He will do it by his own hand. He will board the ferry across the Styx with a lie on his lips, with the only hope that religion is a myth and death annihilation.

It is too painful for him to go into the details of the crime. It is simply a Jekyll and Hyde existence. By a freak of nature, he was not made as other men ... this girl was not the first ... in this case there was no intention of murder – the victim unexpectedly collapsed. The hands of the woman, in her frenzy, did the rest.

May it be some satisfaction to yourself, your devoted mother, and the memories of your family to know that at least one of the legion of the damned, who is the cause of your death, is suffering the pangs of hell. He may not ask for forgiveness or sympathy, but he asks your understanding.

It now seems certain that an innocent man was hanged, with DNA evidence proving that Ross did not kill Alma Tirtschke.

DOCTOR DEATH

A Melbourne doctor addicted to drugs and gambling kills three of his children and a servant before killing himself.

To all intents and purposes, Dr George Cranstoun was a pillar of society in the Melbourne bayside suburb of Hampton. He and his family lived in an extremely comfortable Queen Anne villa in Station Street, just 50 yards from the Hampton railway station, and had a thriving medical practice. His wife regularly attended the local Congregational Church and their five children went to Sunday school.

Dr Cranstoun, 45, was a pharmacist until he graduated in medicine at the University of Melbourne in 1914; he practised in Gippsland for several years before establishing the practice in Hampton. He was well liked and another Hampton medical practitioner, Dr Garnet Leary, said he "never met a more charming personality". He added: "Everyone who met him liked him."

However, Dr Leary shared one of Dr Cranstoun's darker secrets as just a month after the former pharmacist opened his practice in Hampton, Dr Leary had to treat him for an over-injection of morphia. Dr Cranstoun was unconscious for 16 hours, but then made a full recovery – only to continue his drug addiction.

Dr Leary could not possibly have known what Dr Cranstoun's drug addiction would lead to and, on the morning of August 14, 1922, Melbourne newspapers trumpeted what they described as the worst domestic tragedy in the history of Victoria. Dr Cranstoun had killed three of his children and a servant and had tried to kill his wife and their other two children before suiciding. The victims were servant Gladys Baylis (22), John Cranstoun (15), Robert (10) and Colin (eight). Mrs Cranstoun and daughters Margaret (13) and Belle (six) survived Dr Cranstoun's deadly attacks by hypodermic needle.

The discovery of this enormous domestic tragedy was made by one of the doctor's patients. After she had telephoned with no answer, she decided to make a personal call and arrived at the Cranstoun house, where she peeped through a letter-box and saw the pyjama-clad doctor lying in the hall. Police were called and they found a hypodermic needle on the floor near Dr Cranstoun, who was still alive. They found the other bodies, with Mrs Cranstoun and the two daughters very ill. Dr Cranstoun died in hospital before he could be questioned, but police investigations revealed he had injected his family and Miss Baylis with strychnine, which can be used as a stimulant, but is lethal in large doses.

Apart from his drug problem, Dr Cranstoun was heavily in debt and form guides and race programs were found in his surgery after his death. Police also learned that he had been to the Caulfield races the Saturday before killing his three sons and the family servant.

TAKING THE RAP?

When career criminal Angus Murray was executed in Melbourne following the shooting of a bank employee during a hold-up, some thought he might have been taking the rap for the notorious Leslie "Squizzy" Taylor.

Bank clerk Thomas Berriman was carrying almost 2000 pounds in notes in the Melbourne suburb of Hawthorn in October, 1923, when was confronted by two men. When Berriman refused to hand over the money he was carrying, he was shot dead. Career criminal Angus Murray was arrested and charged with Berriman's murder but the other man,

Richard Buckley, managed to avoid custody for more than seven years.

There were some who believed that Murray might have taking the rap for the notorious Leslie "Squizzy" Taylor or, a least, Taylor had planned the robbery. Regardless, Murray was found guilty of the murder of Berriman and was sentenced to death.

If Taylor had been directly or indirectly involved, Murray did not let on, not even in the final minutes before his execution at the Melbourne Gaol on April 14, 1924. The *Sun News-Pictorial* reported: "He (Murray) might have gone on to revile his misfortune or to blame a confederate. He did not. He turned to his executioners as they fastened the noose around him: 'Pull it tight,' he said. This was his second remark to them. In his cell, when he first met the masked faces that, by their appearance before him, conveyed to him the final hopelessness of reprieve, he made to them his last request in life – 'make it quick, friends'. Perhaps they were. Murray's death was as instantaneous at their hands as the switching on of an electric light."

The newspaper reported that 1000 people knelt in prayer outside Melbourne Gaol in the lead-up to Murray's execution. Then, as the crowd waited for the "clang of prison bell" to announce Murray's death, they knelt and recited the Lord's Prayer. An inquest into Murray's death was held immediately and, with unintentional black humour, it concluded that he did not suffer from brain disease.

Buckley, meanwhile, eventually was apprehended by police and convicted for his part in the fatal hold-up. He was sentenced to life imprisonment, but was released after just 15 years. "Squizzy" Taylor and another underworld identity,

"Snowy" Cutmore killed each other in a gunfight in the inner Melbourne suburb of Carlton in 1927.

Murray was the last man hanged at the Melbourne Gaol and executions in Melbourne then took place at Pentridge. However, the first man executed at Pentridge was not a murderer, but a sex offender. David Bennett had been convicted of criminal assault on a four-year-old girl and was executed on September 26, 1932. Bennett proclaimed his innocence to the last and his final word was "goodbye". The other 200 prisoners at Pentridge had to wait in their cells until Bennett's body was been cut down from the gallows.

DEATH OF A HERO

A police officer who won a Military Medal for bravery in World War I is shot and killed at Swan Hill, northern Victoria.

Constable Joseph Delaney, of the Victorian mounted police, was one of the most highly respected members of the Swan Hill community. A tall man, Constable Delaney dispensed justice along the Murray River with tremendous authority and the backing of a thankful rural community. In fact, Constable Delaney was regarded as something of a hero as he had been awarded the Military Medal in France during World War I. He and another soldier were engaged in laying lines at Villers-Bretonneux when they were surprised by the enemy. The other soldier was shot, but Delaney completed the task and then carried his mate to the safety of the trenches.

Police had been called to a farmhouse at Tyntynder, about eight miles from Swan Hill, on August 28, 1923. There had been a break-in during the absence of the owner, Mr William Crick. Police suspected a young farmhand from a neighbouring property had taken advantage of Mr Crick's absence and he was questioned over the break-in. However, Constable Delaney decided to interview the suspect himself on August 30. He went straight to the house where the youth was living and, once inside, noticed a movement from behind a door. The police officer then was shot in the chest from point-blank range.

The youth was seen running out of the house and neighbours who went to investigate found Constable Delaney lying in a pool of blood. He was still alive and conscious and told the men who found him what had happened. One man stayed with him while the other jumped onto Constable Delaney's horse to notify other police. A doctor and a police officer arrived two hours later after being bogged in a quagmire and feared they would be too late. However, Constable Delaney was still alive and arrangements were made to have him taken to Swan Hill and later, at the Swan Hill Public Hospital, his condition was reported as "serious". Police scoured the country for the gunman and finally tracked him down to a farmhouse a few miles from the scene of the shooting. Later, at the Swan Hill police station, police charged 15-year-old Frederick Smith, a ward of the state, with intent to murder.

Meanwhile, the police surgeon, Mr G.A. Syme, was flown from Melbourne to Swan Hill to perform an emergency operation on the wounded constable. However, Constable

Delaney's death was announced on the morning of September 4. The whole of Swan Hill went into mourning and Constable Delaney was given a hero's farewell, with his coffin draped by the Union Jack. Smith eventually faced trial at Bendigo for the police officer's killing and the court was told that the 15-year-old had waited behind a bedroom door before ordering Delaney to "put his hands up". Instead, Smith claimed, Delaney rushed him and that the shooting was an accident.

Smith was found guilty of the lesser charge of manslaughter, although Justice McArthur indicated that he believed Smith had lied to the court. He added: "The court must declare that the promiscuous firing of guns – whether by young or old – has to be put down with a firm hand." He sentenced Smith to five years' jail and a private whipping of at least 10 lashes of the birch.

DEATH AT SEA

A naval rating has his forehead bashed in with a hammer and has his throat slashed, with another rating's body later found hanging in a refrigerator chamber.

Murders have been committed in every imaginable situation and place, in pubs, alleys, theatres and even at sea. There have been several cases of murder at sea involving ships plying coastal Australia and at least one documented case aboard an Australian Navy vessel. It was the sad case of two naval ratings who quarrelled aboard HMAS Brisbane in 1924. The vessel was anchored off Garden Island, Sydney, on April 19 when the body of 17-year-old seaman David Rich, from the western Melbourne suburb of Yarraville, was found in his hammock. His head had been hammered in and his throat had been slashed.

Police were called immediately and, meanwhile, the ship's officers called for a muster. All hands were accounted for, except one. The missing seaman was an assistant cook, George Brown, from Brisbane. A search for Brown resulted in the discovery of a second death aboard HMAS Brisbane as his body was found hanging in a refrigerator chamber. Brown obviously had killed Rich before suiciding, but police were unable to determine a precise motive, although ratings did tell police and naval officers that Brown often had quarrelled with his shipmates.

Brown had bashed in Rich's forehead with a hammer, which later was found under the 17-year-old's hammock. Rich had joined the navy in search of adventure, but was killed by a shipmate in a cruel and vicious attack barely months after embarking on his chosen career at sea.

THE THREE LITTLE ANGELS

A distraught father, a Sydney piano teacher, cuts his three daughters' throats and later is hanged for murder.

Few Australian cases have been as sad as the slaying of three innocent little girls in Sydney in 1924. The case shocked, revolted and saddened the nation and when the bodies were discovered there was an enormous outcry. The killings occurred in the Sydney suburb of Paddington, which was then a slum suburb.

Edward Williams, a 52-year-old piano teacher, struggled to raise his three daughters, Rosalie (five), Mary (three) and Cecilia (two) by himself. His wife was an inmate at the Callan Park asylum and Williams and his three girls visited her there almost every weekend. It was a tough, difficult life for Williams and he eventually cracked under the strain. On the night of February 24, 1924, he told Rosalie, the eldest of his innocents, that he would help her get to heaven. Rosalie earlier had told her father that she would like to go to heaven and this was one of the contributing factors to his actions. He cut the throats of his daughters with a razor, bundled their bodies on top of their double bed and placed newspapers under the bed to catch and mop up the dripping blood.

He then left Sydney, but not before arranging to see some furniture. When the dealer arrived to collect the furniture, he failed to discover the bodies of the three little angels. The gruesome discovery was made by landlady Mrs Florence Mahon, who was horrified. Meanwhile, Williams handed himself in to police at Newcastle and he was charged with murder. The piano teacher, at Sydney Central Court, made a pathetic figure as he tried to explain his actions and described the killings as "acts of love" and wanted to save his girls from their mother's fate.

On the night of the killings, he believed he saw his wife's crooked eyes in those of Rosalie and therefore decided to kill her. Then, with twisted logic, he decided that if killed one he would have to kill all three daughters. He also said: "I seek neither favour nor mercy. I only ask for justice. I am entitled to a fair trial, and I know I shall receive it from you. If I am to be hanged, then let me be hanged. Take no notice of the plea of insanity. I myself do not raise it. As for it being temporary insanity, I can't say myself." As a Catholic, Williams would not resort to suicide to appease his conscience, but little to save himself from the hangman's noose. He was found guilty of murder and was hanged on April 29, 1924, just two months after he killed his little girls.

THE PICNIC PARTY KILLER

A gunman open fires on a group enjoying a bush picnic near the Murray River.

It was a perfect summer's day, ideal for a bush picnic. Sunday, February 10, 1924, dawned hot and still and Mr and Mrs Charles McGrath made early preparation for a picnic they would hold on the banks of the Jingellic Creek, a small tributary of the Murray River. A group of country neighbours had been invited to the picnic, just 200 yards from the McGrath homestead and guests were asked to assemble from about 1 o'clock.

Dairy farmer Charles Barber and his wife Ruth were the first to arrive, followed by Mr and Mrs McGrath, tobacco grower Richard King, butter factory manager David Shephard and his wife and child, farmer Charles Gainer and his wife and eight-year-old George Pointz. The group ate a lazy luncheon under the willows draping the creek, unaware that someone on the opposite bank had been watching every mouthful, every gesture, every movement.

Barber decided at 2.30pm that it was time for the men to go for a walk, but moved only 100 yards from the women and children when they heard a loud cracking noise from the opposite bank. King fell to the ground, seriously wounded in the chest. The men looked up and saw a man in a black hat taking aim for a second shot. Barber immediately recognised the man as his farmhand, Claude Valentine Batson, regarded as one of the best shots in New South Wales. The men were sitting ducks as Batson fired the second shot, which hit Gainer in the right knee. Shephard then took a bullet through the body as Barber shouted to the women and children to take cover.

Barber, showing great courage, ran to a horse and rode off, while former army major McGrath decided Batson had to be shot down. He made a dash for his homestead but was hit by four bullets. Although critically wounded, McGrath managed to scramble back to the creek bank with a gun in his hand. Meanwhile, Barber's daring ride alerted the entire region and a massive manhunt was launched in search of the gunman.

Shephard died in hospital the next day and the search party became even more determined than ever to apprehend Batson, a 23-year-old who had spent his entire life in the bush and knew every source of food and shelter in the area. On the second day of the search, Batson was confronted by two police officers at an orchard near Lankeys Creek. Shots were exchanged, but Batson managed to escape and he later left a note at a farm which said he had taken cyanide. However, police knew this was a ruse as cyanide killed instantly and Batson would not have been able to write a note.

Finally, on February 15, Batson walked up to two men on a dairy farm just outside Jingellic and, when farmhands Robert Emerson and William Hore asked him about the shootings, he replied: "I was driven to it. I hope they put me on trial. I will tell them something." Batson then was arrested by two police officers who had been called to the farmhouse.

Batson was committed for trial on one charge of murder and three charges of felonious wounding with intent to murder. However, he never stood trial as he was committed to a mental institution. Batson obviously had had a mental breakdown and no one now will ever know why he shot at innocent picnickers.

THE BATTERED BRIDE

A "newly-married" woman is battered and has her throat slashed at a honeymoon cottage at Lake Macquarie.

Pretty Mona Beacher was radiant as she prepared for her "marriage" to James Turner. Uniwittingly, she was also preparing for her death at the hands of her young "husband", who used the wedding ceremony as the first step in an elaborate plan to free himself of the entanglements of love.

The young couple was married at the Catholic church in the Newcastle suburb of Tighes Hill on the afternoon of

Friday, May 15, 1925. Mona and Jim told everyone, including the bride's parents, they would be honeymooning in Melbourne. In reality, they headed straight for their newly rented home at Lake Macquarie, an extremely popular honeymoon destination between the two world wars. Jim convinced Mona that this would give them even greater privacy and would also help them settle into married life not far from where he worked in Newcastle.

Mona booked the cottage on a six-month rental agreement through an advertisement in a Newcastle newspaper. The cottage owners, Mrs and Mts Arthur Williams, lived in Newcastle but used the cottage as a holiday home and were delighted to rent it to the young couple. Although Mona made the initial inspection and agreement, Jim Turner made a follow-up inspection and was delighted with his fiancee's choice.

Mr Williams, keen to see how his tenants had settled in, made calls on the honeymooners but, although bread, mail and newspapers had been delivered, there was no answer. He therefore prised open a window and saw the blood-splattered body of Mona Beacher, who had given Williams the name of Miss Anderson. An autopsy later revealed she had been battered around the head and had been slashed across the throat.

Every effort had been made to hide the body's identity as clothes had been burned and a broom handle had been used to shove underclothes up a narrow chimney. Police, however, discovered fragments of rosary beads in ash from under the stove and started making enquiries at Catholic churches. Also, police found a brooch with the name "Mona" engraved on the back. Police therefore were able to contact Mona Beacher's parents in Newcastle, but were told Mona was on her honeymoon in Melbourne. Also, Mr and Mrs Beacher told police Mona had not married a man named James Turner, but her long-standing boyfriend Arthur Oakes, a warehouse worker.

Oakes immediately became a wanted man and eventually was apprehended on the evening of May 24 at his home at Tighes Hill. Both he and his wife were preparing to go to bed. Oakes at first denied any knowledge of Mona Beacher, but the evidence was so overwhelming he was charged with the young woman's murder.

Oakes told the jury at his trial before Chief Justice Sir Philip Street that Mona knew he was married, but insisted on a wedding ceremony even though she knew it was bigamous. He also said he went to bed on the night of May 16 and woke up with Mona dead beside him. He panicked and tried to hide any identification of the body. Oakes was found guilty of murder and sentenced to death. However, this sentence was commuted to one of life imprisonment.

THE DANCE OF DEATH

A jilted young woman shoots her former boyfriend dead during a ball at Perth's Government House.

The band had just started an encore of a new and unfamiliar foxtrot, *Follow Yvette*. It was Perth's glittering social event of the year – the St John of God Hospital Ball at

Government House. It was just past the witching hour on August 27, 1925, and as couples started gliding around the polished floor, a tall and beautiful young woman in a blue evening dress walked slowly but purposely towards one of the couples. She touched the man on the shoulder, but he brushed her aside with the sneering comment: "Oh, go away! Can't you see I'm dancing?" The woman responded by pressing the trigger of a revolver she had hidden behind a handkerchief. The dashing young man in the dinner suit crashed to the floor, a crimson stain spreading across his white-starched shirt. Some women screamed, while others rushed to the scene to see what had happened. The young man had been mortally wounded, shot through the heart, and the woman who had killed him stood staring into space.

The shooting of Englishman Cyril Gidley by the woman he had spurned became one of the most celebrated cases in Australian criminal history. Its Government House setting and its aura of melodrama created headlines around the country for months; the public devoured every word written about this sensational killing and, for example, the now-defunct Perth *Mirror* shrieked the headline BALLROOM HORROR.

The shooting, of course, brought the ball to an abrupt end and the band played *God Save the King* as stunned revellers filed out of the ballroom. Perth had never seen anything like the shooting at Government House. Audrey Campbell Jacob had shot her man dead and her photograph was splashed across the front pages of just about every newspaper in Australia. Dark-haired, vivacious and pretty, Audrey Jacob would have been every young Australian's dream girl of the 1920s. But her man had done her wrong, and she had shot him down in front of a dancing throng of revellers.

When a policeman took Miss Jacob by the arm to lead her away, she told him: "It's all right; I know what I have done." She then was placed in a chair before being taken to a nearby lock-up for questioning. Miss Jacob, a mere 20 years of age, was charged with the murder of 25-year-old Gidley, who had arrived in Australia as a fourth engineer on a British steamer in 1923. Although he had a family in the north of England, he decided to leave his British ship to take employment as an engineer on a coast vessel, the *Kangaroo*. It was during one of his many stops at the port of Fremantle that he met the lovely and innocent Miss Jacob.

Gidley, blond and dashing, was a man of the world and Miss Jacob fell head over heels in love with him. In fact, she broke every rule of her convent upbringing to give herself – body and soul – to the man she loved. Although she had been engaged to another man, she broke off the engagement to suit Gidley and even left home so that she could see him whenever he was in port. However, Gidley obviously had a roving eye and there were other women in his life. His carefree attitude cost him his life.

Miss Jacob stood trial before Justice Northmore just six weeks after the shooting. It was the cause celebre of the year, if not the decade, and there were long queues outside the Criminal Court when Miss Jacob was due to give evidence. Miss Jacob told of how Gidley was "the living embodiment of the Sheik" a clear reference to Hollywood movie idol Rudolph Valentino. The former Catholic convent girl also told of how Gidley had told her he would be on his way to Singapore on the night of the ball. A friend convinced her to go to the ball regardless and she immediately saw her lover there. He refused to recognise her, so she went home and undressed.

It was then that she saw a revolver given to her by her previous fiancé for protection, so she decided to dress again and go back to the ball – armed with the revolver. However, on the way back to the ball, Miss Jacob stopped at the Catholic Cathedral and prayed. There was no doubt that the public believed Gidley had inadvertently caused his own death and evidence was presented at Miss Jacob's trial that he was a cruel arrogant womaniser. Miss Jacob, who told the court she never wanted to harm Gidley, was acquitted of murder. It was an enormously popular decision and Miss Jacob left Perth almost immediately, presumably to make a new life for herself under another name in another state.

THE BOILED BODY

An old man is killed in outback New South Wales and his body boiled before being buried.

Old Bill Oliver was a well-known and well-loved character in outback New South Wales. Everyone had a kind word to say about him and he often helped friends in need. However, the local mailman noticed that Old Bill had not been collecting his letters from early January, 1926. Although Old Bill was something of a nomadic bushman, the mailman decided to report him missing as the mail had accumulated for several weeks and Old Bill had never been missing for more than a few days at a time.

Police made a thorough search of bush country around the tiny hamlet of Wanaaring, but there was no sign of the old bushman. The search therefore dragged on until police came across the ruins of an old camp at Yanterbangee. Within minutes of digging, they came across human remains wrapped in an old coat. The body's skull had been smashed in and police were convinced that it was Old Bill's body and that he had been murdered.

The first task was to identify the remains, but this proved difficult as Old Bill's killer had boiled the body before burying it. In fact, the killer even had stripped flesh from the old man's skull in an effort to hinder identification. Besides, the body had been in the makeshift grave for more than a month and was badly decomposed. Flesh had been torn from every limb and effort had been made to foil medical experts. However, forensic pathologists were still able to determine the body's sex, approximate age and physical characteristics. There was no doubt it was Old Bill's body.

Meanwhile, one of Old Bill's cheques had been cashed at Wilcannia and his mail had been collected in a forged order form. Finally, a Wilcannia garage had received a letter instructing it to sell Old Bill's car and to give the proceeds to a man named Walter Harney, who immediately became the number one suspect. Police apprehended him and found Old Bill's watch, spirit level, chain and several documents in his possessions. Police also learned that Harney had tried to raise money in Broken Hill on land deeds owned by Old Bill.

Harney, 30, went to trial at Broken Hill on January 14, 1926, but the jury failed to agree and a new trial was ordered. Harney, a South African, had moved to Australia in 1917 and often had been in trouble with the law. In fact, he was on the run for a shooting in Sydney when Old Bill was killed. After being found guilty of the murder of Old Bill, Judge Bevan told him: "You have been found guilty of a most bloodthirsty murder, and of the murder of a man who had been most kind to you. I agree with the verdict of the jury that the murder could only have been committed with a view to gain … if you have a spark of humanity in you, you must show remorse for your cold-blooded crime." Judge Bevan sentenced Harney to death and the murderer later was hanged.

THE KILLER POET

A young man with a love of poetry shoots dead a young woman with whom he is infatuated and turns the gun on himself.

Mabel Elizabeth James was an attractive young woman with curly blonde hair. She was a country girl living in Melbourne and, like many country girls of the 1920s, was shy and reserved. She had left her home in Maryborough to look for work in the city and secured a position as a housemaid at the St Ive's Guest House, Toorak Road, South Yarra. Poor Mabel James, just 20 years of age when she accepted the position, was not to know that her job would lead to her death at the hands of a crazed suitor.

One of her workmates was Cecil Ronald Leet, who had spent several years in the navy. He was a houseman at the guest house and fell instantly and hopelessly in love with Mabel. His infatuation was so intense that he drove Mabel to despair. He peppered her with declarations of love and wrote her passionate poems and letters. This situation lasted more than two years, until Leet resigned his position and went looking for work in rural New South Wales. Although he got a job as a boundary rider, he continued to bombard Mabel with letters and poems, even though she did her best to dampen his passion. However, Mabel made a fatal mistake in writing back to Leet and signing the letter with the words "your sincere friend". Leet rushed back to Melbourne in the belief he finally could win over young Mabel James.

Leet met up with Mabel in a Melbourne street on July 19, 1927, but the country girl again rejected his overtures. Next evening, Mabel was returning to her room at the back of the guest house when Leet jumped out at her. He was carrying a rifle and, after a struggle, Mabel was shot in the leg. Then, as she struggled to break free, Leet fired a shot into her head before turning the gun on himself. Leet, well-educated and the son of an Edinburgh University graduate, had bought the gun only the previous day. When police went through his pockets, they found the following poem he had written:

> Remember him thou leav'st behind,
> Whose heart is warmly bound to thee;
> Close as the tend'rest link can bind
> A heart as warm as heart could be.

A letter police found read: "The sound of your voice today sent a longing thrill through my feelings … You cannot conceive how deep my regard of you is and so I have your whole interests at heart. My whole thoughts are centred in you. I think of you everlastingly, day and night, until the tears well in my eyes." Leet signed off this undelivered letter to Mabel "God bless you, Chere Ange, Fraternally, Ron". Melbourne coroner Mr Berriman later found that Cecil "Ron" Leet was of "unsound mind" when he killed Mabel James and then himself.

POISON AT THE VICARAGE

A parson's young wife dies in agony in the Gippsland town of Omeo and her husband is charged with murder.

Parson's wife Ethel Constance Griggs died of arsenic poisoning in the tiny Gippsland farming town of Omeo on January 3, 1928 and, within weeks, her death was the subject of considerable speculation, not only in Gippsland, but also in Melbourne. Had Mrs Griggs been murdered, or had she committed suicide? Or was it an accident?

Mrs Griggs was the unhappy wife of Omeo's Methodist parson, Ronald Geeves Griggs, a man who wore his calling like a badge. He started studying for the Methodist ministry as soon as he returned to Australian from the battlefields of World War I and, at the same time, started courting Ethel White, the daughter of a Tasmanian farmer. They had known each other from childhood and, significantly, she was from a religious family. On completion of his theological studies at Queen's College, Melbourne, they were married. That was in 1926, shortly before the Methodist church appointed him licentiate (a preacher yet to be ordained) at Omeo. Griggs, then 26, and his wife, 20, moved into the tidy weatherboard parsonage and, two years later, their names would be known in every household in Victoria.

Although the Griggs' marriage was not an outwardly happy one, there was little reason to suspect that Griggs would fall prey to the sins of the flesh which he denounced with such vigour from the pulpit. However, soon after his arrival in Omeo he became infatuated with 20-year-old farmer's daughter Lottie Condon, a vivacious churchgoer. Griggs and the pretty Miss Condon were often seen together, invariably with the parson riding his motorcycle with the girl as a sidecar passenger. At first there was no hint that Mrs Griggs objected to the friendship and she even invited Miss Condon to stay at the parsonage for the final week of 1926. However, Mrs Griggs soon detected small signs of familiarity and affection and, at the end of the week, ordered the girl out of the parsonage, ending an outburst by describing Miss Condon as "a hussy".

Griggs denied to his wife that he had committed adultery and although he probably was telling the truth, it was not long before he and the delectable Miss Condon became lovers and he often stayed over at her father's farmhouse. This clandestine relationship lasted several months, the couple becoming more and more open and even seen cuddling in the bush surrounding Omeo.

When Mrs Griggs gave birth to a daughter, she hoped her husband would come to his senses, but it had the opposite effect and Griggs even sent mother and baby to Tasmania for a holiday. They were absent for almost six months and, during that time, Mrs Griggs even asked for a divorce. However, she returned with her baby on December 31, 1927, in perfect health. Yet she was dead just three days later. In fact, Mrs Griggs complained of being ill almost as soon as she returned to the parsonage. She vomited and Griggs later prepared her a snack, including a pot of tea, Mrs Griggs drank some of the tea and ate half a sandwich, but would not drink any more of "that tea".

Mrs Griggs' condition worsened and, soaked in sweat, she eventually went into a state of delirium and a doctor was called twice. At one o'clock on the morning of January 3, Griggs knocked on the door of neighbour Herbert Mitchell to ask if he could have a look at his wife as she appeared to be in a very heavy state of sleep. Mrs Griggs was dead and when the doctor arrived, Griggs asked him: "Will you give a death certificate?" He said he could not bear the thought of his wife's body being "cut up" (for an autopsy).

Mrs Griggs was buried without the slightest police suspicion, but the swishing of tongues reached even Melbourne and the police and the Methodist hierarchy became increasingly interested in Mrs Griggs' death. The church acted first and asked Griggs to attend a special committee meeting at which he was asked about his relationship with Miss Condon. Griggs swore he had not committed adultery but, meanwhile, the police started investigating Mrs Griggs' death and sent a vastly experienced officer, Detective Sergeant Daniel Mulfahey, to Omeo. Almost immediately, Miss Condon admitted she and Griggs had been having an affair and she even told the detective the parson had promised to marry her.

Griggs eventually was charged with his wife's murder and Mrs Griggs' body was exhumed to become the subject of scientific testing for arsenic poisoning. The examination was conducted by State pathologist Dr Crawford Mollison, while portions of the body were tested chemically by government analyst Mr C.A. Taylor for traces of arsenic. The poison, apart from being virtually tasteless, can be administered with lethal results through several doses. The amount of arsenic found in Mrs Griggs' body could have killed several oxen.

Although the prosecution had no difficulty proving that Mrs Griggs died of arsenic poisoning, it was another matter to prove that Griggs had deliberately poisoned his wife, especially as police could not find a trace of arsenic at the parsonage. This was a critical point as Griggs claimed that his wife had committed suicide and once had tried to throw herself on to a fire. The problem with this theory was that it would have been impossible for Mrs Griggs, on her deathbed, to remove traces of poison.

The evidence at Griggs' trial in Gippsland was conflicting and the jury, after a long deliberation, returned to say it could not agree on a verdict, although 10 of the 12 were in favour of convicting Griggs. A new trial in Melbourne was ordered and crowds packed the Criminal Court to hear evidence in this sensational case. Again the evidence seemed conflicting, with even a suggestion a pharmacist might have made a mistake with a prescription, and the jury deliberated for six hours and

20 minutes before returning its verdict. Griggs gripped a rail as he turned his head to hear the jury foreman say "not guilty". Griggs' ordeal was over.

Griggs, of course, wanted to marry Miss Condon, but Miss Condon's father shifted the family to New South Wales and the parson never saw his beloved Lottie again. Although Griggs was found not guilty of murdering his wife, his life was almost beyond repair. He tried to enter the Presbyterian Ministry in South Australia under a false name but, after being uncovered, faded from public record, presumably under another assumed name. Griggs might have been found not guilty of poisoning his wife, but his own life had been poisoned and the mystery of Ethel Griggs' death has gone to the grave with her.

THE MOTOR-CYCLE SHOOTING

An Adelaide policeman is shot dead as he and colleagues were moving a motor-cycle for security reasons.

Three Adelaide detectives were called to check on a disturbance on the night of February 23, 1929, when they came across a motor-cycle left in Grenfell Street, in the city. The trio, in attending the disturbance, asked if anyone knew who owned the motor-cycle. No one seemed to know, so the police officers decided that because it was late at night they would move it so that the owner could claim it later. Two of the policemen rode off slowly, but were approached by a man who thought they were stealing it. Constable John Holman started explaining that they were police officers when the man, who claimed it was his bike, fired a shot which hit Constable Holman. Although severely wounded, Holman tried to chase the gunman. More shots were fired and, finally, the gunman went to ground after being hit in the leg by shots fired by another policed officer.

Constable Holman later died in hospital and the gunman, John McGrath was charged with murder. He pleaded not guilty at his trial, claiming he did not know Constable Holman was a policeman. He also claimed that he earlier had been in a row and that he thought someone was out to get him. McGrath also told the court that he always carried a pistol as he was a wharf labourer and needed the firearm for self-defence. McGrath was found guilty and although sentenced to death this later was commuted to life imprisonment.

GOODBYE FROM TOM

Seven charred bodies are found after a fire rages through a timber house near Devonport, Tasmania

A farmer on February 26, 1929, noticed smoke coming from the home of the Archer family in the tiny township of Don, near Devonport, Tasmania. It was early morning and the flames had already turned the timber house into an inferno. Neighbours stood helpless as the flames devoured the building and its contents. Later, after the flames had died to an ember, it was discovered that the entire Archer family of husband, wife and five children had died in the flames. Seven charred bodies were found in the ruins of the homestead.

Andrew Thomas Archer, 49, had shot himself in the head and his body was found on the floor, resting on a shotgun. Olive Archer, also 49, had died in her bed, along with her 10-month-old daughter Nilma. The bodies of the other children, Lexie (11), Phyliss (eight), Murray (six) and Trevor (five) were found in another bedroom. All bodies were charred beyond recognition, but it was presumed that Andrew Archer had shot his family dead before setting the house on fire and then turning the gun on himself.

A note found outside the house in a leather bag was final proof. It was written by Archer, known as Tom, and said simply: "The bag and contents is from Tom. Goodbye." The word "goodbye" trailed off and was unfinished. It later was learned that Archer had visited a doctor two years earlier about fears he would have "mental troubles".

THE SICK KILLER

Arnold Karl Sodeman earns himself a reputation as one of Australia's most notorious serial killers following a string of murders in Melbourne.

A young married man used to sit with his wife by an open fire during the 1930s and stare into the glowing embers. Arnold Karl Sodeman, a quiet family man, would be lost in his own thoughts and his wife Dolly did not think twice about his quiet moods as she knew he was a good husband, an adoring father and a good worker. She also knew her husband liked to have a drink and even came home from work worse for wear, but he never laid a hand on her. Mrs Sodeman could never have guessed that her husband was brooding over murders he had committed.

Sodeman's trail of human destruction started on the afternoon of November 9, 1930. The young labourer had been drinking in the Orrong Hotel, Armadale, before he decided to take a walk. As he walked through Fawkner Park in the inner Melbourne suburb of South Yarra, he saw a group of girls playing and chasing each other. Something clicked in the 30-year-old's mind and he asked 12-year-old Mena Griffiths to run a message with him.

The girl and Sodeman caught a bus to the southern suburb of Ormond and he took her into an empty house in Wheatley Road. He later said: "I took her in there. The back door was open. We walked in and as soon as we got in I seized her by the throat. I then let her go and she fell on the ground. Looking down on her my memory came back and I said, 'My God, she's dead. I have killed her'."

After the killing, Sodeman made his way home to his wife and two-year-old daughter Joan, whom he idolised. He had murdered for the first time and the thought chilled him to the marrow. Meanwhile, Mena's body was discovered the following day and police charged a young man with the murder. Fortunately, this man had an alibi and had to be released.

Sodeman's second victim was 16-year-old Hazel Wilson, whose body was discovered on a vacant allotment in Oakleigh Road, Ormond. The girl had last been seen on the night of January 9, 1931, two month's after Mena Griffiths' death. Hazel's brother found his sister's body the following day and police were horrified as they knew they had a serial killer at loose.

The killings stopped but, on New Year's Day, 1935, Sodeman struck a third time. This time the victim was 12-year-old Ethel Belshaw, who was just one of thousands who had attended a huge picnic at the Gippsland beach resort of Inverloch. Sodeman, who again had been drinking, took her by the throat and strangled her while she was on a walk with the man who already had killed twice. A massive search was launched for the missing girl and her body was discovered the next day.

The next, and final, murder in the Sodeman tragedy was in Leongatha on December 1, 1935, almost a year after Miss Belshaw's death. Sodeman, who was working at a road camp near Dumbalk, strangled six-year-old Jane Rushmer, a friend of his own daughter Joan. Little Jane Rushmer, who knew Sodeman well, had asked him to give her a dink on his bike. Sodeman, who again had been drinking, took the little girl to her death. The body was dumped and a huge police investigation was launched when it was realised the strangler had struck again. This time, however, there were several leads, including the sighting of the little girl being dinked on the bike.

Sodeman returned to his work camp after the killing of Jane Rushmer and heard his workmates talking about the murder. Sodeman flew into a rage and walked off. One of his workmates pondered over this strange behaviour and decided to call the police. Confronted, Sodeman confessed almost immediately and he was charged with murder.

Sodeman's trail was before Justice Gavan Duffy and jury at the Melbourne Criminal Court from February 17, 1936. The case created enormous public interest, with Sodeman pleading insanity, with part of this plea allowing the Crown to refer to the three earlier killings. The jury found Sodeman guilty of murder and Justice Duffy sentenced him to death. Sodeman appealed to the High Court of Australia and the Privy Council, but to no avail. He was hanged at Pentridge on June 1, 1936. A post-mortem examination revealed that Sodeman had been suffering from a brain disease known as leptomeningitis, which partly explained the murders. Simply, Sodeman was unable to account for his actions after a few glasses of beer as delicate brain tissues would be inflamed. This verified what he had written to his wife while he was in jail, that "the drink seems to affect my brain in some way, unknown to me, and this dreadful craze to destroy comes over me". Sodeman should not have been hanged and his letters to Dolly showed that he lived in mental torment, sickened by the knowledge that he had killed during his moods when drinking.

GATHER YE ROSEBUDS

A Victorian farmhand bashes and kills a frail widow and robs her of a small amount of money before fleeing to Melbourne.

Elderly widow Mrs Elizabeth Little was devoted to her grown-up family of a son and two daughters. She lived with one of her children, veterinary surgeon George, on the family's 80-acre farm near the tiny Victorian township of Stratford. Mrs Little was well known in the district as her father had been a prominent Gippsland grazier. The family was well liked and respected by the entire community. It was a happy family and, on the afternoon of October 16, 1930, Mrs Little collected roses from her garden for a visit to one of her daughters. Sadly, Mrs Little, who was not in the best of health, was never able to deliver the roses as she was strangled in the middle of her preparations for the visit.

The alarm was raised by 15-year-old farmhand Daphne O'Brien, who told Sale police that she had been attacked by another farmhand, 18-year-old Herbert Donovan, who had rushed into the farmhouse and demanded to know there Mrs Little kept her money. Miss O'Brien told police that Donovan then went into a bedroom and took three five-pound notes from a bag before attacking her and then forcing her to harness Mrs Little's horse to a buggy. He drove off in a cloud of dust and Miss O'Brien called police.

Mrs Little's body was found in a cowshed on the property. Her hands were tied behind her back by a cow halter and her legs were also tied. There were facial wounds, but police were unable to tell at first how Mrs Little had died. Their immediate concern was to apprehend Donovan, who had abandoned the horse and buggy outside a house in Sale. Police believed he had caught a late afternoon train to Melbourne and police throughout Victoria were given his description.

The first break in the hunt for Donovan was when a taxi driver told police he had driven a young man answering Donovan's description to Melbourne. The driver, Norman Buntine, told police that he found the young man sitting in his cab outside the Star Hotel in Sale at 5.15pm on the day of Mrs Little's death. The young man asked Buntine to drive him to Melbourne and explained that the charge would be one shilling a mile. The youth made no objection to this, but later asked Buntine to pull over at Berwick so that he could hitch a ride to the city. A truck driver, Eric Craig, told police that he had taken the young man to the Dandenong railway station and it was assumed that Donovan caught a train to Melbourne from there.

Police launched a massive manhunt in Melbourne and, at one stage, three police groups were investigating sightings of the wanted young man. Then, on the morning of October 18, two days after the killing, two police officers noticed a dishevelled young man coming out of the Exhibition Gardens close to the city. They watched the youth for several minutes before apprehending him and taking him to police headquarters.

Donovan made a statement confessing to killing Mrs Little and was charged with murder. Evidence was given at his trial at the Criminal Court, Sale, that he struck Mrs Little six times around the head before she died of asphyxiation caused by a handkerchief placed in her mouth. Donovan was found guilty of murder and was sentenced to death. However, this sentence was later commuted to one of life imprisonment after killing a frail widow for just 15 pounds.

BLOOD AND BONES

The discovery of blackened human bones just outside Canberra sets police a puzzle.

Farmer Bernard Cunningham was mustering sheep near Bungendore, about six miles from Canberra, on November 21, 1931, when his dogs yapped and ran into a hollow. Cunningham went to investigate and came across the remains of a huge log fire. He at first thought it was a swaggy's camping site, until he noticed the dogs tugging on bones at the bottom of the ashes. Cunningham bent over, retrieved a bone from one of his dog's mouth and immediately recognised it as human.

Cunningham called police and Detective Sergeant Tom McRae and a team of investigating officers rushed to the scene. They verified that the blackened bones were human and started sifting ashes. Police worked in relay, sifting and re-sifting, looking for even the tiniest clue. Their task looked hopeless, especially when hours of work netted them just a handful of objects, including the molten remains of a gold watch, a belt buckle, a few teeth, a button, several coins and the barrel of a small calibre rifle.

Meanwhile, forensic experts told police the human remains were male and that death had occurred on or around October 27 – more than three weeks before Cunningham's dogs had tugged at the bones. Police had little to work on, so decided to re-sift the ashes and this time they found a small key. More importantly, it carried a code number which, under microscopic examination gave a reading and eventually led to the identification of the body.

However, was it murder or suicide? Police at first thought it was murder as the bones were found under logs used in the fire but, if it was suicide, the man would have had to shoot himself and ask an accomplice to stoke the fire for him. It sounded an implausible theory, but police had to keep an open mind on this intriguing case.

Police eventually discovered that the key had been made in Britain but, undeterred, called in Scotland Yard and police eventually were able to trace the key to the Sydney YMCA, who had given the key to a young man for a locker. It had been used by 21-year-old Sidney James Morrison, captain of the club's basketball team. Significantly, Morrison had not been seen since October. Police, convinced that the remains at

Bungendore were those of Morrison, asked Professor A.N. Birkett of the Sydney University's Aanatomy Department to make a study of the bones. He reported that they were of a young man of approximately six feet and well built – precisely Morrison's physical description.

When detectives started questioning Morrison's friends, they learned that the missing young man had resigned his job as a clerk on October 6, 1931, and had told friend he was going to the bush to prospect for gold. It seemed out of character for Morrison but, even more disturbing Detective Sergeant McRae was told Morrison had been receiving psychiatric treatment. It seemed the young man had an inferiority complex and kept telling relatives he lacked personality.

Police again turned to the suicide theory and suggested that Morrison had lit the huge fire before killing himself so that he would fall back into the flames. This theory gained favour when police investigations proved that Morrison had bought the rifle at a well-known Sydney sports store at the time of his resignation from work. It therefore appeared Morrison might have planned a bizarre suicide. The problem with this theory was that there were logs found across Morrison's blackened bones and traces of blood were found on dry branches several yards from the fire. And what about tyre marks near the scene? Who would have driven a car to and from the death scene?

Police painstakingly continued their investigations, but could not trace Morrison's movements over the last weeks of his life. The only sighting of him in the two weeks before his death was by an old prospector who had seen him with two men in a car about 20 miles from the death scene. Police were never able to trace these men and although an inquest was held into Morrison's death, the coroner returned an open finding. The mystery remains: suicide or murder?

BURIED UNDER CONCRETE

An Adelaide woman disappears, but her body later is found buried under concrete in her own backyard.

Mary Edson was a tall, extremely attractive young woman with dark brown bobbed hair in the fashion of the 1930s. She was 22 years of age, had a 16-month-old daughter and lived in the Adelaide suburb of Knoxville when she disappeared without trace on May 18, 1931. Next-door neighbour Mrs Grace Lindsay was deeply puzzled and repeatedly asked the young woman's husband about the disappearance. Lawrence Edson (known to his friends as Lawrie), a 28-year-old tram conductor, at first told Mrs Lindsay that his wife had run off with another man and that he had been left to care for their daughter, June. Mrs Lindsay thought this strange, although she knew that the Edsons had quarrelled many times over the previous months and that Mary Edson had adopted a "beaten dog" attitude.

Other neighbours started gossiping but Edson merely changed his story and told everyone that his wife had died. After all, he even had a letter which Mrs Edson's sister Dorothy Malycha was alleged to have received from an H. Wilson in Melbourne telling her of her sister's "death" on June

19, 1931. He showed this letter to anyone who cared to read it as "proof" that his wife had died. However, the writer of the letter indicated it was not known at which cemetery Mary Edson was buried.

If neighbours had been suspicious before, they now were determined to get to the bottom of Mrs Edson's mysterious disappearance. They reported the matter to police, who went to Edson's home on July 23 to investigate. Edson, a former police officer, showed police the letter (another two supposedly from Melbourne had been burned, he told them) and then made a statement at the City Watchhouse about how his wife had left him in May and then had died in Melbourne. Police were far from convinced and told Edson they would detain him until officers had had the opportunity to search his home and dig through his garden in Lestrange Street. Edson immediately stepped out of the room in which he was being questioned and on to a landing where he pulled an automatic pistol from his suit pocket and shot himself in the head. He died in hospital two days later without regaining consciousness. Police therefore were left with a riddle, but they knew that the thought of digging up Edson's garden had terrified him.

Naturally, police were convinced that Edson had buried his wife in the garden at their Knoxville home and rushed there to put their theory to the test. Neighbours had told them they had seen Edson working feverishly in the tiny shed at the back of the garden. Edson, who once had kept a pet wallaby in the shed, had been seen taking grapevine cuttings there. They were still there when police investigated, but when they swept them aside they discovered freshly laid concrete. Police used a pick to dig up the thin layer of concrete and found part of a woman's robe. They dug a little further and found a woman's body in a grave just a few inches deep. The body, after preliminary examination, was taken to the Adelaide morgue for identification. This horrendous responsibility fell on Mrs Edson's other sister, Miss Rose Malycha, who made a positive identification.

Police continued their investigations and discovered that at least the first half of the letter allegedly sent from Melbourne had been written by 14-year-old John McMahon, who had identified Edson from a newspaper photograph. McMahon told police that Edson had asked him to write a letter and had provided him with a fountain pen for the task. However, the boy said he stopped writing halfway through the letter as he had become suspicious. Police were unable to determine who wrote the rest of the latter.

Meanwhile, Adelaide newspapers had a major sensation on their hands and pumped it for all their worth. Reporters even tracked down Edson's first wife, even though few people suspected he had been married twice. The first Mrs Edson gave birth to a son in 1922 and Edson used to visit her to pay maintenance money after their divorce in 1928.

An inquest into the deaths of Edson and his wife was held in Adelaide from July 29, 1931. The acting coroner, Mr F.C. Siekman, presided over a case which held South Australia spellbound and, naturally, everyone wanted to know the cause of Mrs Edson's death. There had been reports that Edson had bashed her to death, but although there was some bruising to the body, Mrs Edson had been strangled, possibly with a pyjama coat which appeared to be wrapped around the neck. But why did Edson strangle his wife? No one will ever know, although an Adelaide newspaper reported at the time of his death that he had recently had given a young woman an engagement ring and had promised to marry her. The newspaper reported that detectives had interviewed a woman at Reynella, but there was no mention of this at the inquest and the mystery remains in one of Adelaide's most infamous murder-suicide cases.

DEATH AT THE CHURCH FETE

A group of youths attack a younger group after a church fete and one boy later dies in hospital.

Arthur Head, 16 years of age, was a youth with a future. He had just graduated with honours in the Leaving Certificate from Coburg High School, Victoria, and was only two months into his chosen career of teaching at Moreland State School. He regularly attended Bible classes at Coburg Presbyterian Church and in all ways was regarded as forthright, honest and destined for a brilliant career.

Head had helped organise stalls at a church fete in 1931 and was with several of his friends when a gang of youths pelted them with tomatoes late on the evening of Thursday, March 26. Insults were hurled back and forth and two of the church group ran out of the church grounds, on the corner of Sydney Road and Munro Street, to remonstrate with the tomato throwers. A police constable also was called, but the whole affair was forgotten within minutes – at least by the church group.

Later, around midnight, Head and three companions – 16-year-old Gordon Andrews, 16-year-old Allan Beaver and 14-year-old Oswald Beaver – left to walk home together. However, they had not gone far before they came across an older group of youths. Then, at the corner of Harding and Fowler Streets, one of the youths punched Head to the ground; he had been struck to the back of the head. The others scattered, although Andrews also took a blow to the head.

Andrews, after outrunning his pursuers, climbed a fence and asked the occupant of the house if he could make a telephone call to the police. There was no phone in the house, so he was directed to a neighbour's house, where he failed to make contact because the party line was in use at the time. Andrews therefore decided to return to where he and his friends had been attacked and was shocked to see Head unconscious on the roadway. There was blood coming from his ears and mouth and, although he was rushed to the Melbourne Hospital, he died four hours later. Four youths – Leslie Lewis (17), Allan Ward (18), Richard Jackson (19) and Ralph Fuller (19) – later were charged with murder.

The inquest into Head's death was held before the coroner, Mr D. Grant PM, who was told that one of the group of youths had jumped forward to punch Head on the back of the head. Andrews told the coroner he believed Ward had struck the blow and although Ward at first denied this, he said in a second statement that he wanted to have "first hit" in any fight.

At the trial of the four accused youths, government pathologist Dr C.H. Mollison said Head had taken seven blows to the head and that the skull had been fractured, possibly through falling on the footpath. Chief Justice Sir William Irvine explained to the jury the difference between murder and manslaughter and, when the jury returned from its deliberation of three and a half hours, found Ward and Lewis guilty of manslaughter and Fuller and Jackson not guilty. The jury added a recommendation of mercy and both Ward and Lewis were sentenced to four years' imprisonment, with 20 strokes of the birch each.

A POINTER TO DEATH

A Perth man shoots his family dead over his depression through being unemployed for months.

Roderick Davies, his wife Dorothy and five children in 1931 were living on a dole of two pounds and nine shillings (about $4.90) a week. Davies, 36, had been unemployed for months, but no one knew that this had depressed him to the point of suicide. On August 21, 1931, neighbour Samuel Knifton found a note on the back door of the three-bedroom Davies home in the Perth suburb of Carlisle.

The note read: "Mr Knifton, please open the door." Knifton believed the note was part of an elaborate joke, but once he stepped into the house he realised that the note had been a pointer to death. Mrs Davies, 35, was dead in a bed in the kitchen, a bullet through her head. Next to her, sitting in chair, was the body of her husband, who also had a bullet wound to the head and had a revolver in his right hand. Knifton did not want to see any more and rushed to the police, who discovered the bodies of the five Davies children – Rita (14), Robert (12), Dorothy (10), John (six) and Alfred (five months) – in two of the house's three bedrooms. The bodies of John, Rita and baby Alfred were in one room, with the bodies of Dorothy and Robert on stretchers in another room. All had bullet wounds to the head and there were no signs of struggle.

Detectives concluded that Mr and Mrs Davies had made a suicide pact, with Davies shooting the children and then his wife before turning the gun on himself. Detectives reasoned that Mr and Mrs Davies had dragged a bed from the back porch into the kitchen and the husband then sat by his wife's side before killing her and then himself. Police also believed the children had been drugged before being killed. Police found 19 discharged cartridges in the house but, strangely, not one neighbour had heard a single shot. The nearest house might have been more than 15 metres away, but the shots which wiped out an entire family exploded without notice or comment. The house had been well stocked with food, but the Great Depression had taken its toll on Mr Davies' mental health and pride. Sadly, it was 14-year-old Rita's birthday the day she and her family died.

THE MAD GENERAL

A man known as "the mad general" kills two police officers at Bondi Junction in 1931.

Residents of the Sydney suburb of Waverley knew John Thomas Kennedy as "the mad general" because of his obsession with marching drills and target practice with a .22 rifle. Kennedy twice was rejected for service in the Great War because of varicose veins and this affected him to the degree that he felt persecuted, while neighbours thought he was a returned serviceman who had not recovered from shellshock. On the morning of January 3, 1931, Kennedy, armed with his rifle, refused to pay for a packet of cigarettes in busy Bondi Junction and told the shopkeeper to "charge them to the Governor".

The shopkeeper immediately rushed out to notify traffic policeman Constable Norman Allan that Kennedy not only was armed but appeared to be in a dangerous mood. Constable Allan sprinted after Kennedy and then told him it would be best if he handed over the rifle. Kennedy fired three bullets into the policeman's chest and then warned bystanders to "back off". With Allan dead in the street, police reinforcements were sent to the scene. However, Kennedy raced home and locked the front door before a police officer, Constable Ernest Andrews, unlocked the back door of the cottage and confronted Kennedy. Two shots rang out and, as the policeman clutched his stomach, Kennedy stabbed him to finish him off. A policeman at the front of the cottage spotted Kennedy through the shattered glass of the front door and shot Kennedy in the stomach. "The mad general" died in hospital a few hours later. Thousands lined the streets for the funerals of Constables Allan and Andrews.

DEATH OF A BEAUTY QUEEN

A young man takes a Sydney beauty queen on a picnic and their bodies are discovered separately.

Frank Wilkinson could not help but be attracted to vivacious Dorothy Denzil, a slim, elegant brunette. The attraction seemed mutual and anyone who saw them together would have said they made an ideal couple. Frank, a 26-year-old printer, called for Dorothy at her home in the Sydney suburb of Burwood on April 5, 1932, and the pair headed off in his red Alvis car.

They did not return that night and police, after launching a search, discovered that a man in a red Alvis had been seen buying petrol at Bankstown. Significantly, witnesses earlier had seen a large bundle in the back of the car, but when the driver pulled in for petrol there was no bundle. No trace of either Williams or Denzil was found for six days, with Williams' body discovered on April 11 when a policeman stumbled on an old bush path and noticed blood in a clearing. To his horror, the policeman found three fingers reaching grotesquely out of a dirt mound. Wilkinson wad been buried in a shallow grave, his face bashed in and the back of his head blown open by a shotgun round. Fired from point-blank range.

Police combed the bush area for any trace of Denzil and, four days after the discovery of Wilkinson's body, one of the searchers found a suspicious mound of freshly turned earth in a bush clearing. It was Dorothy Denzil's bush grave and medical evidence revealed that the 21-year-old, who had won a beauty contest just a few weeks before her death, had been raped.

Just as police were wondering how to detect and arrest the killer, they were told that a man known as William Fletcher had called on an acquaintance and had an injured right hand. Witnesses earlier had told them that the man they had seen with Wilkinson's car had an injured right hand and, more importantly, the name William Fletcher was an alias used by well-known petty criminal William Cyril Moxley.

A massive police hunt for Moxley was launched and he finally was arrested after he stole a bicycle and tried to flee from the Sydney area. In fact, he managed to get right across Sydney before police confronted him in the bush. Refusing to surrender, Moxley jumped into a gorge and was captured only after a police officer jumped after him and overpowered the fugitive.

Moxley stood trial in Sydney two months later and pleaded insanity. He said that although he went into the bush with the intention to rob someone, he had not planned rape or murder. He claimed that Wilkinson rushed him during a robbery and was flattened for his bravery. He tied the young couple up and took them to a shack and from there, he claimed, his memory was blank. Moxley's plea failed and he was hanged on August 18, 1932.

THIRD TIME 'LUCKY'

A Melbourne man goes on trial three times on the one murder charge, of killing his mother.

It is most unusual for anyone to face three trials on the one charge – especially a murder charge – as 48-year-old Walter James Henderson did in Melbourne in 1932. Henderson had been a farmer at Lake Boga, but had shifted to the Melbourne bayside suburb of Albert Park at the suggestion of his mother, Mrs Sarah Jane Henderson, in 1932. The home Mrs Henderson found was in one of Melbourne's most fashionable streets, St Vincent's Place, which was close to where Mrs Henderson's daughter lived, in Kerferd Road.

Henderson, who had been married but was living apart from his wife, was at home on the afternoon of July 27, 1932, when he found his mother seriously injured at the foot of the stairs. He called to next door neighbour Mrs Elizabeth Meurillian for help and advised her to get a doctor.

Mrs Henderson died in hospital that evening, but this was no surprise as the 63-year-old had suffered horrific head injuries. Although Henderson said his mother had obviously fallen down the stairs, police were suspicious as a broken, bloodstained hammer was found in the home and there was blood everywhere, with clothing scattered about the floor.

An inquest was told that Mrs Henderson had suffered five lacerations to the left side of the head and there was a laceration of the brain, even though the skull was not fractured. Henderson was sent for trial before Justice Mann and jury at the Criminal Court, and the jury deliberated for more than five hours before sending a message to the judge that it could not agree upon a verdict. Despite asking the jury to persist in trying to come to a decision, it returned an hour later to say there was no agreement.

The retrial was heard in October before Justice Wasley and the evidence presented was almost identical to what was presented at the first trial, with Henderson insisting he had done nothing to cause his mother's death. The jury retired at 1.25pm on October 20 and returned six hours later to say it could not agree on a verdict. Henderson was remanded for a third trial at the Criminal Court the following month.

Henderson's third trial was before Justice Macfarlane and jury, with most of the same evidence paraded again. By this time the Melbourne public had tired of the mother-son case and little of the evidence was reported. After all, the public had read it all before. The third trial lasted three days and, in his summing up, Justice Macfarlane told the jury that it had been the responsibility of the Crown to prove that Mrs

Henderson had died in the way alleged. Henderson again gave evidence and said he had heard his mother fall and had gone to her aid, hence the blood on his clothing. Two highly qualified medical experts also gave evidence that Mrs Henderson's injuries could have been caused by a fall down the stairs. The jury retired at 5.45pm on November 23 and returned three hours later with a "not guilty" verdict.

THE WRONG BODY

A mystery develops after the body of the wrong man is buried following a huge fire at a hut in central Victoria.

William Griffenhagen was a quiet young man who desperately wanted to get married to his sweetheart and settle down at his bush allotment a few miles from the old Victorian mining city of Bendigo. He lived in a hut on the property with his uncle, James Pattison, a well-known local prospector. Griffenhagen, 26, spent most of his time clearing the land of scrub. Pattison, 68, was a dedicated fossicker who lived in the hope he one day would come across a nugget as big as his fist.

Both men were seen on Sunday, October 1, 1933, and Griffenhagen's friends became worried when they had not seen him for several days after that date. Police were informed and two constables went to Griffenhagen's hut, only to find it had been severely damaged by fire. Inside, the constables found a huge pile of ashes in the centre of the log and mud hut. There, under the charred and fallen corrugated iron roof, they found a body. But was it that of Griffenhagen or that of his uncle?

The local police informed the CID and Detective Bill Sloan took charge of the investigation. His first task was to sift the ashes for clues to enable him to identify the body. Police found a pair of badly damaged spectacles, a ring, a watch, a rabbit trap and several misshapen household items. The ring was an obvious clue which several people identified as belonging to the old man. The spectacles, however, puzzled police and locals. Neither Griffenhagen nor his uncle wore glasses. Besides, the old man had only one eye. It therefore was impossible to identify the body as it had been reduced to a blackened skeleton. The discovery of the ring therefore assumed critical importance and, because of its identification as Pattison's, police assumed that the body found in the ashes was that of the old man.

Pattison was buried with all due ceremony, but locals questioned the identification. This prompted Detective Sloan to investigate further, especially as there was no sign of Griffenhagen. Had he, too, been murdered? If so, where was hid his body? Was robbery the motive? Had the old man found a nugget and had Griffenhagen murdered him for financial gain? Or had someone murdered them both? There were many, many questions to be answered, but police first had to positively identify the body.

Detective Sloan made further inquiries and police and 50 volunteers scoured the surrounding countryside and re-sifted the ashes. Their efforts were rewarded with further clues, including the metal buckle from a belt worn by Griffenhagen and three brass caps from shotgun cartridges. Police now were convinced there had been a case of mistaken identity, especially when they learned Griffenhagen did, in fact, wear glasses but had tried to keep this a secret. Finally, Pattison wore false teeth and none had been found in the ashes.

Then, on November 9, Axedale bee-keeper Fred Bennett discovered a man's body in scrub along the banks of the Mosquito River, a few miles from Griffenhagen's hut. The body was identified as that of Pattison. It was badly decomposed, but the thumb and forefinger of the right hand were missing and Pattison lost these digits in an accident many years ago. A suicide note revealed that he had shot himself. But why? Had he killed his nephew in a rage? Pattison, in his suicide note, made no mention of his nephew.

That might have been the end of the "Wrong Body" case if it had not been for a strange confession several months later by a young man who claimed to be Griffenhagen. The young man walked into the Swan Hill police station and told the wife of a senior constable that he was "wanted for murder". She tried to detain him but he rushed out of the police station and said: "I cannot wait any longer; I have to do myself in."

The man claiming to be Griffenhagen went straight to the flooded Murray River, boarded a motor launch and jumped into the river mid-stream. He drowned but police discounted the possibility that the young man was Griffenhagen as there was a big difference in height and build. Griffenhagen almost certainly was shot by his uncle, who then turned his nephew's hut into a funeral pyre. But why? And who was the mysterious young man who drowned himself in the Murray River? These mysteries are unlikely ever to be solved.

THE HUMAN GLOVE

The body of a middle-aged man is discovered in the Murrumbidgee River at Wagga and the body is identified by a "glove" from missing skin.

There have been few more gruesome murder cases in Australia than the notorious "Human Glove" case, which was a sensation during the Depression years. The drama unfolded on Christmas Day, 1933, with the discovery of the body of a middle-aged man in the Murrumbidgee at Wagga. The body, which had been in the water for several weeks, was so badly decomposed that facial identification was almost impossible. The only other hope of early identification seemed blocked when it was discovered that the skin was missing from both hands, making fingerprints impossible.

Police were still trying to solve that problem when they had the luckiest possible breakthrough. They discovered a "human glove" in the same river and immediately concluded it was missing skin from the decomposed body. They were right! A policeman volunteered to use the "glove" over his own hand for a set of fingerprints to be made, police then identifying the body. The dead man was bushman Percy

Smith, who lived with another river identity named Edward Morey.

Police charged Morey with murder and the case was expected to reach an uncomplicated conclusion. However, during Morey's trial, at which evidence was given that Smith was killed with an axe found in Morey's possession, one of the prosecution witnesses was shot dead. The victim was Moncrieff Anderson, who was the husband of a woman in love with Morey. Morey was found guilty of murdering Smith and although sentenced to death, the penalty was not carried out. Mrs Anderson, who claimed that her husband had killed Smith, later was convicted of manslaughter and sentenced to 20 years' jail. Mrs Anderson was trying to protect Morey by claiming that her husband was the real murderer. Her bid to clear him only added to the already tragic aspect of the case.

A GANGLAND MURDER

A career criminal is gunned down in a dark Melbourne alley, victim of a gangland execution.

Well-known criminal James John, who lived in the inner Melbourne suburb of Collingwood, was a gambler and a stand-over man with few friends and many enemies. John, 24 years of age, had been at a gambling club in the city early on the morning of September 22, 1933, and decided to walk to his lodgings through the Exhibition Gardens. He was with a group of men, but two of them left John and another man, Jack Chrisfield, at the top of Nicholson Street.

John and Chrisfield kept walking through the dimly lit streets of grimy Fitzroy when they noticed a cream-coloured car about 100 yards behind them. The car appeared to be cruising behind them and, every time the two men stopped, the car also would stop. John and Chrisfield therefore decided to "lose" themselves in a narrow, tree-lined street which offered them plenty of cover in case there was trouble.

The two men walked into Gore Street and watched in horror as they saw the car's headlight beams turn the corner in their direction. The car moved to within yards of the two men, but Chrisfield decided that discretion was the better part of valour and stepped aside. John was left alone as a man jumped out of the car from the front passenger seat and, with a handkerchief over his face, started firing at him. John had no chance of escape and was riddled with bullets, the gunman even pumping three bullets into John as he lay in the gutter. Chrisfield watched in horror as the gunman climbed back into the car and the driver sped away.

Police were called to the scene, but John was in a critical condition and died under examination at the Melbourne Hospital. Later, at the inquest into his death, government pathologist Dr C.H. Mollison said John had been shot five times. One bullet had pierced his right side and had passed through his chest and liver, another had passed through the middle of his back, the third had lodged in the middle of the back, the fourth had entered the left buttock and the fifth in the right buttock.

Chrisfield told coroner Mr Grant PM that he was unable to identify the gunman or the driver of the car. However, Chrisfield knew he had to be extremely careful about what information he gave to the police and the coroner and, when asked at the inquest whether John had any enemies, he replied: "I do not know." Police already had a suspect, well-known criminal James Robert Walker, and Chrisfield was asked if Walker looked like the gunman. Chrisfield had no hesitation in replying "no".

The inquest was also told salesman Henry Mitchell had made a statement alleging that Walker and a man named Bert Adams had approached him at the Mentone racecourse on September 23 (the day after John's killing) and asked him if he would like to earn 100 pounds. He alleged in the statement that Walker asked him to get rid of a gun, but later recanted that statement. Walker also had an alibi and the coroner had no option but to declare that John's killer could not be identified.

Walker, one of the most infamous criminals of his era, was given a life sentence in 1953 for the shotgun death of a man in St Kilda and, just one year later, shot himself dead during an attempted escape from Pentridge. He left behind numerous notes, a chronicle of crime. In these notes he referred to John's killing and said he confronted the young gambler with "an ice-cold rod in my right hand". Police therefore were able to close the file on John's killing, even though they already knew Walker was the gunman in the cream-coloured car.

SPIRIT VOICES

A woman axes her two children to death in their Melbourne home after hearing "spirit voices" and then slashes her own throat with a razor.

Anyone walking past the Turner home in the quiet suburb of Glen Iris in the east of Melbourne would have rated it one of the prettiest in the neighbourhood. A white weatherboard cottage with a neat picket fence, it could have been a setting for domestic bliss. Instead, the home in Tooronga Road became a slaughterhouse on April 30, 1934.

Boilermaker David Turner left for work early that morning, leaving his wife May at home with their two children. When Turner returned home just after 6pm, the house was in total darkness and the key was missing from its usual hiding place. Turner sensed something was wrong, and on eventually entering the house, saw his wife on the floor in a pool of blood. He ran to a neighbour's to get help but, when he returned, found his daughters Martha (10) and Eliza (eight) with serious head wounds. The two girls, who had been bashed with an axe, died from their wounds and their 35-year-old mother had an extremely deep wound to the throat and slashed wrists.

Mrs Turner was rushed to the Alfred Hospital, but also died of her wounds. At an inquest into the Glen Iris tragedy the following month, the Alfred Hospital's Dr Eric Langley told the coroner, Mr McLean PM, that he had asked Mrs Turner who had attacked her. The dying woman, whose vocal cords had been severed, was unable to answer but wrote a note for the doctor. Mr McLean was handed this note, but refused to release its contents.

Later, Constable M. Murphy told the inquest he had found an exercise book in the Turner home and one entry read: "After being followed all day I wish to die with my children." Another entry said "spirit voices" had been speaking to Mrs Turner every day. Turner told the inquest that he and his wife had migrated to Australia from Scotland eight years earlier and that his wife's mother had died in a mental institution. He also said his wife had become increasingly morbid and fascinated with spiritualism. The coroner found that Martha and Eliza Turner had died of injuries inflicted by their mother "while of unsound mind" and that Mrs Turner had died as a result of self-inflicted wounds.

DEATH OF A PROSTITUTE

A prostitute is battered to death in her Melbourne flat, but her killer has never been brought to justice.

The bludgeoning death of pretty, vivacious prostitute Jean McKenzie in her flat in the bayside Melbourne suburb of St Kilda in 1934 almost certainly will not be solved. McKenzie, 24 years of age and elegantly slim and well dressed, was not your average prostitute. She loved the good life and appeared to live in a fantasy world in which princes came to the rescue of fair young maidens. McKenzie was waiting for her prince to arrive on a white stallion one dark wintry Melbourne night when she was killed in the most brutal of circumstances.

She was at home in her flat on the night of June 7, 1934, when there was a knock at the door. Her landlord, Henry Bloom, later heard McKenzie arguing with a man for more than an hour, but could not catch the words. Earlier, a tall, fair-haired man in an overcoat had been seen entering McKenzie's ground-floor bed-sit. The row died and Bloom saw the tall man leave McKenzie's flat and walk through the front garden. He thought no more of the row until the next morning when there was no sign of McKenzie. Bloom's wife investigated and, when she opened the door to McKenzie's flat, found the young woman dead in the hallway.

McKenzie's head had been battered with a huge piece of wood taken from the fireplace. It was an horrific sight, with McKenzie dressed only in a white singlet. There was blood everywhere and it was obvious McKenzie had struggled with her killer. Furniture had been knocked over and clothing was strewn around the room. Police also disclosed the killer had washed his hands before leaving the flat. He obviously was a cool customer and the nature of the crime suggested to police that McKenzie had been executed.

Police learned that McKenzie had used a number of aliases in her career as a prostitute, but also suggested she might have used these aliases to hide her real identity in fear of someone and was trying to lose herself in the seedier parts of St Kilda. One theory was that McKenzie had been bashed to death by a pimp, but police were unable to prove this. An inquest was held at the Coroner's Court five months after McKenzie's death, but police were forced to admit they did not have enough evidence to identify the killer. The coroner had no alternative but to return a finding of murder against "a person unknown". It is now likely McKenzie's killer has gone to the grave with his secret.

THE PYJAMA GIRL

The burnt body of a young woman is found in a culvert on farmland near Albury and her identity remains a mystery for a decade.

Young farmer Tom Griffiths was walking along the Albury-Howlong Road in the Riverina on the crisp, sunny morning of September 1, 1934, when a prize bull he was leading became restless. As Griffiths approached a culvert, the bull pulled away. It was then that the young man spotted a bundle and, when he went to investigate, he was horrified to see the body of a young woman badly damaged by fire. Police in Albury, just four miles away, rushed to the scene.

The body of the woman had been pushed up the entrance of a water pipe and police knew from the state of the body that identification would not be an easy task. She had been battered about the head and there was a bullet wound near the right eye, apart from the burns. Clues included a burnt bag and towel used to cover the body and, most important of all, cream and green pyjamas with a large dragon motif. It therefore was only natural that the dead woman became known as "the Pyjama Girl".

Police knew the woman was in her mid-20s, well-nourished and had had considerable dental work on her teeth. However, police just could not identify the body, despite seeking the assistance of forces around the world. Police even moved the body to Sydney University and had it placed in a special formalin bath for preservation. Hundreds inspected the body, but there were no positive leads. Several people told police the dead woman resembled Linda Agostini, nee Platt, the wife of Italian migrant Antonio (Tony) Agostini. Although Agostini admitted his wife was missing, he said the body was not that of Linda.

A coroner's inquest was held at Albury in January, 1938, and information on the dead woman was provided by Professor A.N. Burkitt, professor of anatomy at Sydney University, who said the Pyjama Girl was probably English or European and aged about 25. After hearing the evidence, the coroner, Mr C.W. Swiney, said: "I find that between August 28, 1934, and August 31, 1934, a woman whose name is unknown, aged about 25 years of slight build, height around

5ft 1in, with brown hair and bluish-grey eyes, whose partly-burnt body was found at a culvert on the Albury-Corowa Road, about four miles from Albury on September 1, 1934, died from injuries to the skull and brain apparently maliciously and feloniously inflicted upon her, but where and by whom such injuries were inflicted does not enable me to say."

The break in the case came 10 years after the discovery of the body when Police Commissioner William J. Mackay assigned a new team of detectives to re-examine the file on the murder mystery. An old photograph of a group of women led to the name of Linda Agostini resurfacing and in March, 1944, Police Commissioner Mackay now believed Tony Agostini, a waiter at the fashionable Romano's restaurant, had some involvement in the Pyjama Girl mystery. Mackay asked Agostini to see him and the waiter went to police headquarters as soon as he finished work. When confronted, Agostini, who had arrived in Australia in 1927 and had married English woman Linda Platt three years later, admitted he had been keeping a secret for 10 years. He made a statement which said he and his wife had argued and after he had gone to bed, she produced a gun and held it to his head. There was a struggle and the gun went off. Agostini said he panicked and decided to drive off with the body, with "no plans ... just running".

However, the statement did not say how Linda Agostini suffered such serious head wounds and, after being taken to the culvert in Albury where the body was found, Agostini said he had dropped the body, hence the injuries. A second coroner's inquest was held at Albury and, despite claims that the body was that of a woman named Anna Morgan, Agostini was committed for trial.

That trial opened in the Supreme Court of Victoria in Melbourne on June 19, 1944, before Justice Lowe. Agostini's defence was that he did not intend killing his wife , but that she died accidentally. The jury deliberated for two hours and found Agostini not guilty of murder, but guilty of manslaughter. He was sentenced to six years' jail, but the judge commented: "I think the jury were merciful to you." Linda Agostini finally was laid to rest at the Preston Cemetery on July 13, 1944, just 13 days after her husband was sentenced to prison. Agostini served three years and nine months of his sentence and then was deported to Italy.

RELEASED TO KILL AGAIN

A mentally disturbed Melbourne wharf labourer slaughters his family 10 years after killing his first wife.

When wharf labourer George Bromell found the bodies of an entire family in a small, weatherboard shack in the inner Melbourne suburb of Richmond on May 30, 1934, he could hardly have suspected he would be unlocking the door to one of the greatest controversies of the era. Bromell had not seen his workmate and neighbour Frank O'Brien for several days and decided to enlist the help of another neighbour to break into the house in Bosisto Street. Bromell feared the worst as O'Brien had been severely depressed and had told his wife that he did not have enough money to buy food for his wife and three small children. However, Bromell was not prepared for the ghastly scenes he saw in O'Brien's house. O'Brien, 59, his wife Rose, 39, and their three children were all dead – their throats slashed.

All the bodies were found in the tiny bedroom at the front of the house. The bodies of O'Brien and his wife were fully dressed in their double bed and the bodies of the three tiny children – Owen (three), Joan (two) and Marie (nine months) – were found in their bloodstained cots. The scene was heart-rending. O'Brien obviously had wiped out his entire family in desperation over his fear that he was not able to support them and left a suicide note in which he feared he soon would not be able to work.

Melburnians were still trying to come to terms with the tragedy when the Melbourne *Herald* on June 1 broke the news that O'Brien appeared to be the same man who had killed his wife 10 years earlier. The newspaper suggested that a photograph of O'Brien's body had been taken at the city morgue and that officials from the Mont Park Mental Home had "expressed the belief that he was identical" to the man who had killed his wife.

Fingerprints were taken of the dead man and these later matched those on police files. O'Brien therefore was the man who had killed his wife 10 years earlier, and the slaying of his family and his subsequent suicide opened a very nasty can of worms for Victorian government officials. The Inspector General for the Insane, Dr W.E. Jones, admitted that O'Brien had been charged with murder in 1924 and had been committed to an asylum (Mont Park) during the Governor's pleasure. O'Brien had been found to be suffering from "transitory confusional insanity". He was a highly educated man and, according to reports, his mental and physical conditions improved dramatically at Mont Park.

O'Brien, in fact, had been a school teacher who was found not guilty of the murder of his wife at Mildura in 1924 because of insanity. He was released from Mont Park three years and eight months after being committed on the approval of the Attorney-General, the condition being that he reported monthly to Dr Jones.

At the inquest into the deaths of the O'Briens, the Coroner (Mr McLean PM) was told that Rose O'Brien herself had been a patient at Mont Park, but was "perfectly normal" after her marriage to O'Brien. However, the sensation of the inquest was when the medical superintendent of Mont Park, Dr John Catarinich, said he made a report on O'Brien in 1924 which read: "Under no circumstances would I suggest O'Brien ever again live with his children (from his first marriage), nor do I consider it safe to give O'Brien his liberty, even with restrictions."

Yet O'Brien was released, only to kill again in horrific circumstances and the coroner said: "In my opinion, the public is entitled to expect that when a person has been found not guilty of murder on the grounds of insanity, and has been committed to custody during the Governor's pleasure, ample precaution is taken to guard against any repetition of the homicidal act."

THE SHARK ARM CASE

A murder investigation is launched after a captured shark disgorges a human arm at a Sydney aquarium.

Brothers Ron and Bert Hobson wanted a star attraction for their aquarium at the seaside Sydney suburb of Coogee and decided that what they needed was a shark – a big shark. They therefore set up lines off Maroubra on April 17, 1935, and waited. Within 14 hours they had hooked a monster of the seas – a four-metre tiger shark, so big that it had to be lifted out of the sea by block and tackle.

The shark went on display at the Hobson aquarium but, a week later, a young man named Narcisse Young was watching the huge shark become distressed and making what appeared to be coughing movements. The shark then shuddered hugely and disgorged an object and considerable brownish liquid. The shark had vomited up a human arm.

The arm, severed from the shoulder, had a rope knotted with a clove hitch around its wrists. The arm was tattooed, with the figures of two boxers outlined in red and blue and this tattoo convinced police that identification would be relatively easy. But, just to make sure, police scientists took a "human glove" from the hand. The fingerprints from this "glove" proved beyond doubt that the arm was from well-known criminal James Smith. The problem for police was whether Smith was dead or alive as the arm was not conclusive proof of his death.

Police eventually learned that Smith had been holidaying near Port Hacking with a man named Patrick Brady, a shearer and noted forger. They were convinced Smith, who ran an SP book in Sydney, had been involved in criminal activites and had been "silenced". A boat-builder named Reginald Holmes told police Smith had had a row with Brady over a forged cheque and that Brady had said "I have done for him". When Holmes asked Brady about the body, he replied: "They won't get that. I dumped him in a tin trunk outside Port Hacking."

Brady, on May 17, 1935, was charged with Smith's murder, but three days later there was another sensation when police were asked to intercept a motor launch which had been running out of control on Sydney Harbour. They investigated, boarded the boat and found Holmes at the helm with a bullet wound to his head. However, the wound was not serious and Holmes later told police that he had tried to commit suicide.

An inquest was held into the shark arm case and Holmes' evidence would have been critical – except that he was shot dead in a car near the Sydney Harbour Bridge less than 12 hours before the opening of the inquest on June 12. He had been shot three times in a circle around his heart. Two men were charged with his murder, but both were acquitted in the great side-show of the Shark Arm Case.

The inquest was conducted by the Sydney City Coroner, Mr Oram, and evidence was given that the arm had not been amputated by a surgeon, but done roughly. Following the inquest, Brady was sent for trial. However, Justice Jordan said a conviction on the evidence presented could never be allowed to stand and directed an acquittal. Brady died in 1965 at 71 years of age, still insisting he did not kill Smith. The most logical explanation is that someone killed Smith and stuffed his body into a sea trunk, with not enough room for the entire body. The left arm therefore was hacked off, tied to the chest and thrown into the sea. The huge tiger shark then gobbled up the arm with glee, ripping it from the trunk. It certainly was a one in a million chance that the shark would be captured, let alone vomit up the arm of a murdered man. The gruesome mystery remains.

DEATH AT THE VICARAGE

A convicted housebreaker bashes an Anglican vicar to death during a robbery gone wrong.

Parishioners at St Saviour's Anglican Church, Collingwood, loved their vicar, the Reverend Harold Cecil. He truly was a man of the people and worked tirelessly for the many poor in his parish. The quietly-spoken, bespectacled Reverend Cecil tended his flock like the best of shepherds and even went without to help the more unfortunate. He lived an extremely modest life at the vicarage facing Smith Street, in one of Melbourne's toughest neighbourhoods. However, there had been persistent rumours that the Rev. Cecil was a very wealthy man and that he had a fortune hidden at the vicarage.

The rumours were only partly true as although the Rev. Cecil had invested wisely in a farming venture in the 1920s, there was very little money at the vicarage, let alone a fortune in hidden gold. However, every petty criminal in the neighbourhood in 1935 knew that the Rev. Cecil was making his annual Christmas appeal and that there had been a number of donations.

Of course, the Collingwood parish was a poor one and the donations amounted to no more than 35 pounds in cash and cheques. But they were desperate times and the Rev. Cecil should have been more careful when he opened his door to a stranger on December 12, 1935. The Rev. Cecil's body was discovered by church officials the next day.

The vicar had been bashed over the head with a heavy object. The autopsy revealed 17 separate wounds to the head, with a number of other cuts and abrasions to the body. Robbery was the obvious motive as the vicar's wallet was missing, the pockets had been torn from his trousers and two watches (on chains) and a gold chain were missing. One of the watches had an unusual design and police reasoned that if the murderer tried to "hock" it they would make an early arrest. The only significant clue at the ransacked vicarage was a signed notice-of-marriage certificate dated December 12. It was almost certain that the killer had used the notification of marriage to get into the vicarage, and it had been signed Francis Edward Loyne or Layne.

Police next day found a blood-splattered spanner wedged between the brick chimney and the weatherboards at the old vicarage. A pattern on the spanner matched perfectly with the Rev. Cecil's head wounds. The murder weapon and the marriage certificate were to become vital clues in the apprehension of the killer. However, police investigations ran into a dead-end, even though the signature on the certificate was photographed and printed in Melbourne newspapers. Police even checked with signatures at Pentridge in the hope they would be able to match one with the one on the certificate.

The investigation stalled for several weeks, until a detective recalled that a petty criminal once signed the Pentridge record as Frank Lane. Police therefore kept a close eye on 29-year-old Edward Cornelius, who often used the name Frank Lane as an alias. Besides, a South Yarra jeweller had bought the Rev. Cecil's missing gold chain from a young man whose description fitted that of Cornelius. More importantly, the handwriting on the receipt book was similar to the signature on the wedding certificate at the vicarage.

Cornelius was arrested at his home in East Melbourne on February 12, 1936. He had been released from Pentridge only a short time before the vicarage murder after serving three years for housebreaking. Cornelius broke down under police questioning and confessed to the murder of the Rev. Cecil. He told police he went to the vicarage to ask about a wedding certificate purely as an excuse to prepare for a future housebreaking but, after walking away, remembered that the vicar had not closed the front door. Cornelius returned and was rifling through doors when the vicar confronted him. The pretty criminal said there was a struggle and he hit the vicar several times with a spanner.

Cornelius was found guilty of murder and sentenced to death. Although he appealed the sentence, he was hanged at Pentridge on June 22, 1936. He spent much of his time at Pentridge in the exercise yard with serial killer Arnold Karl Sodeman (see 1930 – The Sick Killer).

SUFFER THE LITTLE CHILD

A mother inexplicably kills her nine-year-old son with an axe during what appears to be a nervous breakdown.

Little Allan Richter, just nine years of age, was allowed to stay at his home in the Melbourne suburb of Moonee Ponds one day in March, 1935, because he was too ill to go to school. He spent the morning with his mother and grandmother, but neighbours heard piercing screams from the Richter laundry just before noon. One neighbour rushed to investigate and found the grandmother, invalid pensioner Mrs Mary Egan, in a terrible state of confusion. She told the neighbour that Mrs Alma Richter had confessed to killing her son. The neighbour immediately called police, who found the boy's body in a pool of blood in the laundry shed at the back of the house. He had been hit several times across the neck and head with an axe and he had all but been decapitated.

The bloodstained axe was found in the laundry shed. Mrs Richter was sobbing uncontrollably in her bedroom, where she was interviewed by police. At the inquest into Allan's death, before Deputy Coroner Mr Haser PM, Mr John Richter said that for several months his wife had been approaching a nervous breakdown. He said she had suffered from delusions and was worried that "something terrible" would happen to her sons (the Richters also had an 11-year-old boy, Leonard).

Mrs Richter had been having medical treatment, but her husband never suspected that she would have such a tragic and total mental breakdown. Neighbours told Mr Hauser that Mrs Richter had been a devoted mother and was particularly house-proud. Mr Hauser found that Allan Richter had died from injuries inflicted by his mother at a time when she was "of unsound mind". Mrs Richter was later placed in a mental hospital.

THE LIMBS IN THE YARRA

Two boys find two legs and two arms in a sugar sack floating down Melbourne's Yarra River.

It was described in a Melbourne newspaper headline of the time as a "Ghastly Discovery". It was March 29, 1937, and Melbourne buzzed with excitement for several weeks after the finding of a woman's severed arms and legs in the Yarra River. Two boys were playing on the banks of the river near the Morell Bridge, Richmond, when they noticed something floating in the water near a stormwater drain. The boys investigated and were horrified when they noticed a human leg protruding from a sugar sack. They ran screaming for help and hailed down passing motorist Mr Elvin Heyre, who took one look at the decomposing contents of the sack and drove to the city, where he stopped traffic policeman Constable J. Wardle, who later pulled the sack and its grisly contents from the water.

The sack contained two arms and two legs, and an immediate inspection revealed that the dismemberment had been expertly done with a sharp instrument. The arms had been amputated at the shoulder joints and the two legs at the knees. Police took the limbs to the city morgue, where they were examined by the government pathologist, Dr R.J. Wright-Smith. Police had no idea of whether they would find the head or the torso, and this made their task of identification almost entirely reliant on Dr Wright-Smith's work. His preliminary investigation revealed that the limbs were from a woman aged between 30 and 40. Dr Wright-Smith also concluded that she was well nourished and had four vaccination marks at the top of her right arm. The pathologist told detectives working on the case that the woman had been dead about three weeks and that the body had been dismembered about a week after death. Dr Wright-Smith also told police that the body had been drained of blood and this in itself made his task extremely difficult. However, the doctor was able to remove a "glove" of skin from the right hand for fingerprinting, although the left hand was too badly decomposed for prints.

Police dragged the Yarra but hauled in only the corpses of cats, dogs and rats. The case eventually was referred to the Melbourne City Coroner, Mr Tingate PM, who gave the police as much time as possible to solve the mystery. However, an inquest finally was held on June 3, 1937, and although police evidence was presented, it was impossible to identify the body or cause of death. It also was the first time in Victorian legal history that an inquest was held without either the head or torse being "viewed" by the coroner. The inquest was adjourned indefinitely and the mystery remains.

TRACKED DOWN

A young labourer is tracked down after he sexually assaults and kills a 12-year-old girl in South Australia.

When the body of 12-year-old schoolgirl Elizabeth Mary Nielson was found in scrub at Monash, South Australia, on June 5, 1938, there was enormous public outrage. The body had been pushed into a sack after the girl had been sexually assaulted and strangled. Police investigated every possible angle, but without result – until they called in a black-tracker, Jimmy James.

The black-tracker had almost immediate success, being able to trace 27-year-old labourer James Mark Watherston to his home. The police hunt and investigation was over as Watherston confessed to killing Elizabeth Nielson and was sent to trial for murder.

The young labourer was found guilty and sentenced to death. He was hanged at the Adelaide Gaol at 9am on August 11, 1938, and the Adelaide *Advertiser* reported: "As is usual when an execution takes place, there were a few morbid sightseers outside the gaol … they comprised men and youths, and a young woman who had arrived there on a bicycle and was chatting to two mounted constables on duty about 100 yards from the gaol gates."

THE HAUNTED HOTEL

Two men are axed to death at an old derelict hotel in the Victorian gold town of Dunolly.

The derelict Windsor Hotel in the old gold-mining town of Dunolly in central Victoria was the near-perfect "doss" house. Its walls might have been cracked, its timber flooring might have been uprooted in places and many of its windows broken, but it was home to a colony of tramps. In October, 1938, at least five men were living there, despite the lack of running water or anything resembling comforts. It was little more than a roof over the head and some Dunolly residents claimed the hotel, which was de-licensed in 1914, was haunted.

Those living at the derelict hotel included pensioners Frederick Douglas, Charles Bunney and Robert Gray, along with a younger man, Thomas Johnson. On Monday, October 3, 1938, 61-year-old Bunney (a World War I veteran) and 73-year-old Gray were seen alive for the last time. The following day, Douglas suggested to Johnson that "something has happened" to Bunney. They later made a search for him and found a trail of blood on a landing outside one of the rooms. However, the door to the room was padlocked so, in a state of near panic, Douglas ran to a young local to ask him to climb a wall to peep through the room's window.

The young man climbed up to the window and, peering through the dust and gloom, was able to see what appeared to be two men lying on the floor. He yelled to the men in the room. But there was not the slightest movement from them. Police were called immediately and when the door was broken down, found the bodies of Bunney and Gray. Both men had been bludgeoned to death with an axe, which was still in the corner of the room. The wounds were horrific, with both men having their skulls split wide open.

Police soon deduced that Bunney had been killed on the landing and had been dragged into the room where the body was discovered. Bunney had taken one savage blow to the head and police found his bloodstained felt hat on the landing. He obviously had been wearing the hat when attacked as it had a long gash across its crown. Gray was killed in the room and had taken two heavy blows to the head. The axe, covered in blood, was the most obvious clue and suspicion fell first on its owner, fellow squatter Lancelot Cazneau. However, Cazneau told police he had lent the axe to Johnson and, further, that Johnson had tried to borrow money from several of the men. Suspicion therefore fell on Johnson, who had disappeared.

Police immediately launched a manhunt for Johnson, but were still in the process of distributing a description of him when he walked into a police station at Dandenong, on the other side of Melbourne, and confessed. He told police that he was asleep at the old hotel when Gray woke him by hammering at some floorboards. Johnson said he picked up the axe and smashed the old man over the head. Bunney, who went to investigate, copped the same vicious treatment.

Johnson, 40, stood trial at Ballarat before Justice Lowe and jury, and the court was packed as Johnson, wearing a dark brown suit, was led to the dock. Johnson's only explanation for attacking his fellow residents was that he had lost his temper, killed Gray and then attacked Bunney, who had witnessed Gray's killing. The jury found Johnson guilty of murder and he was sentenced to death. Although the case provoked considerable public debate and the Victorian government was urged to have Johnson undergo psychiatric examination in an effort to have the sentence commuted to one of life imprisonment, he was hanged at Pentridge early on the morning of January 23, 1939.

THE PAYROLL KILLING

The owner of a shoe factory is shot dead in a bankroll robbery in an inner Melbourne suburb.

Brothers Frederick and Clarence Sherry had started a small shoe-making business in the inner Melbourne suburb of Abbotsford in 1924 and, despite the Great Depression, this business flourished and, by 1938, the Sherry Shoe Company had more than 30 employees. This, of course meant a substantial payroll in an era before pay cheques, direct entry or even security services. On the other hand, Melbourne was a much quieter, more peaceful city in those days and armed robbery was relatively rare. The Sherry brothers were confident they would be able to draw the wages from their bank and deliver it to employees without any trouble. That view changed dramatically in March, 1938, when two masked men tried to hijack the Sherry wages. One of the men drove a car alongside the Sherry car and the other masked man leaned out of a window and pointed a pistol at Clarence Sherry, "Hand over your money," the bandit shouted as he waved the gun. Sheery sped away and, for several months, a police escort was used for the delivery of wages.

Time passed and the brothers felt the attempted hold-up had been a one-off incident and they therefore decided to discontinue the use of the police escort. It proved to be a fatal mistake for 46-year-old Frederick Sherry, a father of six. On September 1, 1938, Sherry and company secretary Henry Thomas drove to the Northcote branch of the Commercial Bank and withdrew more than 600 pounds. Thomas stuffed the notes into his coat pocket and threw a large number of coins into a bag. Sherry and Thomas left the bank and were confronted by a youth. However, neither was aware there would be another hold-up and got into their small brown car. They were followed by a blue tourer with two men in the front.

Sherry drove his car down High Street and around a curve along a railway line into Queen's Parade, not far from the factory. The blue tourer pulled alongside and Sherry and Thomas saw two men with handkerchiefs pulled over their faces. The two shoe factory men must have thought they were in some weird Hollywood drama, with the men in the car playing the baddies in a Western movie. They were forced to pull over and asked to hand over the bag. When Thomas pressed his hand on the horn to attract attention, the man holding the pistol fired a shot which pierced the window and cut Thomas about the face. Sherry bravely grabbed the gunman's hand and struggled for several seconds before opening a car door and running down a street.

The gunman followed him and, when Sherry fell, shot him through the heart from almost point-blank range. The bandit turned to a gathering crowd and, waving the pistol, warned them to keep away. He then rushed back to the blue tourer, insisted Thomas hand over the bag and made his escape with the driver. Sherry had been fatally wounded and, after struggling a few paces, fell onto the pavement with blood spurting from his chest wound. The blue tourer later was discovered in a northern suburb, torched to destroy clues.

Police had a fair idea of the identity of the bandits and, five days later, made their first move. A 22-year-old, Selwyn Wallace, admitted he had been involved in the hold-up, but insisted he had not been responsible for shooting Sherry. Then, with Wallace's help, they tracked down a man in Queensland and labourer Herbert Jenner, 23, and Wallace were charged with murder.

They stood trial before Justice Gavan Duffy at the Criminal Court just three months after the shooting. Although Jenner was the man who fired the fatal shot and

Wallace was still in the car at the time of the cold-blooded shooting, both men were found guilty of murder and sentenced to death. However, the judge told the jury that its recommendation of mercy because of the youth of Jenner and Wallace would be conveyed to the Executive Council. Both sentences were commuted to life imprisonment, with no benefit of remission. Both men spent almost 20 years in maximum security at Pentridge before Jenner was transferred to the Corriemungle prison camp in Western Victoria, while Wallace was transferred to the French Island prison farm in 1958. Both were freed in October, 1959.

AXED TO DEATH

A farmhand attacks a brother and sister with an axe at a New South Wales farmhouse.

When Dulcie Summerlad left her farmhouse at Tenterfield, New South Wales, to visit her mother in January, 1939, she had no idea she would return a few days later to a scene of absolute horror. Miss Summerlad returned to her orchard property on the morning of February 4 and was surprised when no one approached her with the usual family greetings. It was deathly quiet. Miss Summerlad lived with her brother Eric, 26, and sister Marjorie, 33, with Eric running the property and Marjorie acting as her brother's housekeeper.

Dulcie Summerlad opened the front door of the farmhouse and stepped inside. She immediately saw the blood-stained body of her sister and, in horror and fear, started calling for her brother. There was no answer. Fearing the worst, Dulcie immediately headed for the verandah, which her brother used as a bedroom. There, Eric, was on a bead, his head soaked in blood. The young farmer was not dead, but critically wounded. Dulcie called the police and an ambulance rushed her brother to hospital, where he was admitted in a life-threatening condition.

The murder weapon obviously was an axe found leaning against the front of the house. It also was obvious that the brother and sister had been savagely hit with considerable force, Marjorie dying immediately. It also was thought her brother would not survive the axe attack. Police, meanwhile, soon realised that farmhand John Trevor Kelly was missing, along with the Summerlad utility. Police launched an immediate search for Kelly, 24, and notified police stationed in a wide radius of the murder scene.

Kelly had driven from Tenterfield to Brisbane, where he rented a room in the suburb of Spring Hill. A wanted man, he was too scared to venture from his room, but was arrested just 14 hours after the axe attacks.

Kelly originally told police that Eric Summerlad had sacked him on Friday, February 3, and this led to the axings. However, Kelly later changed his account of events and said he attacked Marjorie first after he had made sexual overtures to her, even though she was engaged to be married to a local farmer. She called for her brother and Kelly hit him with his fists before going outside and returning with an axe.

Summerlad made a remarkable recovery and told police he could not recall the attacks as he was sleeping at the time. Kelly had been drinking on the night of the murder and his plea at his trial was that of insanity. He told the jury: "I am sorry for what I have done." However, he was found guilty and sentenced to death. The case was appealed to the High Court of Australia, but the sentence stood. Kelly's last chance was for the State Cabinet to give him a reprieve, but the Cabinet, under the leadership of Premier Alexander Mair, stood firm. Kelly was hanged at Long Bay jail on August 24, 1939.

THE NARROMINE BONES MYSTERY

Human bones are found in the remains of an old fire in western New South Wales and a trial is held without the discovery of a full body.

In May, 1939, drover Charles Carpenter came across drifter Albert Andrew Moss near Narromine on the western plains of New South Wales and noted a chestnut horse in Moss' possession. Carpenter immediately recognised the horse as one belonging to a friend of his, local identity Tom Robinson. Carpenter tackled Moss about the horse, sparking a row as Moss claimed he had raised the horse from a foal while Carpenter insisted the horse belonged to his friend Robinson.

Carpenter did a little snooping and discovered that Robinson had not touched his pension since January and therefore went to the police. Two police officers went to the Moss camp, but there was no sign of the drifter. He had obviously done a moonlight flit but, even worse, the police were told he had been seen in Robinson's company several months earlier. Before setting out after Moss, police decided to investigate his background and discovered he had been in and out of asylums and had been in trouble with the law, including convictions for forgery and attempted rape.

Police got their first lead in the case through sheer luck when they came across a piece of blotting paper among Moss' possessions and held it to a mirror to reveal the name T. O'Shea. However, there was no trace of another local identity, Tim O'Shea, and police now were worried about the safety of two men. Finally, there was another missing man – William Bartley - and police launched a massive search, raking over every camp fire they could find.

They eventually made a discovery on April 23 when they found fragments of bone at an old fire site three miles north of Narromine. Moss was charged with the murders of Robinson, O'Shea and Bartley but was tried before Justice Owen and jury only on the charge of having murdered O'Shea. The trial was sensational, apart from being one of murder without the discovery of a full body.

Moss earlier had attempted to convince police that he was mad and would pick thistles and pretend they were lettuces. The jury, however, took just 45 minutes to reach its verdict – guilty. The judge then sentenced Moss to death before praising police officers in charge of the investigation, saying their efforts had been responsible for having a daring criminal brought to justice. Moss' sentence was commuted to one of life imprisonment and he died in Long Bay jail in January, 1958.

ASHES DOWN THE SHAFT

A boring contractor in far west Queensland kills an old swaggy, burns the body, crushed the bones and scatters the ashes down a shaft.

Outback building contractor James Patrick Callaghan thought he had committed the perfect murder in 1940. He was convinced that it would be impossible for anyone to find the body, let alone press a charge of murder.

Callaghan employed an old swaggy, Bill Groves, to work on artesian bores on the Boorara Station, in far west Queensland. It was hot, dirty work and the nearest "civilisation" was hours away at Cunnamulla, where Groves sometimes went to slake his fierce thirst. Groves was something of a grizzler and would bend anyone's ear at any time about one complaint or another. His latest complaint, in July, 1940, was that he had been "diddled" by his boss, Callaghan. Groves complained that he had been underpaid and that he would have to do something about it.

No one in Cunnamulla took Groves' complaints seriously and the old man headed back to the Boorara Station to continue his work with Callaghan. He threw his swag on his back and marched into the dusty red outback, never to be seen alive again.

Meanwhile, Groves had complained to the Australian Workers' Union about not being paid for his work at Boorara Station. He told the union that he was owed more than 100 pounds and the union decided to investigate on behalf of their comrade. However, Groves did not reply to the union's letters and it was decided to send a representative to the Boorara Station.

Callaghan was surprised to see the union man, but told him that Groves had left the camp several weeks earlier with two men in a utility. Callaghan suggested that Groves was heading for Charleville. However, Groves had not been seen at Charleville for months and the union official became suspicious, especially as Groves had been owed a considerable amount in wages.

The union called in the police and Detectives Jack Mahoney and Frank Bischoff headed for the outback in an effort solve the mysterious disappearance of the old grizzler. Callaghan, to their surprise, welcomed them to his camp and then told the two detectives about how he had been glad to see the last of Groves, whom he described as "quarrelsome".

Callaghan was so convincing that most police officers would have closed the files, but Detectives Mahoney and Bischoff decided to make a thorough search of the camp. They began by raking over every old fire within miles. They dug up suspicious mounds and even sifted through the unburnt red soil for the slightest trace of Groves or any of his belongings. The search proved fruitless, until they found shreds of old clothing in a bore several days after they had started their search.

The detectives pumped deep down a bore and carefully collected all the sand and soil in a wooden frame and painstakingly sifted through every load. They were rewarded with the discovery of what appeared to be minute fragments of bone and ashes. However, the most important discovery was a pair of metal buckles which matched a pair from overalls Groves had bought at the Eulo general store near the Boorara Station.

Callaghan was arrested and immediately broke down and confessed to killing Groves. He insisted, however, that the old man's death was an accident and that he had acted in self-defence. He claimed that Groves had accused him of withholding his wages and then had attacked him. Callaghan said that in defending himself he struck Groves a fatal blow. Callaghan then stoked a fire to generate enormous heat and then pounded the dead man's bones on an anvil to reduce them to mere fragments before dropping all the remains down the bore.

The detectives gathered the fragments of bone, which were examined by the Queensland government pathologist and they were identified as human remains. The buckles helped identify Groves as the victim and Callaghan was convicted of murder and sentenced to life imprisonment.

THE TRAGIC LITTLE DIGGER

A returned serviceman stabs to death another veteran in a fight at Melbourne's Treasury Gardens.

Alfred Bye was as harmless as a fly, and not much bigger. He stood just 160cm (5ft 3in) and could have ridden as a lightweight jockey at just 45kg (seven stone). In fact, Bye once worked as a stablehand at Flemington racecourse for James Scobie, who had trained 1927 Melbourne Cup winner Trivalve. However, this was just one of many jobs Bye had during an almost nomadic existence between the two world wars.

Bye was born in the Victorian town of Yan Yean in 1899, the fifth in a family of 10 children. His father was a railway ganger and the family shifted home in the Gippsland area several times. Bye therefore never had a settled childhood and seemed to be dogged by bad luck. He was just four years of age when a horse kicked him in the head, leaving him with permanent damage to his left ear. Bye was also knocked unconscious at 10 years of age when struck on the head by a stone during childhood skylarking.

He left school at 14 years of age, barely able to read and write, and lived in Melbourne's western suburbs. He enlisted in the AIF in 1917 and served on the Western Front until gassed by the Germans and then repatriated to a hospital in England. On return to Australia, he again worked at a variety of jobs in Melbourne's west. Then, in 1930, he met the girl of his dreams, Amelia Ogier. They were engaged for some time, but the wedding eventually was called off because of Bye's fiancée complaining about his gambling. However, they remained good friends.

Bye enlisted in the Second AIF in 1939 for service with the Home Defence Force and literally bumped into his former fiancé in a Melbourne street in 1941. She was with another man, Gallipoli veteran Thomas Edward Walker, who also had enlisted in the Home Defence Force. Bye saw Walker as his rival for Miss Ogier's affection and he begged her to stop seeing her new boyfriend. Then, on September 27, 1941, Bye again saw Miss Ogier with Walker walking along Swanston Street on their way to the Princess Theatre. There was an altercation between Bye and Walker and, after Walker had seen Miss Ogier and her two nieces into the theatre, he went outside for a "smoke". It was the last she saw of him and he was stabbed to death several minutes after he left the theatre.

A pedestrian walking through the Treasury Gardens late that evening found Walker lying in a pool of blood in the middle of a public pathway leading from Gisborne Street to Gipps Street. The area, with its trees and tall shrubs, was badly lit – the perfect setting for a murder. Police were in the Treasury Gardens within minutes of the discovery of the body. The dead man obviously had prepared for a fight as his army jacket, bearing the 1915 Gallipoli ribbon, was underneath the body. Police also ruled out robbery as a motive as 18 shillings and sixpence in coins were found in Walker's pockets.

It did not take police long to work out who had killed Walker and Bye was arrested within 24 hours. At his trial in the Criminal Court, Bye, 42 years of age, denied he had killed Walker in a jealous rage and, instead, insisted the Gallipoli veteran had "rolled onto" the knife in their fight. Bye, seeing Walker mortally wounded, then went to a horse trough to wash blood from his trousers before catching a train to Bacchus Marsh, where he was arrested. Bye's trial lasted two days and the jury took just 45 minutes to consider its verdict – guilty.

Bye, who had never previously been in trouble with the law, was sentenced to death. Although there were considerable efforts to have this sentence commuted to one of life imprisonment, Bye was hanged at Pentridge at 8am on Monday, December 22, 1941.

THE BROWN-OUT KILLINGS

Melbourne is gripped by terror as a serial killer stalks the city during the darkest days of World War II.

Melbourne was a dark city in the autumn of 1942, the city's residents preparing for what they believed would be a long, cold war-time winter. It was during the autumn of 1942 that what came to be known as the "Brown-out Killings" started on May 3, the body of a middle-aged woman was found in the doorway of a house in Victoria Avenue, Albert Park, a beach suburb only three miles from the heart of the city. The woman had been bashed and strangled. Part-time barman Henry Billings, who discovered the body, later said: "At about 3am I saw an American soldier stooping in the doorway of a shop next to the hotel. He might have heard me because he got up and walked towards the corner, turning into Beaconsfield Parade. When I came to the doorway, I saw what I thought was a woman lying there. I struck a match. It was a woman. She was naked. Clothes had been ripped from her body and her legs folded back. I then roused the hotel and telephoned the police."

The police were horrified. The body was a pitiful sight, the poor woman being terribly wounded. Her legs were bruised and left temple had been fractured. The dead woman was identified as Mrs Ivy McLeod, 40, a woman described by friends as easy-going and happy. Mrs McLeod had been visiting friends in Albert Park and was on her way to East Melbourne, on the other side of the city. She was waiting for an all-night bus in Victoria Avenue when the killer struck.

Police were still puzzling over the murder when they were confronted by a second killing. This time the body was found almost in the heart of the city, in the doorway of a residential building in Spring Street, Melbourne, on the morning of May 9. Nightwatchman Henry McGowan noticed a bundle in the doorway at about 5.30am and immediately investigated. His horror can be imagined as he realised that the bundle was the corpse of a woman. As in the killing of Mrs McLeod, the second victim's clothing had been ripped and the dead woman was identified as Mrs Pauline Coral Thompson, 32, the wife of a Bendigo police constable. Mrs Thompson had seen her husband off to Bendigo that night and later was seen in the company of American servicemen.

Police investigating the killings now had a real lead, although finding the killer still was like looking for the proverbial needle in the haystack. There were thousands of American servicemen in Melbourne and the best lead police had was that the man they wanted to interview was "baby-faced". Then, the killer struck for a third – and last – time, on the night of May 18, nine days after the previous murder. The body of 40-year-old Gladys Hosking was discovered in Royal Park, just outside the city proper. Again, the dead woman's clothing had been ripped. The victim, who worked at the University of Melbourne as a secretary with the School of Chemistry, had been strangled.

Hosking's body was lying on its face, which was half-buried in yellow mud and slush produced by rain on heavy clay-like soil. This proved to be an excellent lead and an American solider had been apprehended at a camp entrance at Camp Pell, Royal Park, with yellow mud on his uniform. Police went to interview Private Edward Joseph Leonski, a 24-year-old who was quiet and unassuming when sober, but everyone's buddy when drinking. The baby-faced Leonski was something of a mother's boy and his family had a history of mental problems. Also, Leonski had been charged with rape in San Antonio, Texas, and although found not guilty, that acquittal led to his freedom and therefore indirectly led to the death of three women halfway across the world.

Leonski's court martial was not as dramatic as might be imagined. There were no histrionics and only the press and invited guests were allowed to attend. Leonski admitted to the killings, but his defence hinged on a plea of insanity. It was argued that he behaved perfectly when sober, but was the opposite when drunk. The court martial therefore was suspended for 30 days while three US Army psychiatrists examined Leonski to determine whether he was sane. However, he was found guilty and sentenced to death. He was hanged by American authorities at Pentridge on November 9, 1942. A report in the Melbourne *Herald* read: "Leonski came onto the scaffold and a black cap was put over his head, while his legs and hands were shackled. He maintained such an attitude of calm indifference to the end as to leave everyone associated with him aghast and amazed, Certainly no other murderer in the memory of Australian students of criminology was so obviously uninterested in his own fate." Leonski's body was shipped to the United States for burial.

THE TAXI MURDER MYSTERY

Melbourne cabbie Francis Phelan is shot three times after picking up passengers and his body dumped in a street.

Francis John Phelan was a driver with Red Top taxis and knew the ropes well. In fact, it was rumoured that Phelan had contacts in the black market and sly-grog rackets. Phelan, a former wharf labourer, was 32 and married with four children when he went on duty on February 6, 1943.

He seemed to be doing well early that evening and had been seen driving two American servicemen and at least one woman at about 8.30pm. Phelan's cab was later seen in St Edmund's Road, Prahran, an inner Melbourne suburb. The cab was stationary when shots were fired, with local residents reporting "loud bangs". The taxi sped off but stopped in Izett Street, Prahran, where Phelan's body was dumped. The cab then stopped at the corner of Commercial and Punt Roads, a distance of about half a mile. The cab was then abandoned and a solid man was seen getting out.

Phelan had been shot three times from behind. One shot went through his left shoulder, while the other two shots went through his chest, one passing through his heart. A newspaper report said: "Phelan's body was first seen at 9.30pm by a passer-by who told Prahran police that a drunken man was lying in the street. When two constables went to Izett Street they lifted the body and found Phelan's clothing saturated with blood and the corpse still warm. There was no sign of a struggle and nothing to indicate that Phelan had been shot where his body was found."

Police found empty shells on the front floor of the cab and were struck by one incredible coincidence. The sign "L.Phelan" had been painted in white on a front fence opposite to where Phelan's body had been discovered. However, the sign proved to be nothing more than a macabre coincidence, having nothing to do with the killing. Police were baffled, especially as they found 11 pounds, 15 shillings and sixpence in one of the dead man's pockets.

However, there was one significant clue – an American service cap found in the back of the murder vehicle. Police even had two names to work on as the cap bore two names, of Sergeant Robert Willard French and Sergeant John Freeman Martin, who were both at Camp Murphy, Melbourne. French told police he had sold the cap to Martin in 1941, while

Martin said he had lost the cap in America. Both Americans had alibis and police were forced to abandon that line of investigation.

Phelan's widow, Mrs Joyce Phelan, told the City Coroner, Mr Tingate, that her husband did not carry a gun and did not own one. She also said that her husband sometimes had trouble with his customers and, in such cases, did not hesitate in going to the police. Mr Tingate found that Phelan had been willfully and maliciously murdered by some person unknown. The taxi murder mystery has never been solved.

KICKED TO DEATH

An American paratrooper kicks and batters a women to death in a Brisbane laneway during World War II.

When two young Brisbane men, Stan Smith and Neville Hansen, entered a dark alley on the night of June 19, 1944, to retrieve a bike, they were horrified at what they saw stretched on the ground. It was the half-naked body of a young woman and it was obvious she had been bashed or even kicked to death as her face had been badly battered. Meanwhile, her killer had left behind a vital clue — a American paratrooper cap. The woman quickly was identified as Doris Roberts, who had been seen in the company of several American serviceman at a nearby café . A Private Avelino Fernandez, who had been seen without his cap, was apprehended just a few hours after the discovery of Roberts' body. He admitted he had been with a woman for sex in the laneway but added that he was leaving when he saw another man and woman enter the lane.

Finally, however, Fernandez admitted "hitting the dame". He even admitted to kicking and belting Roberts "all over" because she had made him feel cheap in asking for money. Private Fernandez was tried by court martial and although he insisted he was affected by alcohol, he was found guilty of the murder of Doris May Roberts. Fernandez' heavy military boots were produced at the court martial to show how much damage could be caused by repeated kicking while wearing these boots.

Although he was sentenced to death, Alverez believed he would escape the noose as capital punishment had been abolished in Queensland in 1922. However, he was transferred to New Guinea, away from Queensland jurisdiction, and was told on the evening of November 14, 1944, that he would be hanged at dawn. Alvarez later that night attempted to commit suicide by cutting his throat with a dinner knife. However, the wound was stitched and he was executed the following morning.

THE CHALK-PIT MURDER

A former leading politician is found guilty of murder after a body is found in a chalk-pit in England.

"Connoisseurs" of murder might be puzzled by the title of this segment, for the "Chalk-Pit Murder" is one of England's most infamous cases. However, it deserves its place in this book of Australian murders because one of the accused was a leading Australian politician. Thomas John Ley was a former New South Wales Minister for Justice and a controversial character in the world of political intrigue during the 1920s.

Ley, known as "Lemonade Ley" because of his temperance beliefs, left Australia at the end of his political career and took up residence in England. He lived in semi-retirement with his long-suffering mistresss Mrs Maggie Brook, who was considerably fitter than the grossly overweight Ley. Both were aged 66 but Mrs Brook was a relatively attractive woman, whereas Ley was a mountain of fat. This caused Ley much heartache as he became insanely jealous, regarding Mrs Brook as something of a personal possession. It might have been due to Ley's eventual impotence but, whatever the cause, the obsession led to murder.

The former politician believed that several young men were interested in Mrs Brook but particularly accused 35-year-old barman John Mudie, who had the gross misfortune to share the same lodging house with Mrs Brook at one stage in 1946. Mudie left the lodgings by the time Ley's jealousy had flared, but the former Australian political figure traced the harmless young barman to his new work place at Reigate, Surrey.

Ley then lured Mudie to a "party" in London on November 28, 1946. Mudie attended the "party", but discovered he was the only guest. Ley and two paid thugs, John Smith and John Buckingham, attacked Mudie, covering his head with a blanket before being left at Ley's mercy. A rope around Mudie's head apparently killed him, although it was not certain whether this was by design or by accident. Regardless, Mudie's body was placed in a shallow trench in a chalk-pit near Woldingham and the body was discovered two days later.

Ley and Smith were later charged with murder and both were sentenced to death. However, Ley by this time was desperately ill and escaped the hangman after being declared insane. He died a few months after his trial, while Smith's death sentence was commuted to life imprisonment.

THE "DINKY" KILLING

A five-year-old boy is taken from a street while riding his "dinky" bike and then is choked, kicked and bashed to death.

Little Alan Cooper, just five years of age, liked riding his "dinky" bike in a lane behind his house in the Sydney suburb of Crow's Nest. Alan was riding his "dinky" on August 9, 1946, when approached by a youth who later took the little boy to a nearby house. The youth, 18-year-old Alexander William Tipping, took Alan into his bedroom and attacked him, apparently without motive. According to evidence at Tipping's trial, the 18-year-old tried to choke the little boy, later bashing him with a flower pot and then kicking and punching him. Little Alan did not die instantly and was rushed to the Misericordiae Hospital after Tipping himself rang police. Alan was found suffering from severe head wounds under Tipping's house.

Tipping at first told police that he heard moaning and groaning from under the house and, when he investigated, discovered the badly injured boy. However, he then stated: "I'll tell you all about it – I done it. I bashed the kid. When I was lying on my bed I was thinking I would like to do something big and get away with it. I brought the little boy in from his "dinky", sat him on the bed and tried to choke him. But he was too tough. I took him under the house, bashed him with a flower pot and went upstairs. I heard him still moaning, so I went down again and punished him. Then I rang the police."

A jury could not agree on a verdict at Tipping's trial, but the jury at a second trial handed down a verdict of "insanity" and Tipping was detained at "the governor's pleasure". Evidence was given at the inquest into little Alan's death that Tipping had suffered from brain trouble from the age of three and four doctors told the jury at the second trial that the 18-year-old had contracted encephalitis at the age of three. Child Welfare Clinic psychiatrist Dr Irene Sabire told the court a person in Tipping's condition would not be able to distinguish between right and wrong.

MY CONSCIENCE IS CLEAR

A married Brisbane office worker becomes infatuated with a secretary, kills her and then hangs himself.

Convicted Queensland murderer Reginald Spence Wingfield Brown died insisting that he was not a killer. However, he did not die at the gallows, but hanged himself in Brisbane's Boggo Road jail just nine days after being sentenced

James Kenniff.

Patrick Kenniff.

William Pill - tortured to death.
THE HURSTBRIDGE TORTURE MURDER - Page 287

William Moxley.

Dorothy Denzel, the beauty queen killed by William Moxley.

Frank Wilkinson - one of William Moxley's victims.

Wade Frankum.
THE SHOPPING MALL MASSACRE - Page 408

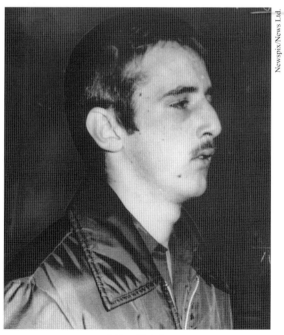

Julian Knight.
THE HODDLE STREET MASSACRE - Page 392

Ivan Milat with a WWI vintage machine gun.
THE BACKPACKER MURDERS - Page 410

Paul Charles Denyer.
THE WOMAN-HATING KILLER - Page 415

Tony Kellisar and his wife Svetlana Podgoyetsky.
THE BODY IN THE ACID - Page 432

Newspix/News Ltd.

Newspix/News Ltd.

Sef Gonzales at the graves of his victims.
THE GRIEVING SON - Page 480

Mark Valera.
THE HEAD IN THE SINK - Page 448

A chilling piece of evidence presented at Mark Valera's murder trial.
THE HEAD IN THE SINK - Page 448

Nicole Patterson - murdered by Peter Dupas.
THE MUTILATING MONSTER - Page 458

John Sharpe with his daughter, Gracie.
THE SPEAR-GUN MONSTER - Page 518

to life imprisonment. Brown hanged himself with a belt from a window grille in the cell in which he would have spent years for the killing of 19-year-old Bronia Armstrong.

The Armstrong case was notorious in Brisbane and was known as the Brisbane Arcade Murder. It was infamous for a number of reasons but mainly because Miss Armstrong was killed during working hours in an arcade office in the middle of the city. The fact that a murder could take place behind the hustle and bustle of a city's working day, with passers-by hearing the victim's screams, was almost too much for the solid citizens of Brisbane, the Armstrong case therefore attracting enormous attention.

Pretty Bronia Armstrong worked as a stenographer for the Brisbane Associated Friendly Societies Medical Institute, with Brown the Institute secretary. Brown, 49 and married with three grown-up children, was hardly a typical killer. He was hard-working, devoted to his job and a typical white-collar worker of his generation. Bronia Armstrong was hardly a likely murder victim, either. A typical teenager, she liked outings and sport and generally enjoyed life as much as any 19-year-old girl. She had no real problems and she came from a good family. In fact, Bronia knew the Brown family quite well, being a former schoolfriend of Brown's daughter.

Brown obviously became infatuated with Miss Armstrong, his interest causing her some discomfort. Brown did not push himself onto the attractive teenager but Bronia told friends that she suspected Brown had not passed on messages from boyfriends. Miss Armstrong could not tolerate the uncomfortable situation any longer and resigned her position. She was due to leave the position on January 17, 1946, but did not live that long. She was murdered a week before that date.

Bronia Armstrong went to work as normal on Friday, January 10, and was seen by a number of people. However, she did not return home from work that night and her worried family contacted Brown, who told them that his stenographer had received a telephone call from a boyfriend. In fact, Miss Armstrong already was dead. Her body was discovered in an Institute waiting room first thing on the Saturday morning, with Brown being called in almost immediately. Police noticed that the girl was wearing only a brassiere and slip and the body was bruised and bloodied. Cause of death later was given as asphyxiation.

Incredibly, Brown tried to make the murder look like a case of suicide. He even told police that Bronia was unhappy at home and that he had told her suicide would be foolish. He claimed that Miss Armstrong talked of jumping off a bridge, but he said: "I told her that if she did, the prawns and crabs would pick her eyes out."

Several clues pointed to Brown as the killer, with the most damning being blood stains found in the office. Brown claimed he had cut his finger on the night of Miss Armstrong's death, but police concluded that he had injured the finger during the struggle with his stenographer. Police concluded that Brown had killed Miss Armstrong in his office and then dragged her body into the waiting room when the coast was clear. There was a long scratch running from his office to the waiting room and this proved damning evidence at Brown's trial.

Brown stood trial in the Supreme Court of Queensland, the public waiting on every word of evidence. The case had created enormous interest and the public wanted to know what would happen to Brown, who vehemently stuck to his claim of innocence. In fact, Brown insisted he had been framed. However, he was found guilty of murder and sentenced to life imprisonment. He hanged himself still proclaiming his innocence and a suicide note read: "I did not kill Bronia Armstrong. My conscience is clear."

DEATH AMONG THE TOMBSTONES

An 11-year-old girl is abducted while on an errand for her mother and her mutilated body later is found in a Sydney cemetery.

Joan Norris, 11 years of age, was a charming, pleasant girl who liked to help her mother with the household chores. Early on the evening of June 12, 1946, Joan's mother asked her to go down the street to buy some bread for her stepfather's breakfast the next morning. Joan skipped out of the house on the simplest of errands and her mother never saw her alive again.

As Joan was a punctual girl, her mother contacted police as soon as she realised her daughter was missing, and one of the biggest Sydney searches for years was launched in an effort to find Joan. Police nightmares turned to reality early the next morning when Joan's mutilated body was found among mossy old tombstones at a disused Camperdown cemetery. Joan was lying on her back, with a piece of her own singlet knotted around her throat. Police were horrified and described the attack as one of the most brutal they had seen.

The cemetery, badly overgrown and dotted with rotting tombstones was – strangely enough – a favourite playground for local children. However, children were terrified of going anywhere near the cemetery at night and police suspected that Joan had been taken into the cemetery through one of many holes in the surrounding fence as her body was found about 50 metres from the cemetery entrance. There was no lighting where the body was discovered.

An examination by the government medical officer revealed that Joan had been dead for about 10 hours when her body was found. She had been strangled and there were marks on the body that were so severe that the killer was described as "a degenerate of the worst type". Meanwhile, police retraced Joan's movements from the time she left her home in Enmore Road, Newtown. Apart from trying to buy the bread her mother had wanted, Joan had called in to the home of her second cousin, Mrs Hazel Geary, in King Street, Newtown. Mrs Geary directed her to a local milk bar, but also told the girl to get home as soon as possible because it was getting dark.

Joan also was seen in a hamburger shop and there were reports she had been seen in a telephone box with a man wearing a military greatcoat. He was described as being 27 or 28 years of age, of medium height and build and wearing a light-coloured open neck shirt and grey trousers. The phone booth was outside the cemetery and police believed this lead was vital. They inspected the booth and found that its light had recently been smashed, with glass scattered around the floor. Police now worked on the theory that the killer had taken Joan to the phone booth and knocked her unconscious before killing her at the cemetery.

The inquest into Joan's death was held in November, 1946, and Detective-Sergeant Denis Hughes told the coroner that police believed the dead girl must have known her killer. Mrs Norris, who broke down during the inquest, said she did not believe her daughter would approach anyone she did now know. Joan's killer has never been identified and her murder remains a mystery.

MURDER AT THE MILL

A timber mill worker in South Australia bashes a workmate, douses him with kerosene and sets him alight.

Paddy O'Leary was a tough customer, and he knew it. Charles Patrick O'Leary had spent time in the merchant navy and the army during World War II and took a job as a sawmill hand after the war. In 1946, O'Leary was working at a government forest at Nangwarry in south-east South Australia. It was a tough life and the men who worked with O'Leary liked a drink, with a weekend spree eventually leading to the death of 59-year-old Walter Edward Ballard on July 6, 1946.

O'Leary and some of his workmates went on a drinking spree on the Saturday morning, their drinking lasting until well into the night. O'Leary, 34, was involved in a number of scuffles but no one could have guessed that the night would end in death for the inoffensive Ballard. O'Leary, well after Ballard had gone "merry" to bed, bashed and killed him, according to the Crown at O'Leary's trial at the Mt Gambier Criminal Circuit Court. The Crown Prosecutor, Mr R.R. Chamberlain, alleged that O'Leary visited a cubicle occupied by Ballard, bashed him, dumped him on a bunk, poured kerosene over him and set him alight. Ballard died two hours later in hospital.

Medical evidence was given at O'Leary's trial that Ballard had been bashed eight times across the head with a beer bottle and that the broken end of this bottle was smashed into his face. Although Ballard was still alive when he was pulled from his bunk, O'Leary was heard to say: "Give me an axe and I'll put the poor man out of his misery – let me finish him off." O'Leary, in a sworn statement, denied killing Ballard and, in fact, did all in his power to ease his suffering. However, O'Leary was found guilty of murder and was sentenced to death. Several appeals failed and O'Leary was hanged at the Adelaide Goal on November 14, 1946.

THE INSCRUTABLE ORIENTAL

A Chinese seaman is accused of murder after a man is stabbed to death outside a Fitzroy hotel.

Melbourne newspaper reporters had never seen anyone like Chang Gook Kong in court before. Chang, a Chinese seaman from the docked British freighter *Fort Abitibi*, was charged with the murder of 23-year-old labourer Douglas Vivian Alcock outside a hotel in the inner Melbourne suburb of Fitzroy on March 29, 1947. Chang, who did not speak much English, sat almost motionless throughout his trial two months later and reporters were treated to the near-perfect example of the inscrutable Oriental. Chang appeared to have little idea about the proceedings of the court and spoke only rarely, through an interpreter. Even when the Criminal Court jury gave its verdict Chang showed little or no sign of emotion.

He had found himself in court as a result of an incident outside the Perseverance Hotel, Brunswick Street. Alcock was stabbed twice in the stomach, with medical evidence stating that either wound would have been fatal. He died an hour later in the nearby St Vincent's Hospital. Chang claimed, through his interpreter, that he was attacked and knocked down by three men, including Alcock. He defended himself with his knife, which had a spring-blade operated by a brass stud, striking one of the men (Alcock) as they closed in on him.

Chang said he believed the men were going to rob him and told police: "These men fight me, knock me down. I didn't want fight. I say, 'I do not want fight'. I have knife, I kill." Chang then ran away from the fight scene. The jury obviously believed his claim of self-defence and Chang was acquitted of both murder and manslaughter. Chang walked from the dock as inscrutable as ever, a free man.

THE MULTIPLE KILLER

Eric Turner kills his girlfriend and her father and, 25 years later, kills his mother-in-law and his stepson.

Eric Thomas Turner won notoriety as one of Australia's worst and most depraved killers when, on October 23, 1948, he killed his girlfriend Clair Sullivan and then her father Frank Sullivan. The 20-year-old Turner strangled 15-year-old Clair as she lay on a settee at her family home in the Sydney suburb of Liverpool. Turner then axed her father to death.

Turner, who claimed he was drunk when he killed the Sullivans, was sentenced to death, but this was commuted to life imprisonment. He was released from jail in 1970 and, just three years later, killed again in a fit of rage, also while he was under the influence of alcohol.

Turner, a man who could not control his rage when crossed, savaged his mother-in-law Harriet Field with a carving knife. Even more tragic was the killing of Turner's 11-year-old stepson John Pilz, who was stabbed while attempting to defend his grandmother. Turner was sentenced to two terms of life imprisonment and, at the time of this book's publication, had spent 54 of the past 57 years in jail, with four deaths from two drunken rages on his conscience.

THE TAMAN SHUD RIDDLE

The body of a man found on a beach in South Australia has never been identified, despite several clues.

A simple headstone in the West Torrens cemetery, Adelaide, says simply: "Here Lies the Unknown Man Who Was Found at Somerton Beach – 1st Dec. 1948." The body of the middle-aged man was buried in the grave in June, 1949, more than six months after being discovered on the Somerton sands. The body had been embalmed and this more than anything else suggested that South Australian police were unwilling to give up early on this mystery, known either as the Somerton Sands Mystery or the Taman Shud Riddle.

The body was embalmed so that it could be examined on any future exhumation. It was said at the time the body was buried that it would be well preserved for many years. However, there has been no lead in police investigations to warrant an exhumation and the mystery remains and no one even knows whether the man died of natural causes or was murdered.

The mystery developed on December 1, 1948, when Adelaide jeweller John Lyons was walking along Somerton beach. He had been there the previous night and had seen a man slumped against the esplanade steps. Mr Lyons therefore was shocked to see the man still there the next morning. In fact, the man was dead and the police were called. However, there was nothing to identify the body – no letters, no passport, no note. There was just a scrap of paper bearing the words "Taman Shud". Police had no idea of what it meant and originally believed it was part of a foreign language.

Dr John Dwyer, a vastly experienced pathologist, examined the body at the Adelaide morgue and was struck by the man's superb physical condition. The subject was about 45 years of age, about 5ft 11in, strongly built and apparently in perfect health before he died. All organs were normal and Dr Dwyer concluded that death was caused by heart failure, but that in itself presented another mystery as there seemed no reason why the man's heart should fail and there was no trace of poison, although he noted that not all poisons could be traced in the body.

Police, meanwhile, concentrated on their Taman Shud clue, being told that the words were from Omar Khayyam's *Rubaiyat*. The words had a macabre significance as they meant "the end". Once the meaning was discovered, a doctor came forward to say that he had found a copy of the *Rubaiyat* on the back seat of his car while it was parked at Somerton on the night of November 30. The page bearing the words Taman Shud was torn from the book and matched the paper found on the dead man, who must have realised he was near his own end. The book found by the doctor also had a series of capital letters pencilled on the last page and they read:

MRGOADARD

MTBIMPANETP

MLIABOAIAQC

ITTMTSASTGAB

There was a cross over the letter O on the third line, but what did it all mean? Police called in code experts, but no one was able to unravel the message if, indeed, it was a message.

Finally, a tailor told police that the man's clothing had been made in America and when police found a suitcase at the Adelaide rail station, the clothes inside matched those on the dead man. There was also a laundry mark bearing the name Kean or Keane, but all police leads petered out.

At an inquest into the mystery man's death, coroner T.E. Cleland concluded that murder could not be ruled out and that (1) The identity of the man was unknown (2) Death was not natural (3) Death was probably caused by poison and (4) Death almost certainly was not accidental. The coroner also concluded that there was not sufficient evidence to warrant a finding. However, police later noticed that a woman dressed in black placed flowers on the grave every December for years. Police interviewed her but although she claimed to have known the man, they were not convinced. So, the riddle remains.

A BONZER KID

A 17-year-old Sydney boy tackles his father about family support and stabs him to death.

Charles Louis Havelock le Gallion, 52, ran a successful motor engineering business in the Sydney suburb of Crow's Nest. A big, burly man, Charles le Gallion was separated from his wife and family of four sons , but the successful engineer still paid his family's living expenses, even the grocery bills. The youngest of le Gallion's four sons, 17-year-old Charles believed his father should have been providing more money and went to see him about this on the night of September 30, 1948.

Young Charles told his father: "Mum is sick and you should provide for her." However, his father replied: "Mind your own business. I'm after a divorce." He then indicated that he had made a will and would leave everything to le Gallion's typist, Betty de Groen.

Police discovered le Gallion's body later that night after Miss de Groen had tried to telephone him. The engineering wizard had been stabbed and was slumped against a table in the office. The post mortem revealed that he had been drinking before he had been killed and that death was caused by a wound on the left side of the chest which had penetrated the chest wall and into the front of the heart. Police arrested young Charles on October 4 and the 17-year-old was committed for trial. He pleaded not guilty at the Central Criminal Court although he admitted visiting to ask about household payments. However, he said his father had grabbed him by the throat and that his father was stabbed in a scuffle. The boy said his wounded father told him to go home and not to worry about a doctor. Young Charles then broke down when shown the pen knife that killed his father.

The jury deliberated for 105 minutes before handing down its verdict – guilty. Mrs Heather le Gallion gasped at the announcement and later described her son to newspaper reporters as "a bonzer kid". The "bonzer kid" was sentenced to life imprisonment, but was released in August, 1960. However, the le Gallion tragedy did not end there as Mrs Heather le Gallion died in a blaze at a Melbourne milk bar she had bought just two weeks before her death on July 30, 1965.

THE LAST WOMAN HANGED

Jean Lee is infamous as the last woman hanged in Victoria, for her involvement in the killing of bookmaker Bill Kent.

Attractive Jean Lee was not alone in the murder of old, overweight starting-price bookmaker Bill Kent in Carlton, an inner Melbourne suburb, in November, 1949. Robert Clayton, her lover, and another accomplice, Norman Andrews, also were found guilty of murdering Kent. But Lee's name stands out because she was the last woman hanged in Victoria. In fact, Lee believed her sex would save her from the gallows. However, the murder of Kent was so brutal that even the Victorian State Cabinet turned down a mercy plea and she was hanged on February 19, 1951, only 15 months after Kent was tortured to death.

Lee's early life was to give little hint of the life of crime she would lead after leaving school in Sydney aged 16. She was brought up with a regard for law and order but knew what she wanted – and that was the good life. She married when aged 18 and that temporarily ended her life as one of Sydney's Depression butterflies. She had a daughter, but drifted away from her family into prostitution during World War II.

It was during her "busy" days entertaining American and Australian troops that Lee met Clayton, who was to become her pimp. Lee and Clayton worked a racket in which Lee was found by Clayton in a compromising position with "another man". Clayton then would threaten violence if the "other man" did not compensate for luring his "wife" into sex. This racket worked so successfully over several years that Lee and Clayton decided to branch out in Victoria and therefore headed south in quest of even more suckers. That was in 1949 and, about that time, they met up with Andrews. The three hit it off almost immediately and they worked their racket in Melbourne, with the bigger Andrews now threatening the violence, usually as Lee's "husband" or Clayton's "brother".

Pickings were good but not as good as when the unholy trio came across old Bill Kent in a Lygon Street, Carlton, hotel. Kent, well known throughout Carlton, had a fistful of notes and Lee, Clayton and Andrews devised a plan to get that bankroll, with Lee as the attractive bait. She sidled up to Kent and plied him with drinks before she, her two friends and Kent headed off to Old Bill's home in nearby Dorritt Street. Lee told her two friends she would "entertain" Kent, so the others headed off temporarily. However, Kent, as drunk as he was, was certainly no fool. He had his money tucked into his fob pocket and Lee, no matter how hard she tried, could not get it.

When Andrews and Clayton returned she gave them the bad news and declared that she would have to get the old SP to take his trousers down. But this only made Kent more aware of Lee's real passion, and that's when it got violent. Lee smashed Kent over the head with a bottle, battered him with a piece of wood and then tied him up with sheet strippings. The terrible trio then cut Kent's fob pocket from his trousers, but were convinced the bookie had much more money hidden. They bashed, cut and jabbed at Kent with several weapons, including the broken bottle, and left him for dead.

Kent's body was found within an hour when a neighbour grew suspicious about "the quietness of the party". Police were called immediately and it did not take them long to track down the three killers. The gang was celebrating when police confronted them at 4am at their Spencer Street hotel, less than 12 hours after the brutal slaying of Kent. On March 25, 1950, all three were sentenced to death after being convicted of murder. Lee broke down and had to be helped from court. On appeal to the Court of Criminal Appeal two months later, a new trial was ordered, but that did not save Kent's killers. The Australian High Court reversed that decision regarding a potential new trial and the Privy Council in England turned down a further appeal. All three were hanged on the morning of February 19, 1951.

THE BABES IN THE CAVE

Two little boys are abducted at Portland, New South Wales, are taken to a cave, interfered with and killed.

Little John Ward and Albert Speirs, like all young boys, liked carnivals. They were looking forward to a day at the Portland, New South Wales, carnival on October 30, 1950. They were expected to enjoy all the fun of the fair and the two seven-year-old playmates were as excited about the carnival as any children in Portland. The two little boys did not return home from the carnival, their day ending in murder. When the boys failed to return home at a reasonable time after the carnival, John Ward's father, John Alfred Ward, notified police.

A huge search was launched and thousands of miners and quarrymen joined police and other volunteers. It was to become one of the biggest searches in Australian history, searchers even carrying torches at night to investigate the possibility of the boys being lost in a quarry cave. Unbeknown to the searchers, they went within less than 100 metres of a gruesome sight on the first night of the search. Hopes faded quickly of finding the boys alive as the search dragged on to a fifth day. Then, on the morning of November 4, 23-year-old Herbert Hutchinson, acting on a hunch, decided to search a cave where he had looked for pigeon eggs as a boy. Hutchinson was horrified in finding two small bodies.

Police were shocked. The huddled bodies were a tragic sight, partly because of their very youth, but also because the bodies had been partly eaten by rats. Police appeared to have a case of murder on their hands, although there were initial suggestions that the boys had been lost and died of exhaustion. However, expert medical examinations later showed that the boys had died of suffocation, with evidence that shock was a contributing factor.

The man police wanted to interview was John Kevin Seach, a 26-year-old quarryman with the reputation of being a heavy drinker. Seach had left the town of Portland soon after the boys were reported missing and John Ward's elder brother, nine-year-old Richard, also identified Seach as the man he had seen walking away from the sports ground with his brother and little Albert Speirs on October 30. Seach had headed for Tamworth, taking a job under the assumed name of John Larsen for the short time that he was missing. Police questioned him at Tamworth and he confessed to killing the two boys.

Seach had told the boys he would take them home, but took them to the quarry cave instead. He interfered with them and immediately panicked. A statement he made read: "I grabbed the little bloke and smothered him by putting a handkerchief over his nose and mouth. As soon as he went limp I just let him fall back. I grabbed the other one and did the same to him." He added: "I was frightened to let them go because they would have told what I had done."

Seach stood trial at the Central Criminal Court in March, 1951, and pleaded not guilty to murder on the ground of insanity. However, a jury took just half an hour to find him guilty of killing John Ward. Seach was sentenced to death, with Justice Street saying: "It needs no words of mine to speak of the abhorrent and detestable crime of which you have been found so rightly convicted. There is only one possible sentence. You are sentenced to death."

THE INFERIORITY COMPLEX KILLER

A 21-year-old leaves Melbourne and embarks on a crime spree in Sydney in which two people are left dead.

Good-looking Ronald Newman Cribbin was educated at one of Melbourne's best Catholic colleges, but ended up a cold-blooded killer. Young Cribbin started his criminal career as a hold-up man, robbing taxi drivers of their hard-earned fares. He got away with this for some time, but eventually was caught red-handed and sentenced to 18 months' jail, serving his time at Pentridge.

Cribbin left jail with an enormous chip on his shoulder and the 21-year-old, who already had exhibited an inferiority complex, soon showed an extreme tendency to believe that everyone considered him worthless. He always had the impression that people were laughing at him. This wasn't true but Cribbin nurtured these feelings and they festered inside him. Those feelings helped turn him into a killer.

Cribbin's short-lived career as a killer started in Sydney on December 14, 1950. After being released from Pentridge, Cribbin headed for New South Wales, obviously intent on leading a life of crime. He struck pay dirt almost immediately when he robbed 72-year-old widow Mrs Edith Hill of 15,000 pounds worth of jewels and killed her in the process. Mrs Hill, who lived alone in a flat in Macquarie Street, Sydney, was bashed and, severely wounded, was discovered on the evening of December 14 by her daughter, Mrs Sibella Brooker. However, Mrs Hill later died of her wounds.

Just two days after killing Mrs Hill, Cribbin hailed a taxi driven by 36-year-old father of five, Norman Cecil Dickson. Cribbin told Dickson to stop after a short journey and immediately produced a gun. Dickson resisted and was shot for his trouble. Cribbin later claimed the gun "went off" but he also admitted that he then "shot at his head to put him out of pain".

Cribbin then drove the taxi, with Dickson's body in the back seat, due west. He was only a few miles out of Bathurst when a motorcycle policeman stopped the taxi because he could not notice any passengers. Senior Constable Reg Lowe then dodged a bullet as Cribbin fired at him from the driver's seat. Lowe fired back, but Cribbin was able to escape in the taxi.

Cribbin later crashed the taxi but immediately sped off on foot, leaving Dickson's body in the back. It was a frantic rush for freedom and Cribbin even swam across a river in his bid to escape his pursuers. However, his efforts proved futile and police arrested him at gunpoint. Police obviously wanted to talk to Cribbin about the death of the cab driver and therefore were horrified when he confessed to the murder of Mrs Hill.

The 21-year-old was found guilty of Mrs Hill's murder despite pleading insanity. It was obvious he had planned the robbery in great detail and although he claimed he struck the widow with a rifle because she "kept fighting" him, the jury obviously believed he knew exactly what he was doing. Cribbin was sentenced to death, but this was commuted to life imprisonment.

THE EAST BRIGHTON STRANGLING

A 19-year-old girl is strangled in a quiet suburban street in Melbourne by her former fiancé.

It seemed like just another Sunday morning for plasterer Richard Hall as he hopped into his truck to go to a job. However, Sunday, May 14, 1950, was to prove no ordinary day. As he drove down Glencairn Avenue, East Brighton, a fashionable bayside Melbourne suburb, Hall noticed a pair of shoes protruding from long grass. Hall stopped to investigate and saw the body of a young woman with a neatly folded newspaper covering the back of her head.

Several Glencairn Avenue residents failed to identify the girl, who had been beaten about the face and strangled. Even Hall could not recognise the girl, although he later realised he knew her well. A description of the girl was broadcast on a Melbourne radio station and Mr Roy Walters, who lived with his wife, daughter and two sons in Glencairn Avenue, heard the special broadcast and thought they knew the identity of the dead girl. However, Mr Walters could not identify the body as he had been blinded while serving with the RAAF in World War II, so sent his brother-in-law to identify the body. The dead girl was Mr Walters' daughter Carmen, just 19. She had not returned home on the Saturday night, but Mr and Mrs Walters had assumed their daughter was spending the night with friends.

Carmen, a quiet, steady girl who worked as a porter at the nearby Hampton rail station, was seen on a bus on the Saturday night with a tall, thin young man and, naturally, police wanted to interview him. In particular, they wanted to interview Carmen's former fiancé , Morris Sutton Ramsden Brewer, 24, of the northern Melbourne suburb of Reservoir. Finally, on May 17, Brewer gave himself up three days after Carmen's death and was charged with murder. In a statement to police, Brewer said he was trying to patch up his relationship with Carmen, but she had told him she blamed his parents for what had happened between them. He took exception to this and "everything seemed to clog up in my mind". He stranged her, walked away, caught a taxi to Oakleigh and then hitch-hiked to Gippsland.

Brewer pleaded not guilty on the grounds of insanity at his trial at the Melbourne Central Criminal Court in September, 1950, and much of the court's time was taken up with hearing evidence from medical experts. The jury took five and a half hours to hand down its verdict – not guilty on the grounds of insanity. Justice Barry ordered Brewer to be detained "at the Governor's pleasure". Barry was released from Pentridge on November 27, 1957.

THE CHILD BRIDE

A young newlywed couple is shot and their bodies burned in a house fire at Casino, on the New South Wales coast.

Orma and Donald Warner were married as teenagers, with pretty dark-haired Orma little more than a child bride. She was just 17 years of age when she married 19-year-old timber mill worker Donald in early 1951. Neither was to know they would be married for just five months. Farmer Athol Lyon was driving past the Warners' weatherboard and fibro house near Casino, on the north coast of New South Wales, at about 9.45pm on July 15, 1951, when he noticed the house was ablaze. There was nothing he could do as the flames already had taken hold.

Police were called and shocked to find two charred bodies in the ashes left by the huge blaze. Even more horrifying, police also found the remains of a couple of rifles, a revolver and two shotgun cartridges. They immediately sensed that the newlyweds had been shot to death and the house then torched. A post-mortem quickly revealed that both Orma and Donald Warner had shotgun wounds to the body. There were numerous pellets in both bodies and, as proof that the house had been torched, police found the charred remains of three kerosene tins. Police did not have to question too many locals as there were persistent rumours that Orma had been nervous of a local stock inspector. However, 29-year-old William Henry Abbott, married with two children, had had an impeccable record during World War II and had even been awarded the Distinguished Conduct Medal for his bravery.

Police then learned that Donald Warner had complained to Abbott about "pestering" his young wife and that the newlywed husband had spoken about getting Abbott shifted from the district in his job. This was just three days before the deaths of Donald and Orma Warner and police, naturally, were now suspicious of the stock inspector. Abbott was unable to provide an alibi and when detectives found a shotgun at his home they knew they were close to breaking the case. Ballistic tests proved that the shotgun found in the Abbott home had been used to shoot the Warners.

Finally, police found bloodstained clothes at Abbott's home and although he at first insisted that the blood was from cattle, police suspected otherwise. He was charged with murder and, at his trial, claimed police had threatened to bash him to get a confession. However, he was found guilty and sentenced to death, this sentence later commuted to one of life imprisonment.

DEATH AT THE CRICKET

A deranged gunman opens fire during a cricket match in Adelaide and kills a fieldsman.

It would be impossible to describe a more typical Australian summer scene. It was Wednesday, February 13, 1952. The sun was shining, cicadas were singing in chorus and the flannelled fools were at their game of cricket. The match was between the South-East and Upper-North at the Railway Oval, 10 minutes from the city streets of Adelaide, as part of South Australia's Country Week. South-East batsman George Kay was about to play a shot from the bowling of Les

Patroney when the handful of spectators noticed that the fieldsman at point, Captain Arthur Francis Henderson, 31, had fallen to ground.

They at first thought Henderson, who had served in the Middle East and New Guinea in World War II, was skylarking. However, they soon noticed blood from a wound over his heart. Captain Henderson was dead. Almost immediately spectators heard the crack of a rifle and another fieldsman, 22-year-old builder Ron Reed, fell with a severe wound to an arm. A bullet had severed an artery.

Cricketers made a dash for the pavilion as further shots whistled through the air from the tree-lined eastern end of the ground. Witnesses saw a small dark-haired man running in a crouched position from one tree to another and then watched in horror as the gunman held the rifle in a firing position and aimed a shot at a pedestrian. Incredibly, the pedestrian seemed unaware of what was happening, even after the shot had been fired. A bullet thudded into the ground just in front of him, setting alight long grass.

Meanwhile, one of the spectators had telephoned the police, who were at the oval within minutes from Thebarton station. One of the officers, Detective Brian Giles, showing remarkable courage, decided to confront the gunman. He abandoned his crouched position and walked straight up to the gunman – 100 yards, 90 yards, 80 yards, 70 yards – he kept walking until he was within 60 yards of the gunman and the barrel of a .303 rifle. The gunman lifted the rifle and aimed it at Giles' heart, but not even this deterred the detective. Finally, with the rifle still pointed at Giles, a police officer moved from behind the gunman to disarm him.

The arrested man was 24-year-old Lebanese migrant Elias Gaha, a former patient at two Melbourne mental institutions.

Gaha appeared to have an inferiority complex and was convinced that Australians looked down on him. Doctors said he was suffering from a mental disorder known as paraphrenia. Gaha had moved to Adelaide and got a job as a railway cleaner, with workmates describing him as a quiet and apparently inoffensive young man. However, he bought the rifle just days before the tragedy and its seemed obvious he wanted to avenge some perceived grudge.

Gaha was charged with the murder of Captain Henderson, the father of three young children, but did not stand trial. He was sent for medical examination at the Parkside Mental Hospital, where doctors certified him as insane. He later was deported to Lebanon, with Detective Giles as one of his escorts. Detective Giles was awarded the George Medal for his courage and the wounded man, Reed, made a full recovery.

THE RAMPAGING RUMANIAN

A Rumanian immigrant runs amok in Adelaide and finally confesses to five killings.

Zora Kusic had the face of a woman who had seen the seamier side of life. She was, in fact, a slut. Zora Kusic frequented Adelaide's darker salons and bars, selling her body virtually to anyone who would buy her a day's drinking. She lived with a Bulgarian named Ivan Nankintseff in a tiny shanty behind a house in North Parade, Torrensville, and sometimes took men to this hut. On the night of December 5, 1952, Nankintseff returned to the hut after a drinking session and found Kusic on their bed. He did not realise it at first, but his companion was dead. In fact, she had been killed in the most revolting of circumstances and Nankintseff soon realised he had come across a dead and mutilated body. He fled in terror and police immediately launched a murder investigation.

Zora Kusic's throat had been cut almost from ear to ear and her stomach had been ripped open. Her chest was slashed and there was blood everywhere in the little tin shanty. In fact, there was a dish containing blood-stained water, while a knife was found on the floor. Nankintseff had last seen Kusic alive at seven o'clock that morning when he left for work and although he arranged to meet her at 4pm, she did not turn up. Nankintseff discovered the body at 6.30pm, police estimating Kusic had been dead for two to three hours. Police were convinced she had been killed by a psychopath and no stone was left unturned in the search for the killer. Because Kusic frequented New Australian clubs and bars, police called in a team of translators to help them and hundreds of migrants were interviewed in clubs around Adelaide.

The prime suspect was a 28-year-old Rumanian immigrant who had been seen with Kusic shortly before her death. However, the man denied he had been with her and police were told their suspect led a quiet, respectable life. Then, however, discrepancies appeared in the man's statements and police finally charged John (real name Joan, pronounced Jo-anne) Balaban with the murder of Kusic.

However, the charge was dismissed in sensational circumstances after a five-day hearing in the Adelaide City Court when it was argued that suspicion was not enough and that there was not enough evidence against Balaban, an industrial chemist with qualifications from a Rumanian university. Balaban admitted that he had been drinking with Kusac, but was not involved in her death. Although this seemed the end of the matter, the Balaban saga was in its infancy as he soon went on a rampage of destruction for about an hour soon after 1.30pm on April 12, 1953.

Passers-by heard screams from Balaban's Sunshine Café in Gouger Street, Adelaide, but could not have guessed the horror that had erupted upstairs in the unfashionable café and snack bar. They then saw a woman fall 20 feet from an upper café window. The woman, Verne Manie, a waitress at the club, was critically injured, suffering back and head injuries. She later lapsed into unconsciousness, although she recovered in hospital. Meanwhile, police forced their way into the café and discovered one of the most blood-curdling sights in South Australian criminal history.

Balaban's wife Thelma, 30, was dead in her bed, her face smashed to pulp. Her mother, 66-year-old Mrs Susan Ackland, was critically injured in another bedroom, but later died in hospital. Even more tragically, police discovered the mortally wounded six-year-old son of Mrs Balaban by a previous marriage. Little Phillip Cadd died 11 days later in hospital. Police were stunned as it was one of Adelaide's worst murder cases. The search therefore was on for Balaban, who had been discharged only three months earlier. The rampaging Rumanian finally was found outside the café and was charged with the murder of his wife – and Kusic.

Balaban stood trial at the Criminal Court in July, 1953, and pleaded insanity. The most interesting part of his trial was that he was charged with the murder of a woman (Kusic) for which he already had been in the dock. His trial was a sensation from start to finish, but the most incredible was Balaban's statement, made in a halting voice, in which he admitted to FIVE killings, including one in Paris. Of this killing he said:

> On February 10 (1947) I met a woman called Iva Kwas in a subway tram. She worked at a chemistry laboratory. We were talking and I walked home with her. We sat up so late talking that I missed the last tram. She showed me a couch to sleep on. I went to her bedroom and made love to her. After about an hour I became furious with her. I felt very powerful and strong. I put my hands around her neck and strangled her. I did not have any intention of killing her but I had a feeling I had to. I had not been drinking beforehand. I stayed in her room until about five o'clock in the morning and then I decided to come to Australia.

Of killing Kusic, he said that after the woman asked for a payment of five pounds, he looked at her and saw how common and dirty she was. He said:

> I became very disgusted and angry with her and put my hand on her neck and started to strangle her. She struggled for a minute and then lay still. I continued to strangle her. I then took a knife off the dressing table and cut her throat. I then cut her up and down the body and across her chest … I did not feel sorry for Kusic. I thought I was quite justified for doing so because anybody could tell she was a low woman and deserved to die.

Of the other killings, he said he decided "instantly" he would kill his wife when he returned to the Sunshine Café after he had hit a man with an iron bar after seeing him making love with a woman on the banks of the Torrens river. He said:

I went into her bedroom. I did not switch on the light. I hit her on the head. I don't know how many times. Then I thought I would kill Mrs Ackland. Mrs Ackland had made my wife's first husband, Mr Cadd, unhappy and I thought she would also make us unhappy. Phillip sat up and cried and I hit him. I thought it better that he die too. I would like to die, too, myself. I went out to the sleepout where Verna Manie slept. I went out to kill her because she had been stealing money from the shop, and she had been siding with my wife against me. She had been insolent. I hit her on the head and told Verna that I wanted her, and put her on the bed. I had intercourse with her. I went back and had a look at the bodies and hit them again and then came back to the sleepout and saw that Verna was on the ground. I took some money and climbed over the roofs into Thomas Street. I only killed the people from the Sunshine Café because they deserved to die.

Balaban, who pleaded insanity, was unmoved when the jury foreman announced the verdict of guilty. Balaban turned to Justice Abbott and said: "According to the law, I want to obey the law, and I think I am not guilty." The judge then sentenced him to death and an appeal to the South Australian Full Court failed. Balaban spent his last few days playing chess and cards and was executed on August 26, 1953.

THE BODY IN THE BARWON

A decapitated body is found in sacks and a kerosene tin in the Barwon River, Geelong.

Tall and elegant Mr H.A. Winneke QC (later Sir Henry Winneke, Governor of Victoria), chose his words carefully. Mr Winneke was making an opening address in one of the most sensational murder trials in Victorian criminal history. Mr Winneke said: "Someone has committed a foul and ghastly murder. On May 13 (1953) the dead man left his home after his evening meal, giving no indication he was not returning. Nothing more was heard of him until a diver recovered the decapitated body from the Barwon River, Geelong, on August 1. When the body was recovered the head was sawn off the trunk, and each hand had been sawn off above the wrist. The trunk was in two sacks wired to a 126-pound stone, and the head and hands in a kerosene tin punctured with holes. A post-mortem examination showed the body to be very, very extensively damaged. The trunk had been mutilated – there were six main wounds on the skull and there were underlying fractures beneath three of them caused by heavy blows."

On trial before Justice Martin in the Supreme Court of Victoria at Geelong were Andrew Gordon Kilpatrick, 33, and Russell William Hill, 22, both of Colac, a prosperous rural city in Victoria's Western District. Both had pleaded not guilty to a charge of murdering Donald Brooke Maxfield, also of Colac, on or about May 13, 1953. The case was widely known as "The Body in the Barwon" murder and it captured headlines in Victoria for years. Yet, incredibly, only a determined policeman's hunch led to a murder investigation.

The policeman was Detective Sergeant Fred Adam, a well-known member of Victoria's Homicide Squad. Detective Adam had been sent to Colac to investigate a number of mysterious break-ins in the district. It was not a murder investigation and there was not even a hint of murder, at first. Detective Adam's job was to prosecute Kilpatrick and Hill on a charge of assaulting a local constable with a weapon. That case alone drew considerable publicity in Melbourne as Kilpatrick and Hill eventually were found guilty of assaulting Constable George Ross Chester and sentenced to a year's jail each. They gave notice of appeal and were released on bail.

However, Adam felt something was wrong and filed a report to police headquarters suggesting there was a conspiracy of crime in Colac which needed investigation. Adam was ordered to proceed with the investigation and, believed that by putting pressure on the younger Hill, he would get further than by questioning Kilpatrick. Hill was young, impressionable and not as worldly smart as Kilpatrick, who had been educated at the exclusive and expensive Geelong Grammar School. In preparing for the investigation, Adam also noted that another man, 22-year-old Donald Maxfield, had gone missing.

Adam looked at the Maxfield file and said later: "It had murder written all over it." Then, when questioned, Hill blurted out: It's no good denying it. He's dead. He's in the river. We cut him up." Hill then made a confession about how Maxfield was killed because he had told police too much about the break-ins. Kilpatrick had arranged to meet Maxfield in a garage on the night of May 13, 1953, hit him on the back of the head four or five times with an iron bar and threw him into the back of a Pontiac car. Maxfield was still alive when Kilpatrick pulled him out of the car, so Hill finished him off with another blow to the head, this time with a .45 pistol.

Hill's statement then said that the two drove to the Barwon River, where Kilpatrick said that if they cut off the dead man's head and hands no one would be able to identify him. The Hill statement said: "He (Kilpatrick) got out a hacksaw and cut off his hands and then his head." Kilpatrick then ordered Hill to put the head and hands in the kerosene tin, with the body then being thrown into the river from a bridge. Police divers found the body of the unfortunate Maxfield and Kilpatrick and Hill were charged with murder.

The jury at their murder trial deliberated for almost three hours before returning verdicts of guilty. Justice Martin sentenced both men to death and told them: "You have been

1953 - THE DEADLY MISTAKE

found guilty of a horrible and cruel murder, of a crime planned in cold blood and completed in circumstances of the utmost barbarity." Asked by the judge whether they had anything to say, Hill replied in the negative, while Kilpatrick, who claimed he had been framed, said: "I am not guilty, sir." The death sentences were never carried out. Hill had his sentence commuted to one of 20 years' jail, while Kilpatrick's was commuted to one of life imprisonment.

THE DEADLY MISTAKE

A Melbourne teenager is abducted, sexually assaulted and killed after making a mistake about which railway station she had to meet someone who was to take her to a party.

Shirley Collins, just 14, might still be alive if it had not been for one tragic mistake. Instead, she suffered a terrible death at the hands of a monster. Worse, that monster has never been brought to justice for his savage crime. Shirley Collins, whose real name was Shirley Hughes, lived with Mr and Mrs Alfred Collins in the northern Melbourne suburb of Reservoir. Her real mother, Mrs Leila Hughes, had shifted to Queensland and although Shirley kept in touch with her, she referred to Mrs Collins as her mother.

A quiet, shy girl, Shirley took a job as a shop assistant in the city when old enough to leave school. An invitation from a store employee, Ronald Holmes, 21, to attend a party at Richmond on the night of Saturday, September 12, 1953, was the first innocent step to tragedy. Shirley, with Mrs Collins' blessing, accepted the invitation and Holmes arranged to meet the young girl at the Richmond rail station. Unfortunately, Shirley was confused about the meeting place as there were several other rail stations in Melbourne bearing the name Richmond. Shirley, used to travelling to work in the city on the Reservoir line, passed through the West Richmond station each working day and obviously believed she had to meet Holmes at the West Richmond station, and not the Richmond station. It was a fatal mistake.

Holmes waited at the Richmond station for Shirley, parking his car nearby. However, Shirley did not turn up and after a long wait Holmes went to the party believing she had decided not to go to the party after all. However, Shirley had left her home shortly after 7pm to catch a train. Shirley Collins was murdered that night, but her body was not discovered until the following Tuesday morning.

Incredibly, the girl was murdered some 40 miles from Richmond, at the popular seaside resort of Mt Martha. The body was discovered by Mr Lionel Evelyn-Lairdet, who was out walking his dog. Other passers-by had seen the body in the driveway of a vacant holiday cottage, but believed it was a girl suntanning herself. Meanwhile, Shirley's foster mother had already alerted police over the girl's disappearance as the 14-year-old had been told to be home by midnight.

Police were shocked when they examined the body. It was a terrible sight, the girl being battered to death. Shirley had walked up the drive of the holiday cottage with her murderer and was hit over the head with three full bottles of beer. The murderer then smashed Shirley's face in with heavy slabs of concrete guttering and her features were unrecognisable, her face smashed to pulp. The murderer also removed Shirley's panties, stockings and girdle, leaving the girl's skirt above her shoulders. She was not sexually assaulted but the murder horrified Melbourne.

Police were told a light-coloured car had been spotted near West Richmond station on the night Shirley disappeared, but would Shirley have entered the car willingly? One theory was that she knew the driver, but nothing was conclusive. Police also traced the batch numbers on the the labels of the beer bottles, but without any significant lead. The police even reconstructed the abduction, using a model, with the now-defunct *Argus* newspaper running a photograph to try and prompt someone's memory. Again, there were no leads and this horrific murder remains a mystery.

THE POISONOUS GRANNIE

Great-grandmother Caroline Grills, a most unlikely killer, uses the poison thallium for her sometimes inexplicable reasons.

The poison thallium became a popular rat killer in Australia in the first half of the nineteenth century and was supposed to be undetectable in the human body. It therefore became popular with those who wanted to kill without detection. Caroline Grills had a rat problem at the Goulburn home she shared with her husband and the poison Thall-rat solved it. Then, when the Grills moved into the Sydney suburb of Gladesville, there were more rats. However, Grills did not stop with killing rodents and used thallium to kill her 87-year-old stepmother Christina Mickelson and then 84-year-old Angelina Thomas. In both cases, Grills benefited from estates, coming into possession of two houses.

The next victim was her husband Richard's brother-in-law John Lundberg, who died in October, 1948. Then followed Grills' dead brother's wife Mary Mickelson. In 1951, her husband's sister, Eveline Lundberg (widow of John), took seriously ill, with the woman known as Aunt Carrie looking after her. However, on May 13, 1953, daughter-in-law Chrissie Downey made Eveline Lundberg a cup of tea, which Grills offered to take out to the sick woman sitting on a verandah. Downey's husband John then saw Grills take something from a pocket. He switched the cups of tea and, on the pretext of wanting more water, poured the contents into a jar; the tea contained thallium. Two bodies were exhumed and found to contain traces of thallium, while two other bodies had been cremated.

Grills was charged with four counts of murder and three attempted murders. Traces of thallium were found in the pocket of a dress she was wearing when she tried to poison Eveline Lundberg and Senior Crown Prosecutor Michael Rooney QC suggested that Grills was "a killer who poisoned for sport, for fun, for the kicks she got out of it, for the hell of it, for the thrill that she alone in the world knew the cause of the victim's suffering". That "suffering" included severe gastric pain, heavy legs, delirium, blindness and, eventually, death. The jury took just 12 minutes to find Grills guilty and she was sentenced to death. However, that sentence was commuted to life imprisonment and she died in 1960 in a Sydney hospital of a ruptured gastric ulcer. Ironically, she must have experienced pain similar to that experienced by her victims.

THE BOMB GENIUS

An engineer makes a bomb and explodes it to kill his wife and her brother before turning a gun on himself.

Residents in and around Paterson Avenue, Kingsgrove, a Sydney suburb, were preparing for a quiet night on August 14, 1956, when the peace of the neighbourhood was shattered by a tremendous explosion. Residents ran from their houses as windows rattled and rooms rocked. Residents in the avenue itself could not believe their eyes when they saw a bomb-wrecked car in their quiet suburban street. The car was a dreadful sight. Its bonnet was 50 metres down the street, all four doors had been blown out and windscreen glass was spread for metres.

People crowded the scene and police and firemen had to link arms to keep the area clear before a detailed investigation could be launched into the bombing. The explosion occurred when Dr Edward Brotchie, 50, turned on the car's ignition. Dr Brotchie died in hospital shortly after the explosion and his passenger, his sister Mrs Elsie Foster, 45, died instantly. They were victims of an expertly planned car bombing. Police knew that whoever planted the bomb knew exactly what he was doing.

In fact, the technical officer of the Explosives Department, Mr S.W.E. Parsons, said soon after examining the wrecked car: "To make a bomb of this strength and type, and to be able to place and connect it, would require considerable knowledge of explosives." The bomb, indeed, was the work of an expert, Mrs Foster's husband Henry Foster, who shot himself through the head soon after the bombing. Police did not discover Foster's body, in Dr Brotchie's surgery 100 metres from the bombing, until the next morning. Incredibly, Foster left behind a swag of notes which painstakingly described the bomb's mechanism. He wanted experts to know exactly how the bomb worked so there would be no confusion after his own death.

Foster's note explained everything, right down to the last detail. It seemed he disliked his brother-in-law for failing to treat him to his satisfaction for a back complaint. But, strangely, it seemed consulting and design engineer Foster loved the wife he killed with the hand-made explosive device. The inventive genius killed and died with the efficiency of an analytical scientist.

THE FIRST STEP
TO THE WEDDING

Three members of a Greek family are shot dead in their Adelaide home following a Romeo and Juliet type drama

The quiet city of Adelaide was shocked in September, 1957, when three members of a Greek family were shot dead in their own home. The Greek community was outraged when one of their own community members was later charged with murder. Community members felt that the killings had brought shame on them. Dead were Mr Tom Galantomos, his wife Anna and daughter Ploheria (Ritsa). A 24-year-old

Greek, Stalianos Athanaisidis, was later charged with murder. The Galantomos killings created enormous interest in Adelaide, with a Romeo and Juliet type drama unfolded in the courts.

Stalianos Athanaisidis had migrated to Australia from the Greek island of Rhodes three years earlier and worked in Adelaide as an electrician. The Galantomos family also came from Rhodes and Athanasiadis started courting 17-yearold Ritsa and then asked for her hand in marriage. The Galantomos' agreed and everyone seemed more than happy. In a 14-page statement to police, which Athanaisidis titled "The First Step to the Wedding", he wrote of everyone's joy and how everything seemed perfect for the wedding.

The couple was married in a registry office on April 27, 1957, and in the eyes of the law they were man and wife. However, they did not live as man and wife because they were awaiting the Greek religious ceremony. Meanwhile, the Galantomos family bought their new son-in-law a Ford Mainline car valued at 2000 pounds, but later was upset when he discovered it had been bought on hire purchase, with 1800 pounds owing. From then, according to his statement, "things automatically changed". He also was convinced Mr and Mrs Galantomos were planning to take their daughter back to Greece to be married to a young student doctor.

Athanaisidis snapped, killed Mr and Mrs Galantomos and then, according to his statement, made a suicide pact with his beloved Ritsa. He pumped 11 bullets into her and then shot himself. Although he had mortally wounded Ritsa, he was rushed to Royal Adelaide Hospital and survived. Athanaisidis was tried twice, being found guilty of murder both times. He was sentenced to death at his first trial, but an appeal to the High Court resulted in a new trial. He again was found guilty and again sentenced to death, which later was commuted to life imprisonment.

THE HURSTBRIDGE TORTURE MURDER

A market farmer is tortured and killed on the outskirts of Melbourne and his body is tied to the foot of an iron bed.

William John Pill was a hard-working market farmer who lived alone and hoarded his money. He was renowned for his excellent tomato crops and made considerable amounts of money through his hard work. Late in 1958, realising he was in ill-health, he sold 13 acres of land and decided to move in with his sister-in-law Mrs Ada Pill. The 64-year-old Pill had lived all his life in two shacks, one of them used as a kitchen and the other as a bedroom.

Pill had sold his land for 800 pounds and although this might have been a tempting figure for robbers, the agents had received only a deposit of 10 per cent and none of this had been passed on to Pill when he was brutally tortured and murdered on December 21, 1958.

Pill had been seen working on his tomatoes on December 21, but was not seen the following day. A neighbour, Herbert Funnell, became suspicious when he noticed a delivered newspaper was untouched outside one of Pill's two shacks. Funnell peeped inside and, after taking one glance, ran to notify police. Pill was dead, tied to the foot of his iron bed. Clothed only in a shirt, he was bound and gagged in a kneeling position at the foot of the bed, with his head on the mattress.

Police were shocked by the brutality of the murder as the old man had been viciously tortured, his killer(s) obviously trying to find where Pill had hidden his money. There were 287 different bruises on Pill's body, the old man lashed with a metal-ended razor strop and burned with strips of lighted sheeting. He must have suffered terribly, but whoever was responsible missed the cache of money (870 pounds) hidden in a cavity behind a fireplace. Police interviewed a number of people in an effort to solve the murder mystery but were unable to charge anyone over Pill's death, even though a 1936 Oldsmobile or Pontiac car was seen parked near the Pill shacks on the night of the murder.

THE BLACK NEGLIGEE

An amateur hypnotist buys a black negligee for the girl he wants to marry and, following rejection, stabs her to death before suiciding.

Eileen Joan Moriarty, a 23-year-old nurse, was not the typical Australian woman of the 1950s. She had had a child in Western Australia before moving to Sydney and then to Tasmania to seek a new life for herself and, during this time, she had at least a couple of lovers. Miss Moriarty's daughter was eight months old in 1959 and was boarded out in Hobart while her mother lived at Wingfield House, part of the Royal

Hobart Hospital complex. It was in the Apple Isle that Miss Moriarty met a most unusual man.

Graham Alan Stewart, a 24-year-old Tasmanian, was an amateur hypnotist whose hobby was the occult. Stewart, a dark, slim man with a goatee beard, carried business cards which suggested he specialised in the hypnotic treatment of nervous disorders. He also performed in nightclubs and decorated his flat with occult signs and symbols. His flat, in north Hobart, had an attic which had a mysterious black circle, with accompanying symbols, painted on the floor. A red light, which blinked on and off, was rigged to the ceiling to highlight the circle and symbols. It was suggested that Stewart regularly held midnight black magic sessions.

Stewart met the pretty, dark-haired Miss Moriarty in 1958 and soon fell in love with her. However, this love was not entirely reciprocated, despite Stewart's best endeavours. He made many approaches but although Miss Moriarty "liked" Stewart, she was wary of his unusual appearance and pursuits. Finally, on April 8, 1959, Stewart proposed marriage and – strangely – Miss Moriarty accepted. Stewart therefore prepared a marriage application, which Miss Moriarty signed. The couple was to have been married the following day but, for some unknown reason, she changed her mind and fixed another wedding date – April 23. Stewart made preparations for the wedding, but was left at the altar. Miss Moriarty had returned to a former lover.

Stewart, infuriated, went on a shopping spree. He bought himself a black-handled stiletto and a black negligee before renting a luxury apartment at the seaside suburb of Sandy Bay. He contacted Miss Moriarty, who then failed to turn up for work at the hospital. The police were contacted three days later and an officer from the Hobart Missing Persons Bureau investigated the girl's disappearance. After learning that Stewart had hired an apartment, they went there and, after entering through an unlocked window, found Stewart and Miss Moriarty dead in a huge pool of blood on a double bed. The dead woman's body was covered only by the black negligee Stewart had bought. The stiletto he had bought was by his side and police determined that Stewart had stabbed Miss Moriarty a number of times in the chest and then thrust the knife deep into his own heart after she rejected him yet again.

THE SEALED
ROOM MURDER

A successful gambler is battered to death in Melbourne after being seen with a large amount of money.

Young Salvatore Tabone left his home in Malta in 1916, determined to make a fortune in Australia. Tabone, who later changed his name to Borg, did not make a fortune but he did build up a profitable business after years of hard work. Sam Borg worked in Queensland's cane fields after arriving in Australia but later built up a café business in Melbourne's Little Lonsdale Street. It was not a fancy café but Borg seemed reasonably happy with his lot. He made a small amount of money and was able to indulge in his favourite pastime – card gambling.

Borg was hooked on cards and often played with migrant friends in Maltese clubs. He also made money by renting a room in his café for gambling purposes. Card games were everything to Borg and he was able to build up substantial bank rolls through his gambling activities. In fact, Borg was regarded as an expert gambler and the only problem was that, like many people his age, he did not trust banks. Instead, he preferred to hide his money in his bedroom. It was a dangerous habit as Borg eventually was killed, with robbery the probable motive.

Borg, 67, was seen flashing 1000 pounds in notes shortly before he was murdered in May, 1960. That was most unlike Borg, who usually was smart enough to keep his winnings to himself, and the last anyone saw of him was when he was leaving a Maltese club in North Melbourne on the night of Saturday, May 28. His body was discovered the following Monday night.

Police were called to Borg's café when a local Maltese identity told them he had not seen Borg for a couple of days. Police immediately went to the café and had to smash in the front door. Borg's battered and bloodied body was found in a bedroom but, incredibly, the door to that bedroom had been nailed – from the inside. Melbourne newspapers immediately tagged the case the "Sealed Room Murder".

Police, in reconstructing the crime, reasoned that Borg had been battered to death with the leg of a heavy wooden table, the body then dragged into a spare bedroom where it was pushed under a bed. The killer, or killers, then climbed out of the room through a skylight which adjoined another room.

The killer(s) then left the building by the front door. Borg's pyjama-clad body was wrapped shroud-like in sheets and blankets and bound by strips of rag. Despite claims that Borg had been seen with 1000 pounds, 450 pounds was found in the bedroom and café .

More than 400 people were interviewed over Borg's death and police believed they had an excellent lead when it was reported a man wearing a dark overcoat had been seen lurking outside Borg's café on the Saturday night. However, the mysterious man never came forward to answer police questions. Members of the Homicide Squad later interviewed two men in Queanbeyan and Sydney but were satisfied they had nothing to do with the murder. The police investigation ran into a dead end and the mystery remains.

THE GRAEME THORNE MURDER

Australia is horrified when a kidnapped eight-year-old, Graeme Thorne, is found murdered in Sydney

Salesman Bazil Thorne thought all this wishes had come true when he won 100,000 pounds in a New South Wales State lottery. It was a mammoth cash sum in that era and, today, it would be worth several million dollars. Thorne and his family might have been wealthy beyond their wildest expectations, but the lottery win was accompanied by one of the most horrific events in Australian criminal history.

Thorne's eight-year-old son Graeme was kidnapped and later found murdered.

Graeme Thorne attended Sydney's Scots College and each day the little boy would walk the same streets from the family's Bondi home before being driven to school by a family friend. On July 7, 1960, he disappeared – little more than a month after his father's huge lottery win. Mrs Freda Thorne had just telephoned police about Graeme's disappearance when she received a phone call demanding 25,000 pounds by late afternoon. The caller, who had a thick European accent, told Mrs Thorne: "I have your boy."

The caller told Mrs Thorne he would call back before that afternoon's deadline, but there was no call and police the next day found Graeme's school bag on the outskirts of Sydney. Police by now feared the worst, especially as kidnapping was regarded as something more likely to occur overseas than in Australia. Mrs Thorne made a plea through the media for any information on her son and the 25,000 ransom even was withdrawn from the bank in case the kidnapper rang back with further information or instructions.

Graeme's school cap and books were found days after the kidnapping and, on August 16, the Thorne family's worst fears were realised when Graeme's little body was found on a vacant block in Seaforth. He had been bashed and strangled and his hands and feet were tied with rope. His body had been wrapped in a blanket and he was still wearing most of his school uniform. The kidnapping investigation now had changed to one of murder, and the Australian public was sickened to its stomach.

Police were told that a blue 1955 Ford Customline had been seen at the time of Graeme's kidnapping and, naturally, police wanted to interview the owner or driver. It was just the lead the police needed as a couple notified them that a neighbour, Stephen Bradley, drove a blue Customline and, even more significantly, he had a thick European accent. Police interviewed him at his work, but told them he could account for his activities on the day Graeme had disappeared as it was the day his family had gone on holiday and he moved house with the help of removalists.

The next break in the investigation was when police learned that Bradley had sold his Customline. Police impounded it and took a number of scrapings from the boot, including specimens of what turned out to be a rare type of cypress (smooth cypress and squarrosa false cypress), with scrapings from Graeme's clothing showing similar traces. Other evidence pointed to Bradley, but he was gone. He, his wife and her 13-year-old son from a previous marriage had sailed from Sydney on the P &O liner, the *Himalaya* on September 26. Bradley eventually was arrested in Colombo, Ceylon (now Sri Lanka) on October 10 and brought back to Australia to face a charge of murdering little Graeme Thorne. He was found guilty and sentenced to life imprisonment. Bradley, who was born in Budapest, Hungary, in 1926, died of a heart attack on October 6, 1968, at 42 years of age.

THE WEALTHY WIDOW MYSTERY

An elderly woman is stabbed to death in her Melbourne flat and her killer has never been apprehended.

Mrs Ennie May Anderson, with her round, chubby face and twinkling smile, was everyone's picture of a typical grandmother. She was 78 years of age, devoted to her grandchildren and interested in church activities. She was the type of woman who would not pick an argument with anyone. Unfortunately, however, rumours had swept the inner suburb of East Melbourne that Mrs Anderson had a lot of money stashed away in her Clarendon Street flat. Mrs Anderson leased the Clarendon Terrace apartments, and sub-let them. Naturally, she collected rent and she often kept money in secret pockets in her clothing. However, she was no hoarder and the money she kept in the flat was not worth her death. Her killer could not have believed that when she was stabbed to death in her flat on October 29, 1961.

Mrs Anderson was wearing a nightgown when the killer struck. She apparently was in bed when disturbed. However, Mrs Anderson had no time to raise an alarm. Certainly, no one heard a scream and there was no sign of a struggle. Mrs Anderson was stabbed just once, a thrust below her left shoulder blade , just near the heart. The killer fled, apparently escaping with 30 pounds. Mrs Anderson's body was not discovered until daylight, tenant Miss Winnie Hayes calling on Mrs Anderson at about 12.30pm. Miss Hayes wanted to know if Mrs Anderson required any shopping. But, because there was no answer and the inside lights were on, Miss Hayes went inside and found the landlady's body across a bed.

The East Melbourne area at that time was notorious for prowlers and burglars and police were confident there would be an early arrest. Their hopes rose dramatically when the murder weapon was found the day after the killing. Milkman Mr Jack Meehan found the kitchen knife in a lane near Clarendon Terrace. The knife had been stolen from a kitchenette only a few feet from the door to Mrs Anderson's flat and was one of a set of four. Police left no stone unturned in their efforts to nab the killer, but were baffled because the killer left many valuables untouched, including a few pounds in cash, an uncashed cheque, bank books and jewellery.

Police then had what they at first thought was their best lead yet when a man rang Russell Street headquarters several times a week. They eventually traced the calls and the mystery man was taken in for questioning. The man even told police that he had murdered Mrs Anderson, giving them details of the killing. However, police soon discovered that the man, a 20-year-old Italian, could not have murdered Mrs Anderson and he was later fined for hindering police. Meanwhile, Mrs Anderson's funeral was held at St Paul's Cathedral, with her killer still free. Now, almost half a century later, the mystery is unlikely ever to be solved.

THE CASE OF THE WALKING CORPSE

The gruesome mutilation murders of men in Sydney sends shock waves through Australian society.

There have been few more shocking murders than the ones committed by a man known initially as "The Mutilator" and then as "The Walking Corpse". William MacDonald's gruesome crimes horrified Australia yet, incredibly, his blood-saturated spree could have continued indefinitely if he had not panicked after killing his final victim. Born Allan Ginsberg in England in 1924, he served in the British army before changing his name to William MacDonald and migrating to Canada and then to Australia. Unable to hold down a job for any length of time, he moved from city to city before settling in Sydney.

Then, on the night of June 4, 1961, the lonely MacDonald started a conversation with vagrant Alfred Greenfield as they sat on a bench in a Darlinghurst park. MacDonald, who was working as a letter sorter with the Post Master General (now Australia Post), suggested to Greenfield that they move on to a more secluded spot to drink some beer. Then, after a walk to a spot near the Domain Baths, MacDonald repeatedly stabbed his unsuspecting victim. It was a frenzied and premeditated attack as MacDonald had slipped into a plastic raincoat before he slashed and slashed Greenfield, severing the arteries in the vagrant's neck.

But there was worse to follow. MacDonald removed Greenfield's trousers and sliced off the dead man's penis and testicles. The Mutilator had struck. Yet the man whose deeds shocked the nation walked calmly away. MacDonald slipped his bood-stained knife into a plastic bag and threw Greenfield's genitals into Sydney Harbour. The discovery of Greenfield's body created uproar. The horrific murder, naturally, was splashed all over the front pages of Sydney's newspapers, with the term "The Mutilator" used for the first time to describe the killer.

The police, despite every effort, were baffled and the NSW government eventually offered a reward of 1000 pounds ($2000) for any information leading to the arrest of the mutilation killer. Every police inquiry led to a dead-end and, six months later, MacDonald struck again. The body of Ernest William Cobbin was found in a blood-splattered public toilet in Moore Park. MacDonald again had used the lure of drinking beer together. The Mutilator slashed Cobbin to the neck, severed his jugular vein and inflicted many other wounds. He then sliced off his victim's penis and testicles. The seemingly cool, calm and collected MacDonald washed himself on the way home and again threw his victim's genitals into the harbour.

The media again referred to "The Mutilator" and the police, despite staking out public toilets in the area and issuing warnings, again were baffled. Another five months passed and, with the police fearing The Mutilator could strike again at any time, MacDonald made their worst nightmares come true. He struck again in Darlinghurst after striking up a conversation with a man named Frank McLean. Again, MacDonald invited his intended victim for a drink but, for the first time, ran into difficulties in carrying out his murderous intention. McLean resisted after being stabbed in the neck and tried to fend off MacDonald's thrusts with the sheath-knife. Despite being much taller than his attacker, McLean was unable to ward off the many blows and was stabbed in the neck, chest and face. MacDonald then cut off McLean's penis and testicles.

However, the mutilation killer was far from cool, calm and collected this time and almost panicked. He fled the scene as quickly as he could and not long after his frenzied attack, McLean's body was discovered. Although police were on the scene almost immediately, MacDonald had made it safely home. Sydney, of course, was in a frenzy over The Mutilator's killing.

Police formed a special task force and the State government increased its offer of a reward to 5000 pounds ($10,000). Meanwhile, MacDonald, who had been working at the PMG under the alias of Allan Brennan, had decided in a change of career and took over a mixed business in the Sydney suburb of Burwood. However, the urge to kill remained and, on the night of June 2, 1962, The Mutilator struck again.

MacDonald's next victim was Irish derelict Patrick Hackett, who has just been released from jail for a minor offence. This time MacDonald took his victim back to his own home and, when Hackett, had passed out from drinking too much, The Mutilator stabbed him in the neck. The Irishman quickly came to his senses and shielded himself from the blows MacDonald rained on him with his knife. In the process, MacDonald slashed his own hand. Finally, however, the multiple killer stabbed Hackett in the heart. MacDonald tried to remove Hackett's genitals, but the knife by now was too blunt for the task. Exhausted, the killer fell asleep, but next morning took himself to hospital to have stitches inserted in his wounded hand. He then set about cleaning up his shop, wiping away pools of blood and tearing up the linoleum on the floor. His final task was to drag Hackett's body under the shop.

Realising he would find it almost impossible to dispose of the body, MacDonald decided to flee the scene. He caught a train to Brisbane and prayed he could change his identity and melt into the background. Although MacDonald daily expected to read headlines about the discovery of Hackett's body, there was no mention in any newspaper or on any radio news service.

Then, several weeks after Hackett's murder, neighbours noticed a terrible odour from MacDonald's shop on Burwood Road. Police discovered Hackett's body, but it was so decomposed that identification was impossible. In fact, police believed the body was that of MacDonald and it was buried under MacDonald's assumed name of Allan Brennan. Coroner F.E. Cox, who returned an open verdict, was not convinced it was the body of the man known as Brennan and said: "It seems extraordinary that the body of Mr Brennan should have been found in the position and the condition in which it was found."

According to the evidence, the deceased had neither his trousers on, nor his boots or shoes, or singlet. He was clad only in his socks, with his coat and trousers alongside him. "Nothing was found to indicate to any degree of certainty that the deceased had taken his own life, even if it were his intention to do so. It seems to me an extraordinary thing that the deceased should have gone under the house to commit an act that would result in his death."

The astute coroner then added that the dead man could have been "the victim of foul play". Although he stressed that he had no evidence of this, he noted: "I cannot exclude that possibility." MacDonald breathed easier in the belief that he was a dead man walking. No one knew he was still alive and he believed the police would never be able to charge him with even one of the murders he had committed. However, he had not counted on fate, in the form of a former workmate.

MacDonald was walking down a Sydney street one day when he bumped into an old work mate who expressed great surprise that "Allan Brennan" was still alive. The work mate, who even had attended the funeral service, could not believe his eyes. The stunned MacDonald fled down the street and almost immediately caught a train to Melbourne. The work mate contacted a Sydney crime reporter with his remarkable near-collision with a ghost and the following day the *Mirror* newspaper ran Morris' account under the headline CASE OF THE WALKING CORPSE.

Police, stunned by the report, re-examined the case of the body under the shop and finally realised they had made a mistake and, in fact, the body was that of Irishman Hackett. The body was exhumed and this time stab and cut marks were found on the body's genitals. The police believed they finally were onto the trail of The Mutilator, albeit almost by accident. The police released an identikit description of MacDonald, and it paid dividends when workers at Melbourne's Spencer Street railway station thought the portrait resembled a new work mate.

They notified the Victoria Police and arrested the man who had moved from Sydney as The Mutilator. MacDonald confessed to his crimes and was brought to trial in Sydney in September, 1963. However, he pleaded not guilty on the grounds of insanity. After all, what sane man would kill for the thrill of it and then remove his victim's genitals? Yet the jury did not see it that way and found MacDonald guilty on four counts of murder. He was sentenced to life imprisonment. However, after bashing an inmate at Long Bay jail, he was removed to the Morriset Pyschiatric Centre for the criminally insane before eventually being returned to protective custody.

THE AMOROUS BARBER

An Italian barber is shot dead in North Melbourne over alleged advances to another man's wife.

Gregario Marazita, widely respected in Melbourne's Italian community, and his brothers ran a flourishing licensed grocery business opposite the Victoria Market. Marazita had a number of friends in the area and these included Salvatore Manusco, who worked as a barber in Victoria Street, North Melbourne, opposite Marazita's grocery shop.

Marazita, 37, treated Manusco, 25, like a brother and the two got on well together. Marazita even took Manusco to his home in West Brunswick, where Manusco used to cut the children's hair. Manusco and Marazita had been friends for about four years in 1962, when the friendship started cooling, after Marazita had heard that Manusco had tried to kiss his wife. The situation exploded into violence on the night of June 18, 1962, after Marazita left the grocery shop and started walking to his car parked nearby. Marazita tangled with Manusco and a scuffle developed. Shots were heard and Marazita was found badly wounded. He was rushed to the nearby Royal Melbourne Hospital with bullet wounds, but died soon after arrival.

Manusco later walked in to the Swan Hill police station in northern Victoria and was later charged with murder and committed for trial. The Crown alleged at Manusco's trial in the Criminal Court that Manusco fired four shots from a revolver at Marazita in Little Cobden Street, North Melbourne, at about 5.40pm on June 18. The Crown also claimed that the shooting followed adverse advances by Manusco towards Marazita's wife. Mrs Rita Marazita told the court that Manusco had repeatedly tried to kiss her and that only five weeks before the shooting her husband had slapped Manusco to the face. She said that her husband had told Manusco over the tea table in West Brunswick: "I have treated you like a brother and you are trying to upset my home."

The court was told that there originally had been three shots, but a witness, Stephen Chiodo, said he then saw Manusco run up behind Marazita, lift a revolver and fire a fourth and fatal shot into Marazita's back. However, Manusco claimed he had never tried to kiss his friend's wife and had not made advances to her. He admitted he walked up to Marazita on the night of the killing, but said Marazita grabbed him by the coat with one hand and punched him with the other. He said that as they struggled, Marazita pulled out a revolver and the gun went off. The jury took an hour and a quarter to find Manusco guilty of murder. He stood motionless as Justice O'Bryan sentenced him to death, that sentence commuted to one of 40 years' jail.

THE 'SON' WHO KILLED

A young man walks into a Melbourne police station and tells them he has the body of a woman in his car and that there is another woman's body at a nearby house.

Officers at the Moonee Ponds police station in suburban Melbourne could not believe their ears when a man claimed on December 2, 1962, that he had a body in his car. Detective Ken Smith spoke to the young man and police then examined a car parked outside the police station. The body of a young woman was lying across the front seat. Police then went to a house in the nearby suburb of Niddrie and discovered the body of a younger woman. The dead women were sisters, and the man who had walked into the police station had been engaged to the older woman. Police had twin killings on their hands but at least they did not have to launch a search for the killer.

The dead sisters were Lynette (19) and Anthea (16) Ainsworth. Douglas Alfred Mauger, 24, was charged with having murdered the sisters. It was a tragic case as Mauger had moved into the Ainsworth family home two and a half years earlier and Mr Bernard Ainsworth, father of the dead girls, said he treated Mauger "like a son". Mr Ainsworth said he believed Mauger had been deprived as a youth and "wanted to give him the things he missed". Mauger and Lynette Ainsworth became engaged in November, 1961. Mauger moved into a pet shop business early the following year, but that venture indirectly led to his troubles as the business failed and he was declared bankrupt. The engagement therefore was called off in October, 1962.

The engagement was an "on-off" affair and the young couple made several attempts to reconcile their differences. However, it seemed they would never really get together again. At least that is how it appeared to Mauger, and he was determined not to lose the girl he loved. The matter came to a head on the night of December 1 when Mauger watched his former fiancée talking to another young man at the Ainsworth home. It was an innocent enough conversation, but it was the turning point for Mauger.

He spoke to Lynette in her bedroom that night and told her he did not want to lose her. But even then Lynette could not have known that Mauger would go to such extremes. He loaded a .22 rifle, went into Lynette's bedroom again but did not pull the trigger. He just could not kill, not at that stage, anyway, Mauger, soon after nine o'clock the next morning, went into Anthea Ainsworth's bedroom and shot her in the body and then in the head. He then battered the girl about the head with a hammer as he was convinced she had had something to do with his broken engagement. Mauger then drove to the Ainsworth garage business, picked up Lynette and drove to an area near Anthea's school in Essendon. A struggle developed and Mauger shot Lynette five times in the head and then drove to the police station.

Mauger pleaded not guilty to two charges of murder and his counsel entered a plea of insanity on his behalf. However, the jury took just an hour and a half to find him guilty. Mauger was sentenced to death, but this was later commuted to 50 years' imprisonment and the State Executive Council ordered that he not be eligible for parole until he had served 40 years.

THE BOGLE-CHANDLER MYSTERY

The Bogle-Chandler case of New Year's Day, 1963, remains one of Australia's greatest mysteries.

The bodies of Dr Gilbert Bogle and Mrs Margaret Chandler were found early on New Year's Day, 1963, in the Sydney suburb of Chatswood. They had been at a party given by a CSIRO scientist and police were baffled as there was no evident cause of death. Both bodies were covered, Dr Chandler's by his jacket and trousers and Mrs Chandler's by cardboard beer cartons. The director of the NSW department of Forensic Medicine, Dr John Lang, testified at the coroner's inquest in May, 1963, that the couple had died from acute circulatory failure, but could not explain why the circulatory systems had failed. There were no marks on either body and no poisonous substances were found in either body's internal organs.

However, government analyst Mr Ernest Ogg did not rule out the possibility of chemical poisoning. He also indicated: "I can see no prospect of this mystery being solved so far as chemical poisons are concerned." It was suggested that Mrs Chandler wanted to take Dr Bogle, an eminent scientist, as her lover, but there was no evidence she had had sexual intercourse just before her death. And her husband, Mr Geoffrey Chandler, had left the party earlier than his wife and had picked up his two children at his in-law's home in Granville. No satisfactory theory has been put forward as a solution to the Bogle-Chandler mystery and no one even knows for sure whether it was a case of murder at all.

THE DEATH WALK

A Melbourne schoolboy vanishes after going for a walk and his body is discovered two weeks later.

Sunday, October 11, 1964, had been a quiet, pleasant day for the Ganino family in the northern Melbourne suburb of Fawkner. It had been like many Sundays, spent in quiet relaxation and family activities. Dominic Ganino, 15, had spent the morning at Mass and Communion, then spent the afternoon looking for bits and pieces of motor cars at a nearby rubbish tip. He returned home in time for an early dinner and washed up the dishes for his mother.

Dominic, a student at Fawkner Technical School, did not feel like watching television with his brother and sister after dinner but elected to take his dog Lassie for a walk. It was still a pleasant spring day and Dominic could not have known that his day would end in death. He stepped into Sydney Road, immediately outside his home, without a worry in the world. Dominic did not return from his walk and his parents became worried almost immediately. It was unlike Dominic to stay away for long without telling his parents. When it became obvious he was not with friends or relatives, the family contacted police.

A description of Dominic was flashed to police patrols soon after 10 p.m. and Dominic Ganino officially became a missing person. What now particularly worried Dominic's family and police was that the boy's dog had returned home by herself soon after 7 p.m. An intensive police search the next day failed to find any trace of the missing boy.

Two weeks later, on Monday, October 26, a security officer at the Ford motor works (six kilometres from the Ganino house) was searching swamp country behind the works. He was looking for hollow logs, and eventually spotted what he might have been after. However, Mr Alexander McCann also discovered the body of Dominic Ganino under a tree trunk. The face was immersed in about ten inches (16cm) of water and the boy's clothing was disarranged. Dominic had been murdered and police immediately launched a massive investigation. Forensic examination later showed that Dominic had died of asphyxiation due to strangling. However, the post mortem also showed that that boy had been homosexually raped. Dominic obviously had struggled with his attacker but because the body was not discovered until two weeks after his disappearance, the trail to the killer was cold.

Police had few clues. There were footprints and car tracks near where the body had been found but they were too old to be of much use. A blue comb also was found near the body, but this also proved to be a negative clue. Police decided that the public had to help in inquiries and thousands of people in the Fawkner and Broadmeadows area were questioned and interviewed. In fact, police launched a doorknock campaign, speaking to everyone in the neighborhood. Residents were asked if they had seen the boy on the night he was murdered. Dominic had been wearing dark jeans, a check shirt and a grey school pullover. He was just 5 ft 3 in (160cm), was slightly built and dark.

Several sightings were given, the most useful being by a 14-year-old neighbour, who told police that he had seen Dominic on Sydney Road but on the opposite side of his home, Dominic obviously crossing busy Sydney Road. It seemed that the whole Italian community of Melbourne mourned the death of Dominic Ganino. His funeral, on November 5, was a mass display of grief, with hundreds of schoolmates, friends, relatives and sympathisers moving from St Matthew's Church, North Fawkner, to the Fawkner Cemetery. Dominic's killer was still free. Police continued their investigations, convinced that someone had abducted the boy and driven him to the lonely swamp country at the back of Ford's. One theory was that the killer offered to give Dominic driving lessons 'away from the traffic'. The boy was interested in cars and desperately wanted to learn to drive.

Although police never arrested anyone over Dominic's killing, it has been alleged that a notorious paedophile Catholic church worker might have been implicated. Robert Charles Blunden, known as 'Bert', was living at the St Matthew's presbytery at the time of Dominic's death and is known to have been abusing children and young men. Police interviewed Blunden soon after Dominic's murder, but had no information at that time of his sexual activities. Indeed, they knew nothing of this until a victim stepped forward in 1996. Blunden was 79 years of age and in poor health when police were told of his background and, in 1997, he was jailed for four years after pleading guilty in the Melbourne County Court to 27 charges of indecent assault and buggery between 1964-70.

Significantly, Blunden used a ruse of offering boys a lift on the pretext that he would give them driving lessons. But, although questioned by police in 1996 about Dominic's death, Blunden refused to make any admissions. Blunden died in 1998 at 81 years of age.

THE HEADLESS BODY

Two boys playing "cowboys and Indians" make the gruesome discovery of a headless body in the inner Melbourne suburb of Fitzroy.

The condemned and abandoned cottage in Greeves Street, Fitzroy, was the perfect hiding place for 10-year-old Edward Irvine, who was playing "cowboys and Indians" with his friends from the George Street State School on February 26, 1964. The grey building, which had no front garden, had its windows covered by corrugated iron for several months.

However, Edward discovered a way to enter the cottage – to his eventual horror. Little Edward stared wide-eyed at what he saw and rushed to tell his friend, nine-year-old Terry Karvalis, who immediately rushed to have a look at Edward's discovery.

The boys, who both lived in nearby Napier Street, went home to tell their parents that they had seen parts of a man's body. However, their parents chastised the boys for returning home late from school. The boys, not wanting to get into deeper trouble, kept their secret to themselves until the following morning when they met a teacher on the way to school. They blurted out the details of what they had seen and the teacher sensibly contacted the police. Detective Sergeant Tom White and two uniformed constables went to the boarded-up cottage and took only seconds to confirm what the boys had been saying.

The head of the Homicide Squad, Detective Inspector Jack Matthews was called in to investigate a discovery that had Melbourne buzzing for days. The two schoolboys had made one of the grisliest discoveries in years as the body was in two parts – the chest and shoulders, and the pelvic part of the torso. The middle part of the torso was missing, as were the limbs and head.

Then, just 24 hours later, 14-year-old John Garoni and 15-year-old Terry Kennedy were riding their bikes around a lot in nearby Gore Street when Kennedy hit a bump and fell off his bike. He reached out and was horrified. He literally had stumbled on two arms (one with a watch on the wrist), thigh sections and part of an abdomen. The human jigsaw was being locked together, but with no head.

The major breakthrough came when a reader of the Melbourne *Herald* responded to information that the name "Molack" had been found on the pocket of trousers found at the cottage. Police finally deducted that the dead man was 32-year-old process worker Imre "Jimmy" Mallach, who had not turned up for work for several days. The dead man's head and right arm finally were found in a reserve off Alfred Crescent, North Fitzroy.

Mallach, a naturalised Australian, had been born in Hungary and had migrated to Australia in 1957. On February 29, 1964, police charged 37-year-old Mrs Vilma Broda with the murder of her estranged de facto husband. The Criminal Court was told that Mallach had turned up at her home drunk and demanded money. They fought and Broda hit him over the head with a hammer before dissecting the body. The jury found Broda not guilty of both murder and manslaughter and she walked away a free woman.

THE LAST MAN TO HANG

In one of Australia's most infamous criminal cases, escaped convict Ronald Ryan is hanged after the shooting of a prison guard during an escape from Melbourne's Pentridge jail.

There have been few manhunts of such magnitude in Australian criminal history as the one that tracked down Pentridge escapees Ronald Ryan and Peter Walker over 17 days from December 19, 1965. The shooting and killing of prison guard George Hodson outraged Victorians and the media went into frenzy over the chase for Australia's most wanted criminals. The case will forever hold a place in infamy as Ryan eventually was found guilty of the murder of Hodson and became the last man to be hanged in Australia. The execution was seen by hundreds of thousands of Australians as an outrage and by many close to the case as a travesty of justice and even as a political exercise.

Ronald Joseph Ryan was born in Melbourne on February 21, 1925, into a working class family. He had three sisters — Violet, Irma and Gloria — and a half-brother, George Thompson (by his mother Cecilia's first husband). Father Jack Ryan could not find work and life was tough for the family. So much so that Cecilia Ryan could not cope and the Ryan children were put into homes, Ronald to the Salesian order's monastery at Sunbury and the girls to a convent in the inner Melbourne suburb of Abbotsford. Ryan apparently was a good student, but ran away from the orphanage when he was just 14 years of age and headed north where he found work as a rail-cutter and general hand. He worked hard and long and, in 1943, returned to Melbourne. By now he was 18 years of age and had money in his pockets.

Ryan took his sisters from the convent and, reunited with his mother, he became the family breadwinner. He led a steady life for several years and, in 1948, married Dorothy George and settled down to raise a family — daughters Janice, Wendy and Rhonda. However, rail-splitting and timber-cutting did not enable Ryan to earn enough money to provide for his family as well as he would have wished and he finally attracted police attention when he passed forged cheques. Ryan was 31 years of age when he was given a bond for these offences but, not long after, he again was caught passing bad cheques. Convicted, he was given a five-year bond and he again seemed to settle down.

However, Ryan three years later was arrested for theft but escaped from custody at the Melbourne City Watch House. Recaptured, he was sent to prison and, instead of settling down on release, drifted back into a life of crime and in 1964 was sent to Pentridge after a brief career as a safe-cracker. Dorothy Ryan divorced her husband and re-married, but Ryan refused to concede that he had lost his family and set about planning his escape from Pentridge.

After studying the sentry catwalks and measuring the thickness of the prison walls, he decided that Sunday, December 19, 1965, provided him with the perfect opportunity to escape. Ryan informed fellow prisoner Peter Walker of his plans and the 24-year-old agreed to join him in the bid for freedom. That Sunday was selected because it was the day of the prison guards' Christmas party and the pair knew there was a skeleton staff on duty. Ryan gave Walker the go-ahead early in the afternoon and they scaled a wall to reach a catwalk. Ryan, with a piece of water pipe as a weapon and Walker behind him, came across prison guard Helmut Lange and grabbed a M1 rifle from a rack. Lange, with the rifle pointed at him, opened a door to the outside while Ryan ejected a live round. Ryan demanded car keys from a passer-by and, when these weren't handed over, knocked the man down.

The alarm by now had been raised and Ryan and Walker ran into busy Sydney Road, Coburg. Ryan tried to hijack a passing car, but noticed that Walker was just about to be nabbed by guard Hodson. A shot rang out and Hodson fell dead on the tram tracks, while the escapees jumped into a car and fled from the scene. Melbourne was abuzz with the escape and killing and, as police scoured the city, Ryan and Walker holed up in the house of a sympathiser in the seaside Melbourne suburb of Elwood. Emboldened by their escape and desperately needing funds, they then held up a bank in the southern suburb of Ormond. By now, the media was in a frenzy and headlines blared every police comment or reported sighting of the outlaws.

In fact, Ryan's mother at one stage appeared on television with an appeal for her son to give himself up. Just five days after their escape, on Christmas Eve, their female sympathiser went to a party and brought home a companion. James Henderson. On meeting Ryan, the young man made the biggest mistake of his life in telling Walker that his companion looked a lot like the escaped criminal Ronald Ryan. Walker shot Henderson dead in a public toilet in Albert Park and he and Ryan were forced to go on the run.

They travelled to Sydney and moved into a flat in the seaside suburb of Coogee. However, Walker could not resist the opposite sex and, after making arrangements for a date, he and Ryan were caught in a police trap after 17 days on the run. The pair was extradited to Melbourne and their trial opened on March 15, 1966, before Mr Justice Starke. The prosecution case relied on numerous eye-witnesses, whereas defence counsel Philip Opas QC was able to point to numerous instances of conflicting evidence. For example, Opas used a leading mathematician to demonstrate that the shot which killed Hodson could not have been fired from ground level. Also, no fired bullet was ever found and, in fact, only one round was unaccounted for, yet Ryan had ejected that round. It begged the question of whether another weapon had been used in the slaying of Hodson.

Opas argued that Hodson's wound was caused by a shot from the prison guard tower. Later, in 1986 and well after Ryan's execution, a prison guard came forward to say that he might have accidentally fired the shot that killed Hodson and feared to say anything at the time in case he got into trouble. He also was convinced Ryan would never be hanged and that the death sentence would be commuted to life imprisonment. Ryan, when he took the stand during his trial, was questioned by his defence counsel and the following is part of that evidence:

> OPAS: Did you murder Prison Officer Hodson?
>
> RYAN: Most emphatically not.
>
> OPAS: Did you fire a shot at all on the nineteenth of December?
>
> RYAN: I did not discharge that gun on the nineteenth of December.

Ryan also was asked about how he came into possession of the prison rifle.

> OPAS: What did you grab the rifle for?
>
> RYAN: So that it couldn't be used against me. I saw the cocking lever on the side of the rifle. Incidentally, I had never seen one of these M1.30s before, I had never handled one, and I pulled the cocking lever back to inject the shell into the rifle or see if there was one in there first. There were none in there, so I pushed the lever forward to inject one, to fit one, and pushed it in.
>
> OPAS: What did you do that for?
>
> RYAN: Oh, to bluff the warder (Lange), let him know that I meant business, to impress upon him that he had better do what I told him to. However, in pushing the lever forward I noticed that the extractors, I suppose you would call them, didn't close over the head of the shell, so I pulled the lever back to force it harder forward. In doing this I picked up another shell and forced it in behind the one which had first gone in. Consequently, my gun jammed.
>
> OPAS: What happened next?

RYAN: Well then, I tested the gun and worked the lever and this all happened very quickly, of course, and I got the shell out; it tipped out on the floor, and I just let the lever go and this unfortunately picked up another shell, and again I was in the same predicament.

Opas later asked Ryan about prison guard Hodson.

OPAS: Did you see what happened to Hodson?

RYAN: No, I didn't see what happened to Hodson. I saw Hodson, who was chasing Walker; he was a pretty big fellow and very stout. He seemed to be just about at the end of his tether. He was pretty distressed, that was my impression, when he was chasing Peter. They ran from my sight behind this Plymouth (motor vehicle). I was approaching, not exactly from the rear but from the driver's side of the rear and consequently that car did obscure my vision of Hodson and Walker. In any case, I presume they were behind a car and I just lost sight of Peter and the officer.

OPAS: What happened with you? Did you hear a shot at any time?

RYAN: I couldn't swear that I heard a shot but I did hear two or three detonations, but this may have been pure auto-suggestion because I was expecting to be fired at by the guard at No. 2 Tower at any stage, but I would not swear that I heard any shots. They could have been shots or they could have been car doors slamming because quite a few people were jumping out of cars at this stage to, well, I assume to lend a hand to the officers.

Ryan, despite sometimes fierce cross-examination, did not deviate from his account of what had happened and there were many who believed he would be given the benefit of the doubt. However, the 12-man jury returned a 'guilty' verdict and Mr Justice Starke had no option but to pronounce the mandatory death sentence. Walker was sentenced to 12 years' imprisonment for manslaughter, with another 12 years for the killing of Henderson. He was released in 1983. However, no one — least of all some of the jurors — expected the death sentence to be carried out. After all, there had been 36 reprieves since the previous execution in 1951. An appeal to the Victorian Court of Criminal Appeal was dismissed and Victorian Premier Sir Henry Bolte announced that Ryan, indeed, would hang. At one stage Bolte, whose government was facing re-election, said: 'There is no possibility of the decision to hang Ryan being reversed. It is quite definite and final.' He was determined to make his point on law and order.

The Bolte government announced that the execution would take place on January 9, 1967, but this was rescheduled after an appeal to the Privy Council in London. This appeal also failed and a new execution date was set, for February 3, 1967. At 10 o'clock the night before the scheduled execution, a special meeting of the State Executive Council rejected Ryan's last minute appeal for mercy. Ryan's solicitor, Mr Ralph Freadman, said: 'We have just received a message from the Crown Solicitor, Mr Mornane, that the Queen, acting through the Governor-in-Council, has rejected the petition to exercise mercy. And that's the end of it.'

Ryan wrote letters to his family on prison toilet paper and said: 'With regard to my guilt I say only that I am innocent of intent and have a clear conscience in this matter.' February 3 broke with the promise of a hot day as more than 3000 protestors, including Ryan's mother Cecilia, stood outside Pentridge as Ryan was hanged at 8am. His last words to the hangman were: 'God bless you, please make it quick.' At the same time, Cecilia Ryan told television journalist Dan Webb:

'He's a good boy, really.' The remains of Ronald Joseph Ryan were buried in quicklime within the grounds of Pentridge.

THE WANDA BEACH MURDERS

Two 15-year-old girls are murdered at Wanda Beach, Sydney, and the mystery remains.

When 15-year-olds Christine Sharrock and Marianne Schmidt went to the Wanda Beach, in Sydney's south, on January 13, 1965, they inadvertently ignited one of Australia's greatest murder mysteries. The girls went to the beach with Marianne's brothers Peter (10), Wolfgang (seven) and Norbert (six) and sister Trixie (nine) and travelled by train to Cronulla. The day had started as fine and hot, but a change in the weather saw the group walking along the beach rather than swimming. Christine and Marianne left the little group and walked towards the Wanda sand dunes, never to be seen alive again.

Marianne's brothers and sister waited for her and Christine to return but, at 5pm, decided to leave the beach and return home, where they were told the two 15-year-olds did not return from a walk. Police were notified and, the following afternoon a man walking along Wanda Beach saw blood in the sand. When he went to investigate, he saw the two dead girls side by side in a shallow grave. There was a considerable amount of blood at the scene and both girls had been sexually assaulted, stabbed and bashed.

Police, naturally, launched an immediate investigation and wanted to speak with a surfer Wolfgang Schmidt had seen in the area. Police also scoured the area for possible clues and discovered a bloodstained knife. However, police were unable to determine whether it was the murder weapon or even if the blood stains were human. In a desperate effort to solve the mystery, police even reconstructed the walk to death, with women police officers dressed as the two girls. However, there were no new leads. An inquest into the death of the two girls was held in April, 1966, but although police had a number of possible suspects, the coroner found that the girls had been murdered by a person or persons unknown. The mystery remains, although one convicted killer remains at the top of the list of suspects.

THE BEAUMONT CHILDREN

In one of Australia's most baffling cases, the Beaumont siblings go missing during a visit to the beach in Adelaide and are never seen again.

Australia day (January 26) broke hot and dry in Adelaide in 1966 and the three children of Jim and Nancy Beaumont were allowed to go to the beach at Glenelg, not far from their suburban home of Somerton Park. The eldest Beaumont child was Jane and although only a shy nine-year-old, she was thought responsible enough to look after herself, seven-year-old sister and four-year-old brother Grant. The

Beaumont children left home at 10.30 in the morning and took a five-minute bus ride to Glenelg. They were expected to return home by noon but, by 3.30pm, their mother was worried.

Police launched a search for the children and were told the Beaumonts had been seen in the company of a tall, blond man in his mid-30s. To worry police even further, a shopkeeper reported that Jane Beaumont had bought cake and a meat pie with a one-pound note, even though her mother had given her only coins for the bus fares and food. One witness, a postman the children knew, had seen the children walking towards home at about three o'clock. The children were never seen again and their disappearance remains a mystery. Public interest in the Beaumont children was phenomenal and all sorts of theories were put forward for their disappearance.

A clairvoyant, Gerard Croiset, even was brought out from Holland and, after examining areas where the children might have been taken, pointed out a site where he believed the Beaumonts had been buried. However, it was a building site and the owners were reluctant to allow excavation until public pressure forced their hand. The search was fruitless, as have many other leads provided to police over almost 40 years. Many theories have been put forward and every suggestion creates headlines, but no proof of where the Beaumonts might be or whether they are still alive.

DEATH ON A TRAIN

A woman returning home by train in suburban Sydney is bashed to death and her handbag, containing just $2 is stolen.

Sales demonstrator Pamela Blair was returning to her St Peters home in Sydney on the night of November 29, 1966, but never reached her destination. Mrs Blair caught a train at Hurstville station at 8.11pm, intending to arrive at the Sydenham station 22 minutes later. However, she was attacked on the last leg of her journey home. She was bashed about the head with a heavy brass door lever, wrenched from a carriage, and left to die. Mrs Blair, who suffered terrible head injuries, was discovered by fellow passenger Cecil Johnson, who tried to help the injured woman by putting a handkerchief to her head wounds. The woman was partly conscious, but largely incoherent and therefore was unable to give Mr Johnson or the train guard any information on her attacker.

Mrs Blair was rushed to hospital but did not recover from her head wounds and died, despite emergency surgery. A mysterious young man was seen on the train on the night of the murder and one witness said that the "aggressive" young man made a sort of "growling noise" as he moved about the train. The killer has never been brought to justice, despite massive police efforts and the New South Wales government offering a reward for information on the woman's death.

THE TAB SHOOTING

A TAB manager is shot dead during a hold-up in the quiet, respectable Melbourne suburb of Mont Albert.

An alarm at the Victorian Totalisator Agency Board's Melbourne headquarters on the night of April 1, 1967, showed there was a hold-up at the agency's Mont Albert branch. Police immediately rushed to the quiet eastern suburb, hoping they would still be in time to nab the bandit. Police had no idea that their call for help was about to lead to a murder investigation. When police arrived at the Mont Albert

TAB, manager Miss Margaret Pavarno was already dead, shot through the chest with a bullet from a .25 revolver.

Miss Pavarno, an attractive 35-year-old, was an experienced small business operator and seemed to love her involvement with the TAB. She was just about to close the agency shortly before 9pm on April 1 when the bandit struck, obviously waiting to be alone without interference from customers. Significantly, all betting on that night's Melbourne Showgrounds trots meeting had closed only a minute before the bandit entered the agency. The bandit was about 5ft 6in, was stocky, wore dark clothes and had a stocking over his face as a mask. Police knew this because there was a witness to the hold-up. A local identity, who was not named at the coroner's inquest into Miss Pavarno's death, walked into the agency soon after the bandit. He saw the bandit and Miss Pavarno near the office safe and told police that the bandit ordered the manager to open the safe, which she refused to do. The witness than made a bolt for the door to raise the alarm. He just managed to escape, but almost immediately heard a shot from the TAB and rushed back to the agency.

The witness was horrified. Miss Pavarno was lying in a pool of blood, mortally wounded. The bandit escaped with $166, a paltry amount for such a horrible crime. However, an armoured escort service had picked up the agency's takings shortly before the hold-up, the bandit obviously unaware of this procedure. Police reasoned that Miss Pavarno died because of her bravery in refusing to open the safe, especially as it was empty. She must have managed to ring the alarm to TAB headquarters before being shot but her steadfast refusal to open the safe obviously angered the bandit, who fired into Miss Pavarno's chest almost from point-blank range. It was a cold-blooded killing but the man who shot Miss Pavarno so callously avoided capture.

THE BUNGLED KIDNAPPING

Australian Muriel McKay is the unfortunate victim of mistaken identity in a horrifying kidnap in the United Kingdom.

Brothers Arthur and Nizamodeen Hosein had delusions of grandeur, way beyond their modest means as pig and chicken farmers in Hertforshire, England. They wanted to be seriously rich, so came up with a plan to kidnap the wife of Australian newspaper magnate Rupert Murdoch. The brothers followed the Murdoch Rolls Royce on December 29, 1969, and abducted the woman driver. However, the limousine had been lent to the Murdoch company deputy chairman Alick McKay and it was his wife Muriel who was at the wheel that fateful day.

The Hoseins initially demanded a ransom of 500,000 pounds and then doubled it as police launched a massive search in snow and sleet for the missing Mrs McKay. Arthur Hosein was arrested near where the ransom money was due to be collected and, although Muriel McKay's body was never found, the Hosein brothers were found guilty of murder, kidnap and blackmail and were sentenced to life imprisonment. It generally was assumed that the Hoseins fed Mrs McKay's body to their farm pigs.

A BIRTHDAY IN COURT

A teenager, after frequent rows with his policeman father, stabs him to death at their Launceston home.

Young Michael Anthony Curran, just 15, was so unhappy at home that he wanted to join the navy. The boy had had frequent rows with his policeman father, sometimes suffering physically for his trouble. Michael's father, 38-year-old Clifford James Curran, wanted his son to stay at school. They argued about the boy's career on the night of April 14, 1969, also arguing about the boy eating his food too fast. It was all too much for Michael, who later went to his parents' bedroom, stabbed his father with a kitchen knife and later slashed his mother with the same knife. Clifford Curran died in the kitchen of the police house in the Launceston, Tasmania, suburb of Mayfield. Mrs Doris Curran was found with stab wounds to the throat and face, was rushed to Launceston General Hospital and recovered from her wounds.

Michael Curran was charged with the murder of his father and stood trial at the Supreme Court in July, 1969. Michael, who turned 16 on the second day of his trial, admitted stabbing both his father and mother, although he made an original statement to police claiming his mother had stabbed his father. A second alleged statement, read to the court by Detective Sergeant B.J. Morgan, said Curran intended killing his father. Curran allegedly wrote: "He was always hitting me and growling at me. And often hit Mum, too." Mrs Curran told the court her son and his father "did not get on". She said her late husband kicked or punched Michael almost every day and was also violent to daughter Julie, 13.

Michael Curran, who pleaded not guilty, told the court his father several times a year threatened to kill him. He also said that on the night of his father's death, his father had held a bread knife to his throat and threatened to kill him if he did not do well in examinations. He said the look on his father's face convinced him he would carry out the threat.

Justice Neasey told the jury it had three alternatives – guilty, not guilty or not guilty but insane. The jury retired for almost four hours and then returned the verdict – not guilty on the grounds of insanity. Justice Neasey told Michael Curran: "Having regard to the jury's verdict and the provisions of the criminal code, I order that you be kept in strict custody in Her Majesty's jail at Risdon until Her

Majesty's pleasure be known." Michael Curran embraced his mother as he was led away.

THE MERCY KILLING

A middle-aged Melbourne man shoots his wife dead to ease her pain and is charged with murder.

When middle-aged Max Enkhardt heard the squeal of car tyres early one night in 1968, he had no idea that the motor accident he had heard a couple of blocks from his Bentleigh home would turn his life into a nightmare. Max Enkhardt's wife Anna was seriously injured in that accident and spent the following 45 days in hospital recovering from head injuries and a broken pelvis. Indirectly, the accident led to her death, with her husband being charged with her murder.

Enkhardt, a German who arrived in Australia in 1928, married Anna in 1936 and, until the accident, they led a blissful life. Then, however, Anna was racked by pain and her condition slipped dramatically. She suffered from stomach upsets and was convinced she had cancer. There was no doubt her husband suffered with her and, 16 months after the accident, Enkhardt acted. On the afternoon of November 3, 1969, he shot his wife dead. Max 59, said later that he killed Anna, 69, because he loved her and that it was a mercy killing.

Enkhardt was charged with murder and was tried at the Criminal Court the following year, the case attracting enormous public interest. Enkhardt said Anna often would tell him she wished she could "end it all" and that he kissed her before shooting her. He said: "I loved her. I only did it for her. Believe me, I didn't come here to grovel for anything. She was my love … my only love for 35 years … she didn't nag me, she loved me. I couldn't bear to see her suffer."

The jury found Enkhardt guilty of murder and Justice McInerney sentenced him to death. However, the Victorian Executive Council later commuted the sentence to 20 years' imprisonment, with a minimum of 15 years. Enkhardt became a model prisoner and won numerous art and public speaking awards while serving his sentence. He was released in August, 1978, after serving eight years and eight months of his sentence. Ironically, he died from injuries he received when hit by a car in Elsternwick in September, 1979. Not long before his death Enkhardt said: "All that's left to say is my conscience is clear. I can meet my Maker, He knows."

THE GIRL IN WHITE

An entrant in the Miss Australia beauty quest is raped and strangled at Geraldton, Western Australia.

Beautiful Anne Zapelli was one of the most popular identities in the West Australian town of Morawa. Anne, 20, had a pleasant personality and was well-liked by all her neighbours in the quiet country town. In fact, the whole of

Morawa had its fingers crossed that Anne would put the town right on the national map by winning the prestigious Miss Australia quest. Anne was due to appear in nearby Geraldton in late September, 1969, for the regional judging and, from all accounts, she had a good chance of going all the way in the quest. However, violence robbed Anne of her dreams – and her life.

Anne went to Geraldton on the Monday before the Miss Australia judging for an examination as part of her job as a telephonist. She was due to return to Morawa before going back to Geraldton for the judging. Anne booked into a guest house in Geraldton on Monday, September 22, with her thoughts entirely on the two big forthcoming events in her young life. Anne went to the local drive-in theatre that night with another telephonist and two young men, one of them a police constable. However, Anne said she was bored with the film and said she was going to walk back to the guest house.

Dressed in white, Anne set off on foot, the other three staying at the drive-in to watch the end of the movie. They did not see Anne alive again. Constable Graham Batt, one of the three with Anne at the drive-in, reported Anne missing early in the morning when he and his friends were surprised to find no trace of her at the guest house. Anne had vanished and a search was launched. Her body was found the following day in brush and scrub 50 yards from a roadway. She had been battered, raped and strangled.

A number of witnesses told police they had seen a girl dressed in a white mini-dress walking from the drive-in that night and some even told police they had seen a suspicious man, or men, in the vicinity. One witness even told police that a light coloured car pulled up near the girl in white. However, no witnesses could be explicit enough and police ran into a dead-end in their investigation. Anne, whose rape and murder shocked Geraldton, was the victim on an unknown killer or killers. Police, who found scuffle marks near the body, reasoned Anne had put up a struggle but was strangled with a rope or cord for her efforts. The murder weapon was missing and, strangely, so too were Anne's pants and pantyhose.

Police tried everything in an effort to bring the killer(s) to justice but all efforts failed. A reconstruction by an ABC television outfit, with a policewoman playing the part of Anne Zapelli, also failed to lead to the killer(s). An inquest was held in 2001, more than 30 years after Anne's death and, for the first time, a possible killer was named. However, with most of the forensic evidence lost or destroyed, WA coroner, Mr Alastair Hope, was unable to make a conclusive finding.

A BEER BOTTLE THROUGH THE HEART

A 14-year-old girl goes missing in Sydney and, after a huge search, her body is found 10 days later, stabbed through the heart with a broken beer bottle.

Maureen Bradley, 14 years of age, was not the type of girl to run away from home. She had regular habits and, before she disappeared on her way home from her Sydney school on the afternoon of December 3, 1971, she had telephoned her mother from Hornsby railway station to say she would not be long. It was the last time Mrs Bradley heard her daughter's voice. Despite every effort and one of the biggest searches in Sydney for many years, no sign of Maureen Bradley was found over the following 10 days.

The naked body of the pretty blonde eventually was found in a disued septic tank at McKell Park, Brooklyn. She had been stabbed through the heart with a broken beer bottle and there was such outrage that the New South Wales government offered a reward of $10,000 for the arrest of Maureen's killer.

Police eventually made an arrest on January 16, 1972, when a 20-year-old man was charged with the attempted rape of a woman at the northern suburb of Cowan. Labourer Bruce Kenneth McKenzie stood trial at the Central Criminal Court from June 5 that year and the court was told he had confessed to murdering Maureen Bradley. Detective-Sergeant Albert MacDonald said McKenzie had told him he had waited near a bush track as Maureen was walking home from school. He then grabbed her by the neck, dragged her to his car and locked her in the boot before driving to Brooklyn, about 14 kilometres away. He then backed the car into the bush and, with the girl's neck locked in his arms, marched her to the septic tank where he made her undress before he indecently assaulted her.

Then, when McKenzie heard someone shout "hey", he thought someone had seen him. He therefore picked up a beer bottle, smashed it and drove it twice into Maureen's chest, piercing her heart. A jury took just 10 minutes to find McKenzie guilty of murder and he was sentenced to life imprisonment. When Justice Slattery asked him if he had anything to say, McKenzie replied: "I am sorry for the trouble I have caused the girl's family and my own, and I just wish to do what is right in the future."

I WANT TO GO TO HEAVEN

The death of a child is tragic, and the murder of a child is even more tragic. However, there can be few deaths as tragic as that of little Charles Benedek, just six years of age.

Charles died because of an overwhelming love and trust of his father and the desire to go to heaven. His father, Edward Tobor Benedek, was the boys' killer but like the pathetic Edward Williams in *The Three Little Angels (1924)* he deserved a great deal of pity, despite the nature of the killing.

Edward Benedek was a deserted father who struggled to make ends meet in the years before 1971. Born in Hungary in 1927, Benedek fled to Australia as a result of the infamous Hungarian uprising of 1956, settled down, worked mainly as a painter and married in 1964. Unfortunately, his wife later spent periods in mental institutions and finally left him. The Hungarian became father and mother to his two children, Charles and Susan. He struggled for three years to raise the children the best way he could, but it was difficult, with jobs hard to come by and money usually stretched to the limit.

Benedek finally made one of the most tragic suicide pacts in Australian history. He took Charles and Susan, four and a half, for a drive along Victoria's scenic Great Ocean Road on July 22, 1971. He previously had spoken to the children about heaven, little Charles reacting because of lessons taught at school. Benedek finally asked the children if they would like to go to heaven with him or live in a police home. Charles, showing unbelievable faith in his father, said he would like to go to heaven, Susan saying that she would prefer to live in a police home.

The distraught father later shot the boy dead and twice tried to take his own life with the same rifle. The girl was taken by a passing bus driver to the safety of a police station. Benedek was treated at hospitals in Geelong and Melbourne, spending several days in a psychiatric ward. "Susan didn't want to go to heaven with me and Charles, and I said to both Susan and Charles to wait in the car until a car or a truck comes by and ask the man to take them to the nearest police station," Benedek said. "With that I missed Susan and Charles and I started walking away from the car towards the rear with my rifle in my hand. Charles ran after me and said, 'I want to go with you, Daddy', and he pointed to his chest and he said, 'shoot me there, Daddy'.

"I fired a shot towards his chest but it couldn't have been vital because he said, 'it hurts Daddy'. With that I put him back on the front seat of the car, covered him up with a blanket, told him to go to sleep, and when he closed his eyes, I fired a second shot in his chest, the one that must have been the fatal shot. Then I kissed Susan once again, told Susan to kiss Charles as well and told her to stay in the car until a car or a truck comes by, then she could go with them to the nearest police station. I walked away about 12 feet from the rear of the car to a grass edge on the road. I leaned over the rifle and fired a shot into my chest where I thought my heart was.

"I became very thirsty and very dizzy as I was sitting in the grass bleeding under the shirt and I asked Susan to bring me the water container so I could have a drink. She did give me the container, then I told her to go back to the back seat of the car, and with that I leaned over the rifle once again and fired a shot into my chest."

Benedek said that the morning before the tragic shooting he told the children about heaven. He said: "I explained to the children about heaven and, to my amazement, Charlie seemed to know a lot about it. I didn't know they taught that in the first grade at school. He asked me if we have any friends in heaven. I said yes and named a few people he knew who had passed away."

Benedek, 44, was found not guilty of murder because of insanity when he stood trial at the Geelong Criminal Court. Justice Menhennit ordered him to be held in the strictest custody at the Governor's pleasure.

AUSTRALIA'S CHARLES MANSON

A man to be tagged "Mad Dog", hearing voices in his head, goes on a killing spree in Sydney

The British public was outraged late in January, 2004, when serial killer Archie McCafferty was fined just 50 pounds for striking a police officer and sentenced to a 12-month community order. It was nothing more than a slap on the wrist for the man known as 'Mad Dog' for his murderous spree and infamous behaviour as a prisoner on the other side of the world in Australia.

McCafferty was born in Scotland, but migrated to Australia with his family when he was just 10 years of age. The McCafferty family first settled in Melbourne, but then moved to Sydney, where young Archie soon found himself in trouble with the police. The tough young Scot's family believed Archie would settle down after his marriage to Janice Redington in 1972, especially when the couple announced they were going to be parents. Son Craig was born in February, 1973, only for the McCafferty joy to be short-lived. Little Craig lived just six weeks, dying on March 17 in truly tragic circumstances when his mother rolled on top of him after falling asleep while breastfeeding him. An inquest exonerated the young mother, but McCafferty accused his wife of killing their son. The death of baby Craig appeared to tip McCafferty over the edge and although he admitted himself to a psychiatric institute, he checked out again a few days later. McCafferty threatened violence against his family, but no one could have known the extent to which he was prepared to go in his lust for blood.

His brief but dreadful reign of terror started on August 24, 1973, when he teamed up with girlfriend Carol Howes, 16-year-old psychiatric patient Julie Todd and teenagers Michael Meredith, Richard Whittington and Rick Webster to kill World War II veteran George Anson. The gang had been looking for someone to 'roll' for easy money, and the drink-affected Anson appeared to be the perfect victim. However, the assault went way beyond a robbery with violence.

McCafferty kicked Anson several times to the head and chest before repeatedly plunging a knife into the 50-year-old's chest and neck. Most of McCafferty's young gang were too shocked to make any comment, but Webster asked the heavily-tattoed Scot why he had gone berserk. McCafferty replied that he had reacted to Anson swearing at him.

Just three nights later, on August 27, McCafferty took his gang to the Leppington Cemetery to show them his little son's grave. The gang then retreated to a nearby pub, only for McCafferty to insist on returning to the grave site. Todd and Meredith went their own way, but McCafferty, Howes, Whittington and Webster went back to the cemetery. Then, at the cemetery, a car pulled over near Craig McCafferty's grave. Todd and Meredith had returned to the group with a victim, 42-year-old Ronald Cox, at gunpoint. They had been hitchhiking in the rain when the miner — on his way home from work — gave them a lift.

McCafferty ran over to where Todd and Meredith were holding Cox and ordered Meredith to kill the terrified father of seven. Both Meredith and McCafferty shot Cox to the back of the head. McCafferty, who later claimed he had heard voices in his head telling him to kill seven people, the following day ordered his gang members to find him another victim. Todd and Whittington went hitchhiking and were given a ride by young driving instructor Evangelos Kollias. However, Whittington then produced a rifle from under his coat and ordered Kollias to lie on the floor while Todd drove back to McCafferty's unit. McCafferty then drove away and ordered Whittington to kill Kollias. The youth did as he was told and shot the driving instructor through the head. Then when ordered to shoot again, Whittington fired into Kollias' head again. The body was dumped in a nearby street.

Meanwhile, McCafferty seemed determined to do what the voices had instructed — 'kill seven' — and high on his hit list was his wife, her mother and one of his gang members, 17-year-old Webster, who had questioned him over the brutal killing of Anson. However, a gang member alerted Webster to McCafferty's plans and he decided to act to save his own life. Webster, an apprentice compositor with the *Sydney Morning Herald*, called the police from his workplace.

Detectives arrived to interview him, but Webster had spotted McCafferty and his gang in a car outside and was too terrified to leave the building. Armed police therefore surrounded the car and arrested McCafferty and Whittington. Although McCafferty admitted to police that he had killed Anson, Cox and Kollias, he pleaded not guilty at a committal hearing, as did Howes, Meredith, Whittington and Webster. The gang was sent to trial, with newspapers referring to McCafferty as 'Australia's Charles Manson', the American hippie leader who organised a gang to commit multiple murders in the late 1960s.

Everything revolved around the question of whether McCafferty was insane or not and, near the end of the trial, he read a statement from the dock which, in part, stated: "I would like to say that at the time of these crimes I was completely insane. The reason why I done (sic) this is for the revenge of my son's death. Before this, I had stated to a doctor that I felt like killing people, but up until my son's death I had not killed anyone. My son's death was the biggest thing that ever happened to me because I loved him so much and he meant the world to me. And after his death I just seemed to go to the pack. I feel no wrong for what I have done because, at the time that I did it, I didn't think it was wrong. I think, if given the chance, I will kill again for the simple reason that I have to kill seven people and I have only killed three, which means I have four to go. And this is how I feel in my mind, and I just can't say that I am not going to kill anyone else, because in my mind I am."

The jury rejected the insanity plea and found McCafferty guilty as charged on all counts. He was sentenced to be imprisoned for life, with Meredith and Whittington sentenced to 18 years in prison and Todd for 10 years for the murders of Cox and Kallios. Webster was given four years for the manslaughter of Cox. Howes, who was pregnant with McCafferty's child when the verdicts were announced, was found not guilty.

McCafferty, who married and then divorced a woman named Mandy Queen while in jail, proved to be one of the most difficult prisoners in NSW penal history and was transferred from one jail to another until, to the horror of NSW police and public, he was given parole. He was deported to his native Scotland in 1997. However, McCafferty could not stay out of trouble and was involved in a number of incidents, including threatening police officers. He settled in Hampshire and remarried Mandy Queen, but then fled to New Zealand when he faced a charge of assaulting a police officer.

McCafferty was arrested immediately he returned to the United Kingdom but, to the amazement of the British public, escaped with that 'slap on the wrist' fine and community order. The court had been told that the man known as 'Australia's Charles Manson' was a changed man and had even taken up painting to 'calm him down'. Indeed, lawyer Simon Moger said his client's work was 'of a very high standard which could sell commercially'. McCafferty, who once had threatened to kill seven people, therefore was left to continue family life, despite once being told he would never be released from jail for the three murders he committed.

THE SKATING GIRL MURDER

A 13-year-old girl disappears after a visit to a roller skating rink and her body later is found in a shallow bush grave.

Michelle Allport was no ordinary skater. When Michelle, 13, pulled on her white skating boots a transformation came over her and she was so good at her hobby that she became the New South Wales Under 13 roller skating champion. However, she was never able to progress her ambitions as she was strangled and buried in a bush grave after disappearing from a roller skating rink at Mittagong on November 1, 1974.

Michelle had gone to the rink, in a shopping centre, with her brother Philip but went off on her own. She told him she would be back soon, but she did not return and was never seen alive again.

Her father, William Allport, reported to police that his daughter was missing and they interviewed children and others who were at the centre that night. The first break came a couple of days later when Michelle's brother-in-law found part of Michelle's yellow slacks near a road outside Mittagong. Police, sensing they were close to solving the mystery disappearance, checked out a bush track about five kilometres from Mittagong. Their worst fears were realised when they discovered a bush grave, concealed by heavy timber, about three kilometres along the track.

A post mortem showed that Michelle had been strangled. Police working on the case said they were lucky in tracing Michelle's body so quickly and added that they believed the killer virtually had left signs telling them where to find the body. They also said a chainsaw had been used to cut down several trees which had been used to hide the bush grave. The killer also threw tree logs and branches over the grave before trying to set them alight. The grave virtually was "marked" for police, who otherwise might have had difficulty in making their gruesome discovery. Michelle's body had been partly burned in the grave. She was buried at the Bowral cemetery on November 7, on the same day police charged Bowral labourer Kenneth William Johnstone with murder.

At the committal hearing at Moss Vale Court, Detective-Sergeant A. McDonald alleged that Johnstone, 36 years of age, had admitted strangling the girl. He told the court that Johnstone had said to him: "I did kill Michelle. I have been having an affair with her for 18 or 19 months. Last Friday she told me she was pregnant and I could not face that at her age or mine. So I strangled her with a bit of rope and tried to burn her. But she would not burn, so I buried her." Johnstone, who knew the Allport family well, pleaded not guilty at his trial at the Central Criminal Court. However, the jury took only one and a half hours to find him guilty and, after the seven-day trial, he was sentenced to life imprisonment.

BURIED UNDER GRASS

A six-year-old Sydney girl is choked, stabbed and sexually assaulted by a neighbour and her body is found two days later under a pile of grass clippings.

Little Svetlana Zetovic (known as Lana), just six years of age, was a strikingly pretty girl with beautiful straw-coloured hair. She lived with her parents and eight-year-old brother Danny in the western Sydney suburb of Guildford. Her family had migrated to Australia from Yugoslavia in 1970 and, four years later, had settled into a quiet routine in their adopted country.

However, Lana did not return home from school on November 7, 1974, and Mrs Barbara Zetovic immediately called police, who launched a massive search for the missing girl. The search was two days old when police made the discovery they hoped they would never make. They found Lana's body under a pile of grass clippings, rags and rubble in the backyard of a house just three doors from the Zetovic home. Lana had been choked, stabbed through the heart and sexually assaulted. Police charged 45-year-old labourer Noel Edward Holden with the murder of the six-year-old girl.

At a committal hearing, police chemist, Inspector J. Goulding, said hairs taken from the girl's body and from a pair of Holden's trousers were the same, "beyond reasonable doubt", while evidence also was given that a knife taken from Holden's house could have been the one used to stab Lana. Holden was sent for trial at the Central Criminal Court before Justice Isaacs and, although he pleaded not guilty, a jury took just 90 minutes before announcing its verdict – guilty. The judge, in sentencing Holden to life imprisonment, described the murder of little Svetlana Zetovic as a "horrible crime".

THE KROPE CASE

The brother of a beauty queen shoots their father dead in a domestic tragedy in Melbourne.

It is difficult to think of a more sensational case than the one involving the family of a reigning Miss Australia beauty queen, Gloria Krope, in December, 1977. The death of Mrs Krope's father, Frederick Krope, in the quiet northern Melbourne suburb of Glenroy made newspaper headlines around Australia for many months. The news of Frederick Krope's death was broken in the December 22, 1977, edition of the Melbourne *Herald*, which ran a huge photograph of Miss Krope in her Miss Australia regalia, was headlined: "17 rifle shots kill Miss Australia's father." The report also carried a photograph of the Krope home, where Frederick Krope was shot to death in a hail of bullets. The home, in Sims Crescent, could have been any humble home in Melbourne suburbia – small, neat and unpretentious. However, it had not been a happy home for the Kropes.

Frederick Krope met his future wife Josephine in Yugoslavia in 1947; they married 18 months later and decided to migrate to Australia in late 1951. The Kropes settled in Melbourne and, in May, 1954, Rosemary, the first of their three chidren, was born. Gloria was born 18 months later and William in May, 1957. The family moved into the Sims Crescent house in July, 1955. Krope worked as a fitter and turner, but the wages from this job were supplemented by sales from small metal production items made in the family garage. Krope was a chronic gambler and the family's financial fortunes fluctuated from week to week, from one race meeting to the next. To make matters worse, Krope had a violent temper and would fly into a rage at the slightest provocation. He was, in fact, a family bully and his wife and three children lived in fear of him. He also used to watch his own daughters through a peephole he had made for himself in the family bathroom.

It was against this background that young William Krope, just 20 years of age, became involved in tragedy. He could no longer tolerate a situation in which he, his mother and sisters were beaten and, late on the evening of Wednesday, December 21, 1977, he shot his father dead with a .22 Ruger semi-automatic. William had waited inside the house with the gun cocked and ready to fire as soon as his father walked through the back door. Earlier, William had been disturbed in the garage while trying to get his father's gun. William believed it was a case of kill or be killed and was convinced his father was carrying a gun. Frederick Krope eventually walked through the door and was shot repeatedly.

Both Mrs Krope and Rosemary were in the house at the time of the shooting (Gloria no longer was living at home) and immediately rushed in to see what had happened. They saw Frederick Krope dead on the floor in a pool of blood. Mrs Krope then walked to the telephone and called police. William gave himself up and told police exactly what had happened. The police inspected the body and noted that Frederick Krope was lying face down. There were numerous bullet wounds, including several to the head. They also found a number of .22 calibre cartridges in the entrance foyer and surrounding area. William made a statement and, with extraordinary courage and character, assumed full responsibility.

William was charged with murder and, in an unsworn statement read at his trial, he told of life under Frederick Krope:

> From an early age I have heard my father calling my mother a bitch and slut and yelling at her. He used to terrify us with stories of how he killed people during the war and at times he had us in tears of fright and I've seen Rosemary run out of the house. From the time I first went to school I wasn't treated like the other boys. I wasn't allowed to bring them home or go out and play with them, except when he wasn't there I did it.

He also told of his father's foul mood on the day of the shooting. He said in the unsworn statement:

> The day he died he was in one of the worst moods I had ever seen. I'd heard my mother asking for extra money for Christmas and I heard him say, 'not for you bloody bastards'. I heard Mum pleading with him, saying we could

have a nice, peaceful Christmas and that she might be able to get Gloria to come home, and his saying things like 'not a bloody cent'. And 'get that bastard to work or I'll have him crawling on the ground like a rat'. I heard my mother pleading with him but he just got in a rage. I heard him telling my mother she was a stupid bitch and if she wanted money to get out and work for it and get me to work …

He came home again about 7pm and my mother gave him his meal, which he ate on his own. He was listening to the wireless and he was using the phone for his betting. He seemed to be in the same bad mood as earlier. I heard him abuse Mum because I hadn't helped her in the garage. He was going on about how useless we all were to him and saying things like as far as we were all concerned we were finished. When I was watching the TV my mother was in the kitchen. I went out on a couple of occasions and put my arm around her, and tried to comfort her and brighten her up. She was still cooking because she said she had to have something to do to keep her mind off things. When I was with her in the kitchen my father came out, gave us one of his mad, threatening looks and said something like: 'I'll figure something out for you.' I was sure he was going to do something to us that night. I thought of his gun and how I could get it away from him. I couldn't bring it in through the house as he would have seen me. That's why I took the flywire off the window, to get out and bring the gun in through the window and hide it in my room. I did this and went to the garage to get his gun to take back.

When I was in the garage I got the gun out of the trunk and just then my father was coming with the torch. I left the gun and walked straight out and ran into the house in fear and got my gun, and got out of the window as I knew once he had seen me with his gun, that would be it. I would be finished. When I got out the back I saw him through the window in the garage where the rifle had been and I thought he was getting it. I got terrified and ran back into the house and hid in the lounge. I heard my father come in from the garage into the house. The lounge light was off and the TV room dimly lit. I was absolutely terrified of him and all the fear I had of him over the past times took control of me and I was just certain he was going to kill me – Mum, me and Rosemary. I believed he had the gun and I thought I had to kill him first. I was that frightened and I shot him. At that time in my mind there was nothing else I could do to save us. I don't know what made me shoot him so often; it must have been fear. I've no clear memory of how often I did it. I was so panicky. I'd often thought over the years that if he attacked me or Mum I would have to kill him. This is the sort of thing that had been going through my mind for years because of his threats and cruelty towards us.

One of the most poignant parts of William's statement was when he said: "No one could believe what we've been through and what sort of man he was. If you had lived in the house with us and him for even only a week you would have known what fear was and how it was with us all the time. I believe that he was truly mad."

The jury deliberated for seven hours to decide whether William was guilty or not of murder and whether Mrs Krope was guilty or not of conspiracy to murder and, when it finally announced verdicts of "not guilty", mother and son hugged each other, their ordeal over. The decisions proved enormously popular with the public and the Kropes finally were able to get on with their lives.

POOR CHRISTOPHER ROBIN

A seven-year-old boy disappears from a camping trip in the Adelaide Hills and his battered body is discovered the following day.

Little Christopher Robin Weltman was looking forward to his first camping experience. He was just seven years of age and the YMCA holiday camp at Loftia Park in the Adelaide Hills would provide him with his first experience of the bush. However, Christopher, a mild asthmatic, disappeared from the camp on the evening of January 12, 1977.

More than 200 police and volunteers took part in the search for Christopher, a quietly spoken boy who often said he wanted to be a policeman when he grew up. Tragically, his body was found by a volunteer on the afternoon of January 13, just 20 hours after the boy had last been seen. The body was found just 50 metres from the camp lavatory block and only 100 metres from the hut Christopher shared with other children.

The boy had been bashed around the head and there was blood around the nose. There was a trail of blood from a nearby track and police correctly assumed the little boy had been attacked on the track and that his body had been dragged into the scrub. Half a brick was found close to the body and, significantly, forensic tests revealed that there were traces of blood and organic material attached to it. There were no indications of a struggle and there was no evidence of sexual assault.

Police, after interviewing the 73 children at the camp, arrested a 12-year-old boy over Christopher's death and he faced the Supreme Court of South Australia in July, 1977. In a sworn statement, the boy told the jury of seven men and five women that he was angry with Christopher for telling other children at the camp that he had "done a poo near a car". Medical evidence was given that Christopher had been struck at least three times to the head and shoulders and that a bruise mark on his chest matches the pattern of the 12-year-old's shoes.

The jury took just 40 minutes to find the boy guilty of Christopher's murder and Justice Mitchell then said that under the South Australian Crimes Act, she could impose only one sentence, for the boy to be detained at the Governor's pleasure. The judge refused an application by the Adelaide *Advertiser* to publish the boy's name.

There was a sad sequel to the case of poor Christopher Robin when, in 1979, his mother, Theresa Dato, armed herself with a knife and went to a reform home "to get the stinking animal who killed my son". Mrs Dato was disarmed, arrested and pleaded guilty in the Adelaide Magistrates' Court of carrying an offensive weapon. She was released on a $250, two-year good behaviour bond.

THE HOUSE OF HORRORS

A shearer and his wife are shot dead at their country home in Jerilderie, New South Wales, over an insurance scam gone wrong.

Mick Lewis was what was known in rural Australia as a "gun shearer". In fact, he was so good at his job that his workmates nicknamed him "Tricky Mickey" and he often sheared more than 200 sheep a day. Mick worked hard, and played hard. He had a big thirst and loved a gamble. In fact, it was said that if he had a good win on the horses he sometimes would have his pockets stuffed with notes. Lewis, 25, was married to a typical country girl, Sue Lewis, a 27-year-old who had a much quieter personality and was devoted to their two children, five-year-old Tania and three-year-old Michael. In October, 1978, the Lewis family was living near the southern New South Wales town of Jerilderie, in an old homestead picturesquely named "Summerfield". It was a typical Australian country homestead, with a high-pitched corrugated iron roof and a surrounding verandah. Early in its days it must have been something of a mansion; in 1978 it became a house of horrors.

On the morning of Tuesday, October 3, 1978, telephonist Mrs Nola Evans was asked if she could check the Lewis telephone line at "Summerfield". A switchboard operator in the nearby town of Hay had been trying to connect a call, but a little girl kept answering the telephone. Mrs Evans rang the number and a sad little voice told her that her mummy and daddy were asleep. Mrs Evans called the Jerilderie police and talked to the girl until they arrived at the homestead.

The police officers, Sergeant Paul Payne and Senior Constable Ken Waterhouse, walked straight into a ghastly scene – they found Lewis dead in the kitchen, his head in a pool of blood. The police officers moved further into the house and turned their noses up at a foul odour from the main bedroom. They walked in and discovered Sue Lewis' decomposing and maggot-infested body in a double bed. The Lewis children, grubby but unharmed, had been caring for themselves in the house where their parents had been killed and left to rot.

Police at first believed Lewis had been bashed around the head, although they were convinced his wife had been shot in the head. They found a spent .22 cartridge in the bedroom, where her body was found, but had not found any bullet wound to her husband's head. They also were puzzled by the different condition of the bodies. Lewis' body showed little sign of decomposition, yet his wife's body was in a terrible state of putrefaction. It finally was realised that Mrs Lewis' electric blanket was turned on the "high" position and this explained the state of her body.

There seemed little doubt the Lewis couple had been executed, but what had been the motive? Police at first thought that Lewis might have had a successful punting spree and been robbed. However, this theory was quickly discounted as the murders appeared to have been extremely well planned. Careful examination of the house of horrors turned up the first clue – a small tear in a flywire door to the kitchen. It was precisely the same size as a .22 bullet hole and a post-mortem examination of Lewis' body showed that he died of a single gunshot wound to the head, behind the right ear. Mrs Lewis had been shot twice in the head.

Forensic tests on the .22 calibre cartridge and a bullet taken from Lewis' skull revealed that the murder weapon was an Australian-made Fieldman rifle. This information proved vital, as the Melbourne manufacturer was able to narrow it down to a batch of 750. Police also pricked their ears at local gossip which suggested that Lewis had been planning to "write off" his car so that he could collect $5000 in insurance money. This information also proved vital and another link in the chain of evidence was forged when police questioned people in Lewis' telephone contact book. One of those listed was a Shepparton painting contractor and part-time insurance representative, John Fairley, who had previously arranged motor insurance for Lewis. When police discovered that one of Fairley's friends had lent him a .22 Fieldman rifle to "shoot a couple of bunnies", they were convinced they were close to solving the gruesome double murder. Fairley's friend, Raymond Rafferty, told police the part-time insurance agent had borrowed the rifle only days before the Lewis couple was shot dead.

Fairly, 40, pleaded guilty at the Central Criminal Court before Justice Yeldham and Detective Sergeant Donald Worsley told the court that Lewis had paid Fairley $295 as part-payment on a premium for his car. However, Fairley had kept the money and Lewis' car therefore was not insured. Lewis expected an insurance payout and Fairley therefore decided that the only solution was to kill Lewis and his wife. He borrowed the rifle and shot Lewis dead before walking through the old homestead to kill Sue Lewis. Fairley, who had never previously been in trouble with the law, was sentenced to two terms of life imprisonment. Worsley, who headed the team, later was presented with a special prize for the most outstanding phase of police duty of 1978.

THE 'DISGUSTING' MONSTER

A Melbourne man is jailed over the deaths of a woman who was a regular at a night club and a six-year-old girl.

Theresa Crowe, to say the least, had a most unusual lifestyle. And, tragically, this led to a most unusual death. The twenty-two-year-old former student teacher was a regular on the Melbourne disco scene and lived almost hermit-like in a tiny room measuring no more than four metres by three metres. This room, which was really a loft above and behind a boat building factory, was off Chapel Street, Prahran, an inner Melbourne suburb.

Crowe's meagre possessions were crammed into this minute living area, jostling for space with a swing seat which hung from the rafters. Crowe would climb into her room from a staircase and enter through a trapdoor. It might have been ever so humble, but it was home, sweet home to Theresa Crowe. Few people ever received an invitation. Theresa, who had attended Strathmore High School and Toorak Teachers' College before accepting, and abandoning a number of jobs, loved the nightlife and was a regular at Chaser's Nightclub, not far from her 'home'. In fact, she was there six nights a week and was such a familiar face there that she was a gold pass member, giving her free admittance.

She almost always wore black and, because of this and her surname, her nickname was 'Blackbird'. If Theresa was not at Chaser's there usually was a good reason, and that was why her friends started asking questions after they had not seen her for several days from June 19, 1980.

Theresa's 'disappearance' was still the subject of discussion at Chaser's when, on June 25, two Prahran men, Simon Greig and Hugo Ottoway, went to her room and made an horrific discovery. They found Theresa's naked body wrapped in a blanket. Police later said that Theresa had been dead several days and that her body had been mutilated. There were numerous cuts on her face and a sharp instrument had been used to slash her body from throat to vagina. Although the initial post-mortem failed to disclose the cause of death, there were bruise marks on Theresa's neck and it was later proven that she had died of asphyxiation. Police were mystified at first and even suggested that Theresa might have been held captive for several days before being killed. They also considered the possibility that the unfortunate young woman had been killed in some weird satanic rite. They based this theory on the fact that medical evidence pointed to Theresa being killed on June 24, which was a beltan — one of four Sabbaths on the Satanists calendar.

However, police later indicated they had a suspect, but not enough evidence to press charges. The Blackbird Case, as it was dubbed by the Melbourne media, faded from the headlines for three years. Police then charged Malcolm Joseph Thomas Clarke, a twenty-eight-year-old assistant projectionist from the inner western suburb of Brunswick, with manslaughter. Clarke had seen Theresa Crowe at Chaser's on the night of her death three years earlier and had later walked with her to her loft. She went upstairs and Clarke left, only to return later. By this time Theresa had stripped for sleep, and when she rejected his overtures, Clarke got angry. However, Clarke insisted that Theresa's death had been accidental and that she had died of asphyxiation when her neck pressed against a rope on her swinging chair. Medical evidence suggested that this could well have been the case. On the other hand, government pathologist Dr James McNamara told the Criminal Court that he had found a bite mark on Theresa's back, apart from the throat-to-vagina mutilation.

Clarke was found guilty of manslaughter and Mr Justice Nathan, in passing sentence of fifteen years' imprisonment, said a "joyful and pleasant" young woman had died because of Clarke's motive of "sexual gratification". He added: "You committed this crime in the most horrific and depraved circumstances because not only did you cause her death, but after death you defiled her body … in the most disgusting of all defilements."

Clarke was ordered to serve twelve years before being eligible for parole but, two years before he was jailed, he had committed a far worse crime, the killing of six-year-old Bonnie Clarke (no relation) at her home in the inner Melbourne suburb of Northcote. Clarke, who was released from jail in 1994 for Theresa Crowe's death and the stabbing and raping of a woman at Brunswick in August, 1983, boarded with Bonnie's mother Marion for eight months at the Westbourne Grove house in 1982.

Bonnie Melissa Clarke was asphyxiated and stabbed on the night of December 21, 1982, but, despite an inquest and intensive police efforts, the crime remained unsolved for 22 years. However, when police re-examined the case in 2001, Clarke eventually became the chief suspect. In a video-taped interview he said the little girl woke when he sexually abused her. He then put a pillow over her face to quieten her. He said: "I was extraordinarily drunk ... and when I come to my senses (after pressing a pillow to the girl's face), I realised that Bonnie was deceased. When I took the pillow off ... she didn't struggle. I just held it down with one hand 'cause she had one hand up. She was lying down and one hand came up when I put it over her face. Her hand came up, then it just dropped. It just dropped. It was like, lifeless. I gave her a bit of a shake, whatever, I realised there was something wrong and I maybe, as I said, in panic did it with the knife."

The Supreme Court of Victoria jury in June, 2004, took just seven hours to find Clarke guilty of murdering little Bonnie. Clarke burst into tears, but others in the court cheered the verdict.

DEATH OF A CONSUL

The Turkish consul-general and his bodyguard are killed in suburban Sydney by assassins on a motor-bike.

It promised to be yet another ordinary day for the Australian Turkish consul-general Sarik Ariyak as he prepared to leave his Sydney home in Portland Street, Dover Heights for his office at Woolahra. Ariyak got into his car while his bodyguard/driver Engin Sever got into another car, one marked with consular plates. As they prepared to drive off, a motor-bike rushed at the two vehicles, stopped and the pillion passenger fired a semi-automatic at the bodyguard and then turned the gun on Ariyak, who was killed almost instantly. Sever died an hour later in hospital.

Police had few clues, although they knew the killers had used a .38 semi-automatic and that 14 rounds had been fired, with Ariyak shot through a car window from almost point-blank range. Even though the New South Wales Government posted a $250,000 reward for information leading to convictions, there were no takers and the killings remain a mystery. However, police remain convinced the consul-general and his bodyguard were the victims of a political attack.

THE HIT-MAN

A man who already was serving time for murdering two prostitutes confesses to being the hit-man in a murder committed 20 years earlier.

Richard Hanmer and his wife Mildred ran a hardware shop at Mordialloc and, as part of the business, also had an agency for the State Savings Bank and a dry cleaning depot. On September 20, 1982, Mrs Hanmer drove her two daughters to school and then opened the family business for trade as her husband was recovering from hernia surgery. She was holding $2569 in bank deposits when, at about 12.50pm, she was shot in a hold-up. A woman next door heard a long "bang", the sound of Mrs Hanmer taking a shot to the right chest between the second and third ribs. The gunman fled, but not before taking the money. Mrs Hanmer rang her husband to say she had been shot and told him: "Dick, I've been robbed and I'm dying" and later she told him "It's all right – here's the ambulance."

Mrs Hanmer was rushed to the Alfred Hospital and, while still conscious was able to describe the gunman as about 25 years of age, Australian, about 5ft 7in and having ginger hair. He was carrying a sawn-off rifle which had been used to shoot her from the front. The coroner, Dr J.H. McNamara, subsequently found that Mrs Hanmer died from a haemorrhage caused by the gunshot wound. There were no witnesses as no one else was in the shop at the time and, despite their best efforts, police were unable to track down the killer.

Then, in August, 2000, a convicted murderer stepped forward to say he had killed Mrs Hanmer. Gregory John Brazel, who was 28 years of age at the time of the shooting, was a career criminal with a terrible record of violence and dishonesty. He had been convicted of the murder of a prostitute at Barongarook, western Victoria, on September 13, 1980, and of the murder of another prostitute at Sorrento, on the Mornington Peninsula, in the same month. He was sentenced to a cumulative term of 30 years but then incurred other sentences while in prison and was not to have been released until February, 2024.

Brazel might have stepped forward to confess to the murder of Mrs Hanmer, but it took police almost two years to verify his claims that he had been paid to kill the woman in the hardware shop. He claimed he was acting as a hit-man after being approached with a $30,000 offer for the killing, half to be paid in advance and the rest on completion of the job. He said that when he went back to the instigator after the killing, he was told "well done".

Justice Cummins, who had sentenced Brazel for the murder of the two prostitutes, said in the Supreme Court of Victoria in April, 2003, that the convicted killer stepped forward "to tell the truth". The judge told him: "It was to seek to purge, partially, your guilt. It was, in your words, to confront your demons. I am satisfied that there was not a collateral or hidden reason for your coming forward. The only benefit you sought to gain was the partial expurgation of your guilt. You well knew that the consequence of your coming forward would be a significantly increased term of imprisonment upon the already lengthy terms you were then serving."

Brazel pleaded guilty to the murder of Mrs Hanmer and Justice Cummins, before passing sentence, told him: "There is a cluster of mitigating factors in your present situation and which is relevant to the proper sentence to be imposed upon you. First, after nearly 20 years you have come forward wholly of your own volition and confessed to the crime. Second, your coming forward and confession was motivated by contrition and true remorse. Third, the authenticity of that motive is not deflected or derogated from by any collateral purpose or seeking by you of advantage. Fourth, your confession has solved a long unsolved crime. Fifth, it has brought some partial finality to the suffering of the living victims; but they will suffer for as long as they live. Sixth, you have pleaded guilty to the crime. Seventh, you have genuine and plenary remorse. Eighth, you have not at any time since you came forward and confessed, sought to avoid full responsibility for your actions. You also waived the benefit of possible indemnity. Ninth, you told the truth to the police, involving as that did the placing of this crime in the most serious category of murder, a paid execution. Tenth, you have been in continuous custody since September, 1990, and face lengthy further imprisonment and you are in a state of poor health."

The judge directed Brazel, who once had been in a serious altercation with the notorious Mark "Chopper" Read, to serve a minimum term of 27 years before being eligible for parole and he now will not be released until at least 2030, when he will be 75 years of age.

THE BIKIE BATTLE

Two bikie gangs face each other in a street battle in Sydney, leaving seven people dead and at least 20 injured.

There was no love lost between the Comancheros and Bandidos bikie gangs, but no one expected the massacre that would occur at Milperra on September 2, 1984. The Bandidos was founded after a faction broke away from the Camancheros and there had been considerable bad blood between the two gangs, with both declaring matters would come to a head that brutal day outside a Sydney pub.

A spare parts meeting had been organised and, with hundreds in attendance when the two gangs faced off. When the shooting and mayhem finished, six men and 14-year-old Leanne Walters, who had been selling raffle tickets, were left dead or dying. Police charged more than 43 men with murder, but some charges were dropped and only nine were found guilty of murder, the rest being found guilty of manslaughter.

The court case following the massacre at the time was one of the biggest and most expensive in Australian criminal history. The leader of the Comancheros, William "Jock" Ross, was accused of being responsible for the decision for gang members to go to the Viking Tavern armed and ready for violence. He was sentenced to life imprisonment, along with seven other bikies. Sixteen other men were sentenced to 14 years' jail for manslaughter.

THE 'HIDEOUS KILLING'

In a killing a judge describes as one of the worst he has encountered, a Sydney teenager sexually assaults and kills his 10-year-old cousin.

Sydney teenager David Jack Glen had recently been introduced to his 10-year-old cousin Kylie Corbett on October 10, 1985, when the little girl left home to go to school. She was carrying a bag of old clothes she had collected for a charity drive at school when she came across 19-year-old Glen, who invited her into his flat on the pretext that he had some clothes for her.

When Glen lured little Kylie into his bedroom he grabbed her by the neck and threatened her with a knife. He pushed her onto a bed, removed her clothes and inserted a finger in her vagina before tying her up with rope. Glen then left her on the bed while he went shopping and playing pinball machines in Parramatta. Then, when he returned, he continued his disgusting attack on the defenceless girl.

Glen took the girl to have a shower to wash her vagina and then allowed her to read her school books before he produced a baton and pushed it under her chin so violently that she choked into unconsciousness. Finally, Glen tied a cotton belt around her neck and hanged her from a bar in his wardrobe before leaving the flat. A search was mounted for the little girl and police found her body in Jack's wardrobe the following day.

A post-mortem revealed horrific injuries, apart from the marks around her neck. Her vaginal walls were lacerated and part of her anal passage was torn and gaping. Death was caused by asphyxia due to hanging and shock, and Glen was arrested almost immediately. When asked whether he intended to kill Kylie with the baton he replied: "No, I did not intend to kill her with the baton. I was going to kill her with a knife, but I couldn't get the courage up to stab her, so I then took the baton and choked her."

At his trial in December, 1985, Glen pleaded not guilty of murder, but guilty of manslaughter. This plea was rejected and Glen, who did not give evidence, made an unsworn statement in which he said: "Ladies and gentlemen of the jury, I am not guilty of murder. I am sorry about what has happened. As I said in my record of interview, I wish this hadn't happened at all.

"When I asked Kylie around to my flat I didn't have any intentions to hurt her. I just wanted to give my wife's maternity clothes to her because my wife left me 12 days before and I thought I wouldn't see her or my daughter again. I don't know why I sexually harassed Kylie. I didn't plan for that to happen. After I did that, I didn't know what to do; that's why I tied her up. I didn't want to hurt Kylie in any way, even though I said 'if you scream or cry, I'll kill you'.

"I had a knife, but I didn't use it to hurt her, but just to cut the rope when she said it was too tight. I didn't put any part of my body or anything into her anus. When I put the baton on her neck I didn't want to kill her or hurt her badly. In fact, I don't know why I did that at the time and I don't know now.

"When I put Kylie in the wardrobe, I tied the cotton belt around her neck to stop her falling off the chair as she was unconscious at that time. I didn't do that to hurt her, to kill her. I didn't think it would cause any more harm. All I can say is that I'm truly sorry for what I have done. I mean that, but I have done what I have done and there is nothing I can say, but to say that I am sorry and I don't know how it happened. Thank you."

Justice Wood described the killing as "hideous" and the "worst case of murder" over which he had presided. Glen, who had a disturbed childhood and entries for offences ranging from burglary to malicious injuring, had been unemployed since he was 16 years of age and was an occasional user of alcohol, cannabis and LSD. He was sentenced to life imprisonment.

THE LONELY HEARTS TOMB

The badly decomposed bodies of a Melbourne woman and a man she had been introduced to through a dating agency are found in the bush six years after they had disappeared.

Veronica Dienhoff, known to her friends as Ronnie, was a slim, attractive 45-year-old who lived in a neat-as-a-pin flat in the inner eastern Melbourne suburb of Armadale. She worked as a secretary and, to help with the mortgage payments, also had a part-time job as a restaurant waitress. Life seemed full for Ronnie Deinhoff, except that she was lonely; so lonely, in fact, that she contacted a Melbourne dating agency in an effort to find a partner. Ronnie had been married three times – the first at just 16 years of age – and had four grown-up children. All three marriages had failed, but Ronnie seemed determined to find Mr Right. And why not? Ronnie, who had been born in Czechoslovakia and had migrated to Australia as a child, had succeeded in every other regard and had even won a brave fight with breast cancer.

Wolfgang Hindenberg, a 30-year-old who worked at a Dandenong engineering firm, also was seeking happiness and had contacted the same club. They were "paired", but Ronnie was never told that her new friend had a history of violent behaviour and, in fact, had once been charged with the attempted murder of a policeman.

Ronnie started dating Hindenberg in 1985, but soon became aware of his violent nature. She became terrified of him and avoided his company at all cost, even changing her telephone number to avoid his calls. Then, on November 28, 1985, Ronnie failed to keep a luncheon date with a friend. Police were called but Ronnie had disappeared. Ominously, Hindenberg had left his employment on November 22 and had never returned. Police issued a description of Hindenberg's car, a white four-wheel vehicle which once had been used as an ambulance, but it too had vanished.

Then, on February 6, 1992, the distinctive white vehicle was found entangled in bush off a country track near Rubicon, 130 kilometres east of Melbourne. The badly decomposed bodies of Hindenberg and Ronnie Dienhoff were found on a mattress in the back of the vehicle, which had been used as a bush tomb for more than six years. A hose had been connected to the exhaust pipe.

THE 'REVOLTING' ASSAULT

A young man kills a woman following a dispute over rent in Sydney and then kills a witness, her three-year-daughter.

Michael John Alexander moved to Sydney from Narrabri to start a new life after battling drugs and alcohol. The 24-year-old moved into a home with 42-year-old Mrs Susan Kirk and her three-year-old daughter. Mrs Kirk, who was separated from her husband, was grateful she had someone to help her with the rent. However, she and Alexander had a row about the rent on August 20, 1985, and he was so enraged he went to a garage, grabbed a length of rope and returned to strangle Mrs Kirk.

Then, just as he was covering the body, he was spotted by three-year-old Stephanie Kirk. Alexander therefore struck her with a length of wood before stabbing her through the heart. The killer hid the murder weapons and went to work, where he confided in a female co-worker that he had committed murder. By coincidence, police visited the factory on a separate and far less serious matter and were told of Alexander's "confession". He passed it off as a joke, but police took him to Mrs Kirk's house, where he told them he did not have any keys.

Alexander was allowed to return to work, but he then went back home and placed the two bodies, wrapped in a curtain, under the house. The police eventually were handed keys by a real estate agent, but found nothing at the house. They then visited Alexander again at work and told him he was being charged with having caused a public mischief. This time he confessed, took the police back to the house and pointed to the bodies.

Alexander pleaded not guilty at his trial before Justice Slattery and a jury and, although he did not contest that he had been responsible for the deaths of Mrs Kirk and her daughter Stephanie, he sought to raise the partial defence of diminished responsibility. This was rejected by the jury and he was found guilty of the murders of mother and daughter.

Justice Slattery pointed out: "The post mortem reports and photographs in evidence disclose the ferocity of his acts. Not content with this sneaky, cool and calmly executed act, he stabbed her (Mrs Kirk) with considerable force in the chest, puncturing her lung and aorta. His attack upon her was vicious and probably executed with all the feelings of frustration and anger that he been brewing within him for days, if not weeks.

"When three-year-old Stephanie innocently came upon him in the garage where he had taken her mother, he bashed her twice in a savage and brutal manner on the forehead and the back of the head. He also stabbed her in the heart. The treatment of the young child was uncaring and brutal. It was a revolting and horrifying assault upon a young, innocent child. Undoubtedly, the reason for her death was because she stood in the way. She was a person who could identify him. He regarded her as a brat who had to be killed along with her mother."

Alexander was found guilty and sentenced to two life terms. Then, in 1995, he and another prisoner escaped from Grafton jail and were at liberty for two days before being captured. In 1999, Alexander applied for redetermination of the two life sentences and, in the Supreme Court of New South Wales, Justice Kirby set a total minimum term of 28 years, with the double killer not being eligible for parole until August, 2006.

THE CYANIDE KILLER

A council worker in New South Wales poisons his wife with cyanide and buries her body in the back yard.

Patrick James Stephens married his Malaysian wife Sandiya in 1980 and the couple lived on his parents' property at Dungay, near Murwillumbah, New South Wales. However, Stephens, 28, started having an affair with another woman and, sensing she would not go out with him if he was married, told her that his wife had been dead for two years. In fact, the last time Stephens made love to the woman was on December 28, 1985, just 10 days after Sandiya's death.

Sandiya complained on December 18 that she had a headache. Stephens therefore went to a shed on the property and reached for some cyanide left over after he had killed dingoes. He had with him a cold relief capsule and pulled the two halves apart. He then emptied the contents and refilled the capsule with cyanide from the bottle in the shed. Stephens then went back to his wife and offered her what she thought was a cold relief tablet and a glass of water. Within half an hour, she was dead, cyanide being an extremely lethal poison.

After discovering his wife dead, Stephens wrapped her in a sheet and buried her in the back yard. However, he told his sister the next day that Sandiya appeared to have died suddenly in her sleep and that he was going to take her to a mosque for burial. He also telegrammed Sandiya's family in Malaysia to tell them of her death and of how she had been ill for some time. Police investigated when a friend of the family in Australia started asking questions and Stephens eventually was charged with murder.

He told police several accounts of what had happened and, at one stage, he said he believed his wife kept a knife hidden in a freezer and was going to use it to attack him. In one statement he said he and his wife often argued and that she once had attacked him with a knife and told him she wanted a divorce. Justice McInerney described this statement as a "self-serving document" and the crane operator for the Tweed Shire Council was found guilty or murder he was sentenced to jail for life. This later was determined at 22 years with a minimum of 16 years.

THE ANITA COBBY CASE

In what is arguably the most infamous case in Australian criminal history, attractive nurse Anita Cobby is tortured and killed in the most horrifying of circumstances.

Anita Cobby was a beauty queen who had the world at her feet. The attractive 26-year-old was a nurse at the Sydney Hospital and could have had her pick of suitors. She had married John Cobby in March, 1982, but the marriage failed and Anita went back to live with her parents Garry and Grace Lynch in the Sydney suburb of Blacktown. She had regular habits, was considerate and worked hard. In fact, whenever she worked late, she would always telephone her parents to stop them worrying.

Anita did not ring her parents immediately after work late on the afternoon of February 2, 1986, as she went to a restaurant with two of her nursing friends. These friends dropped Anita off at the Central Railway station and that was the last anyone saw of her alive. When Anita did not turn up for work the next day, a sister called the Lynch's, who assumed their daughter was with friends. However, Mr Lynch eventually decided to call police, who organised a search for the missing woman.

Then, two days after Anita disappeared, farmer John Reen rang police to tell them he had made a gruesome discovery on his farm at Boiler Paddock. Police rushed to the scene and were horrified by what they saw. The body fitted the description they had been given of Anita and it was a sickening sight as the beautiful young woman had been raped and bashed and had her throat slashed. The wounds were terrible and it was obvious Anita had been tortured. Also, a post-mortem revealed that the woman's throat had been slashed twice and that the head was almost severed from the body. She also had been sodomised and it later transpired that she was forced into oral sex. Bashed, kicked and slashed, the naked Anita was left for dead.

Police set up a task force and the first public reports started pouring in, with several people reporting they had seen a woman being dragged into a car at the Blacktown railway station. The car was described as a white Holden Kingswood, but there was little else for the police to work on in their massive hunt for the killer(s). Public interest was phenomenal as the killing was one of the most brutal ever committed in

Sydney and, finally, police got the call to put them on the right track. The man who called police said they should be looking for a man named John Travers who had stolen a car a couple of days before Anita's killing.

Travers had a shocking reputation and police, believing he could help with their enquiries, made a dawn raid on a property at Wentworthville and found a bloodstained knife . They also found Travers and another man, Mick Murdoch, in bed together and believed they finally were getting somewhere, especially as they also picked up a man named Les Murphy at a house in Doonside. Police then charged Murphy and Murdoch with car theft and released them, hoping they would lead them to vital evidence.

Meanwhile, police set up a "sting" operation to nab Travers, using a woman he had confided in over a rape charge. The police set up a meeting and were confident of success. That confidence was justified as Travers admitted abducting Anita and how he and his pack of animals raped, tortured and killed her. Police then arrested Murphy and Murdoch, while Travers confessed to police, implicating two others, Gary and Mick Murphy, brothers of Les. Police eventually captured Gary and Mick Murphy in the Sydney suburb of Glenfield, and the entire gang now had been apprehended. Travers and his gang eventually faced trial and those in court were disgusted with that they heard of the killing of Anita Cobby.

The gang had been drinking on the day of the abduction on February 2, 1986, and decided on the spot to grab Anita. Travers and Murdoch started undressing her and punching her in the face as she struggled in the back of the stolen car. Travers and Mick Murphy raped her at knifepoint while she was still in the back of the car, while Travers and Gary and Les Murphy raped her after she had been thrown into a ditch. The animals then dragged her through a barbed wire fence and she was forced to have oral sex with Mick Murphy and was sodomised by Les Murphy. Finally, Mick and Les Murphy kicked her in the head and left her for dead. It was then that Travers went back to her and slit her throat so that she could never tell anyone of what had happened and who had done it.

The jury returned its verdicts on June 10, 1987, after a 54-day trial in which every detail sickened the Australian public. The five men – John Travers (18), Michael Murdoch (18), Les (24), Gary (29) and Michael Murphy (33) - were found guilty and Justice Maxwell sentenced them all to life imprisonment, with their files marked "never to be released". The judge told them: "There is no doubt that apart from the humiliation, the degradation and terror inflicted upon this young woman, she was the victim of a prolonged and sadistic physical and sexual assault including repeated sexual assaults – anally, orally and vaginally." The judge compared their behaviour with wild animals and said it was the most horrifying case of sexual assault he had encountered in his 40 years of law.

LATE JUSTICE

A nine-year-old girl disappears in Sydney and the man responsible for her death is not brought to justice for another 16 years.

Samatha Knight was as pretty a nine-year-old as anyone would wish to see, with cute, innocent eyes and long hair. However, she was last seen alive on August 9, 1986, after she had bought a toothbrush while waiting for her mother after school. Samantha and her mother Tess had moved to Bondi in 1986 and they had a permanent arrangement in which Samantha would change at home after school and then play with friends until her mother arrived home from work at about 6pm. However, Samantha was last sighted at 5.30pm on the day she went missing and had been seen in the company of a man.

A massive search was launched for the missing girl, but without result. A number of well-meaning people reported possible sightings, but the case went cold for a number of years – until two seven-year-old girls in February, 1996, told their parents about a man abusing them and taking photographs. Police were called in and interviewed the man, Michael Anthony Guider, who then was 45 years of age. Police searched his home and found child pornography and underwear. He was charged with numerous offences regarding the sexual assault of little girls and was sentenced to 16 years' jail.

Police, however, believed they had discovered only the tip of the iceberg and went to other, rented premises and discovered a scrapbook on the Samantha Knight disappearance, along with photographs taken of her naked. There also were photographs of two of Samantha's friends and when police interviewed these now adult women, they knew they were hot on the trail of a pervert who had caused the death of a little girl as they had learned that Guider's modus operandi was to give girls drinks of Coca Cola laced with drugs. They therefore knew little if anything of the assaults and had no idea of him taking photographs.

Guider was in jail for his sexual offences in 2001 when he told another prisoner he had drugged Samantha and that the little girl had died accidentally. The prisoner told police and although Guider denied he had said anything, police knew they were close to solving a long-standing mystery. They therefore called on the assistance of Guider's brother Tim, who was in prison for planning a robbery. The police told Tim Guider that if he could get his brother to put his hand up for Samantha's death, he would get a pardon himself. Tim Guider refused, but Michael eventually confessed to accidentally killing Samantha, who collapsed after consuming the drugged drink. He claimed he buried her body in bush near Cooper Park, but later dug it up and threw it into a dumpster at Kirribilli. Her body was never recovered and Guider told police:

"I never physically harmed the girl. I intended to take her home; it's a very sad thing. It caught me by surprise that the drug had any effect like that. Naturally, I panicked as I knew I was in trouble. I tried to find some way out of the problem, disposing of the evidence I guess. I've blanked all this out of my mind. I can't be much more specific."

A psychologist who spoke with Guider at the Metropolitan Remand Prison at Long Bay said: "He didn't show any remorse. He blamed the mothers all the time for not caring about their children. They were out having a good time and didn't care who was with their kids." Guider was sentenced to 17 years' jail for the manslaughter of little Samantha Knight and is not eligible for parole until 2014.

THE EVIL COUPLE

A married couple abduct 12-year-old Sian Kingi, who later is strangled, stabbed and has her throat slashed.

If Valmae Fae Beck was an unattractive woman, her husband Barrie John Watts was even less appealing. While Beck was dumpy with a pot belly, Watts was a curly-haired, shrivelled creature with rodent-like features. They might have been opposites in appearance, but shared sexual fantasies. Watts dreamed of raping and killing young virgins, while Beck was more than willing to satisfy this sick and evil fantasy.

They put their plan into operation on November 27, 1987, with Watts telling his wife of one year: 'Today is the day. It's on.' Beck and Watts, like spiders in a web, waited in their car on Queensland's Sunshine Coast for a victim. Tragically, pretty, blonde 12-year-old Sian Kingi was riding her bike at Tewantin, Queensland, when the evil couple called her over to their car to ask her if she had seen a poodle.

They abducted Kingi, with Watts grabbing her from behind and, with her arms bound and mouth taped, was taken to a nearby forest where Watts raped her while Beck watched. Watts then stabbed the innocent young girl a dozen times before slashing her throat and then strangling her with his wife's belt. Watts' lust had been satisfied and, almost unbelievably, he and his wicked wife went home and had a bath before watching television and then going to bed.

The discovery of Kingi's body outraged Queensland and, when Watts and Beck eventually were brought to justice a lynch mob greeted them, with some people carrying banners and placards which read 'Hang Them'. Although Beck and Watts had separate trials, both were sentenced to life imprisonment. During the sentencing of Beck, Justice Jack Kelly said: 'No decent person could not feel revulsion at what you did — and a woman with children of your own (she had six children from previous marriages).' He also described the woman prepared to watch an innocent girl raped and killed just to please her husband's sick fantasies as 'callous and cruel'.

Incredibly, Beck gave evidence at her trial that Kingi 'never cried, never shed a tear, she never uttered a peep, she just did everything we told her'. Watts was described at his trial as 'a thoroughly evil man devoid of any sense of morality'. Even more amazingly, Beck later claimed she was not as evil as she had been painted and had even become a born-again

Christian. She said: 'I am not a repeat serious crime offender. I have no sex or violence offences on my record.' Although she made an appeal to have a lower security rating, this move failed.

However, Beck insisted that she had found God and would be applying for parole, much to the horror of little Sian's parents, Barry and Lynda Kingi. There therefore was outrage in Queensland in 2000 when Beck, (who changed her surname to Cramb) applied for work release, home detention and parole. The application was denied, but a friend said that everyone deserved forgiveness and added: 'If I had a daughter, I hope I would be big enough to try and forgive her, but I probably wouldn't. She was a victim of an obsessive love relationship with her husband.' Queensland Premier Peter Beattie, when told that Beck was seeking parole described the murder of Kingi as 'shocking' and added: 'Just because someone applies for parole does not necessarily mean they will get it.'

THE HODDLE STREET MASSACRE

Teenage gunman Julian Knight opens fire on motorists driving along Hoddle Street in the Melbourne suburb of Clifton Hill.

There was nothing to suggest the evening of August 9, 1987, would be any different to any other cold Melbourne winter's night. Traffic ebbed and flowed along busy Hoddle Street near the Clifton Hill railway station, but that all came to a stop when 19-year-old gunman Julian Knight started firing at innocent motorists and passer-by. He killed seven people and wounded another 19 in a night of infamy.

The shooting started soon after 9pm and, within half an hour, there was carnage along one of Melbourne's busiest roads. Knight, who had showed anti-social tendencies from a young age and had been sent down from the Duntroon Military Academy, claimed to have had a nervous breakdown in the lead-up to the massacre. Regardless, he was charged with seven counts of murder, 39 counts of attempted murder and other alleged offences.

Knight pleaded guilty to all charges and the public learned that on the night of the massacre he packed three guns – a .22 semi-automatic rifle, a .38 semi-automatic rifle and a 12-guage pump-action shotgun – for his murderous mission. He knelt near an advertising billboard and shot at passing motorists and pedestrians. He was sentenced to seven life terms of imprisonment, with a non-parole period of 27 years.

COOKED IN A WOK

Police find a dismembered body, with pieces of flesh in a cooking wok, at a South Melbourne warehouse.

Kyung Bup Lee was a Korean national who arrived in Australia from Japan in 1984 seeking a better life. He spent about three years in Queensland before he contacted a service organisation and moved into a South Melbourne warehouse on May 3, 1977. The following day the 43-year-old was stabbed to death.

Police were not aware of any crime until a woman found a severed penis in the women's toilet at the Flinders Street railway station. The gruesome discovery sparked a prompt and efficient investigation and, soon after, a woman found a scrotum on tram lines in South Melbourne. Police were set a puzzle but a breakthrough came when the New Zealand Customs Department notified the Victoria Police it had intercepted an intriguing letter in which someone had boasted of killing a Korean, with full details.

Police went to a South Melbourne warehouse to question the writer of the letter and walked straight into a chamber of horrors. The man they wanted to question had dismembered a human body. Police found pieces of flesh in a cooking wok, a pile of bones and burnt pieces of body under railway sleepers. They also found numerous weapons, including a blood-stained hunting knife and a rod with a screwdriver attached to it.

New Zealander David William Philip, 32, was remanded in custody and a committal hearing at the Hawthorn Magistrates' Court was told that he had killed Lee and then had cut off the Korean's genitals. The court also was told that Philip had stripped parts of Lee's thighs before cooking the meat in a wok and then eating some of it.

Philip stood trial at the Supreme Court of Victoria and the jury was told he had stabbed Lee in the stomach before cutting his victim's throat. Philip allegedly had told police he had killed Lee because he was "getting slacked off about this lopsided world where the Asians have everything". The jury took just 20 minutes to announce its verdict – not guilty on the grounds of insanity. Justice O'Bryan ordered that Philips be detained at the Arandale Hospital, Ararat.

THE COBBY COPYCATS

A young gang abduct and kill a young woman in similar circumstances to the Anita Cobby murder (see 1986).

Sydneysiders were still getting over the horrific rape and torture killing of Anita Cobby in 1986 when, just two years later, a copycat gang abducted a young woman and subjected her to vile sexual assaults before killing her. The gang, comprising 23-year-old Stephen "Shorty" Jamieson and teenagers Bronson Blessington, Mathew Elliott and Wayne Wilmot decided on September 8, 1988, that it would be a good idea to steal a car. They then decided that the Sutherland railway station would be the idea place to find the right vehicle and, if the opportunity presented, abduct a woman. That woman turned out to be 20-year-old Janine Balding, who was engaged to be married the following March.

The gang abducted her in her own car and Elliott raped her at knifepoint in the back of the car as it travelled along the F4 freeway. The car was driven by 15-year-old Wilmot, with his girlfriend Carol Arrow in the front passenger seat. Balding was raped repeatedly and dragged to the edge of a dam at Minchinbury. Then, their sexual energy spent, the gang tied her up and dragged her to the dam water, where she drowned. All members of the gang eventually were arrested and charged with abduction, rape and murder. However, it was decided that Arrow and Wilmot would go to trial only on charges involving Balding's abduction and the theft of her engagement ring, jewellery and money. Wilmot was sentenced to 10 years' imprisonment, while Arrow was released on a three-year good behaviour bond after spending a year and a half in custody.

A trial against the other three was abandoned when two of the accused claimed police had arrested the wrong "Shorty". Finally, at a second trial, the jury took just two hours to find Jamieson, Blessington and Elliott guilty on all charges and, on September 19, 1990, Justice Newman sentenced them to life imprisonment, with no possibility of parole. He said: "To sentence people so young to long terms of imprisonment is, of course, a heavy task. However, the facts surrounding the commission of this murder are so barbaric that I believe I have no alternative. It is one of the most barbaric killings in the sad criminal history of this State." Jamieson repeatedly has protested his innocence, claiming another man known as "Shorty" was involved.

THE KILLING OF A SON

A father, distraught over the break-up of his marriage, takes his teenage son into the New South Wales bush, shoots him and bashes him to death with a rock.

Norman Edward Wilson, 44, could see his life disintegrating when his wife Janelle left him in June, 1989. The couple had five children but, when Mrs Wilson left the family home at Inverill, New South Wales, only 18-year-old Dean and 14-year-old Melissa were left to live with their father. Just two months later, Dean told his father that he had been successful with an application to join the NSW Police. This appeared to upset Wilson, but this was never raised as a motive for the killing of the teenager who had applied to be a police officer.

On the morning of September 1, 1989, Wilson tricked Dean into accompanying him to a dirt track about 13 kilometres from Inverill. The two argued, mainly about Mrs Wilson leaving him, and the father shot his son in the upper left arm with a .22 rifle. Wilson then attacked his son with a rock, smashing his head so violently that the boy suffered massive brain damage and skull fractures. Wilson then covered his son's body with branches and leaves and drove back to Inverill, where he went shopping with his daughter Melissa.

Wilson reported his son missing and, two days later, asked police if they had heard anything of his son. He then broke down and told them where they could find Dean's body. He said in a statement that he "should have shot myself instead". He said Dean grabbed the gun and that it "went off". He also said: "It just went bang and when I saw blood, I just went mad. I couldn't stop. I just kept going and hitting him, hitting him with anything I could get my hands on, with a rifle, rock, anything." Wilson was convicted of murder in June, 1990, and Justice Finlay imposed a life sentence. Then, in 1999, Justice Dunford re-sentenced him to a minimum term of 15 years from the time of being apprehended on September 5, 1989.

DEATH IN A CARAVAN

A woman is set alight in a caravan at Corowa, New South Wales, and dies three days later.

Raymond John Rosevear had a dispute with his wife on October 19, 1989, and pushed her on to a bed at the caravan they shared at the Rivergum Caravan Park in the southern New South Wales town of Corowa. Rosevear grabbed her by the throat and seemed to black out from there. However, his wife suffered burns to 65 per cent of her body when the caravan caught fire and died three days later in hospital from cardiac failure as a consequence of the shock from her burns. Also, a post mortem revealed that there were findings consistent with attempted strangulation.

Rosevear was charged with murder and, at his trial, police gave evidence that the bed clothes in the caravan had been deliberately lit after being soaked with methylated spirits. Rosevear, an alcoholic who consumed a carton of beer a day, said he did not light the fire, but was found guilty of murder and sentenced to life imprisonment. Rosevear, in the Supreme Court of New South Wales in 1999, sought determination of a minimum term and Justice Studdert set a period of 15 years.

THE HUMAN TORCH

A man is found guilty of setting alight his estranged wife and she later dies in hospital.

Josef Plevac knew precisely what it was like to suffer serious burns. He was seriously injured in a house fire in February 1989. Later, when those burns became infected he had to be admitted to hospital and he was scarred for life, both physically and mentally. Plevac had separated from his wife Dana on October, 1988, almost a year before he suffered those terrible burns. Dana had obtained am Apprehended Violence Order against her estranged husband and he was not allowed to approach her or their five-year-old daughter Natalie.

At about 8.30am on September 22, 1989, Dana Plevac and Natalie left their flat on the fourteenth floor of a Sydney block and made their way to the lifts. A man dressed entirely in black suddenly appeared and threw liquid from a container at Dana and then set her alight. The liquid was petrol and it later was determined that Plevac, a milkman, had bought $10 worth of petrol at a garage just two hours earlier. Natalie, meanwhile, watched in absolute horror as her mother went up in flames, like a human torch. The manager of the block of flats heard the fire alarm, rushed to the fourteenth floor and found Dana a person "that was very much alight at the time and was screaming for help." He also told police: "She came out of the lift, she stopped and she fell over and the flames blew up ... she was pretty much burning."

A resident on the second floor smelt smoke and heard screams for help and, as she went to investigate, saw a man run down the stairs. She noted that he was naked from the waist up and appeared to have burns on his back. Police and firemen raced to the scene and Dana Plevac was rushed to hospital, where she died almost six hours later as a result of full thickness burns to 90 percent of her body. Police found a plastic container smelling of petrol and fire authorities had no doubt petrol had been used to set Dana alight. Meanwhile, a number of witnesses saw the half-naked man running from the scene and he later was identified as Plevac. To make matters worse for him, a hairdresser who gave him a trim later that morning said she noticed what appeared to be black soot-like particles in his hair.

Plevac was arrested that afternoon and a police medical examiner noted that he had fresh burns to his body. The doctor reasoned that the raw, weeping wound was less than 24 hours old, but Plevac insisted he had not killed his wife and that he had last seen her a few nights before her death. Plevac was charged with Dana's murder and, at his trial before Justice Finlay and jury, said he had gone to his wife's address to collect some clothes and took off his shirt to replace it with a clean one. It was then that he heard his wife and daughter scream and, when he opened the doors to the fire stairs, saw a man in a track suit. Plevac said in an unsworn statement: "I jumped towards her because I got bandage on my hand. I pull everything out and I must have been burnt. I don't know, but at that stage I completely lost it. I know now but at that stage I lost, panicked and I ran. I ran to my car." He added: "I didn't kill my wife. I am an innocent man and if they do proper job they will find the real killer."

Plevac was found guilty of murder and Justice Finlay sentenced him to life imprisonment. However, Plevac appealed against his conviction and this appeal was upheld by the Court of Criminal Appeal. He was tried again, this time before Justice McInerney and jury, but with the same result – guilty. The judge imposed the same sentence as Justice Finlay had imposed and an appeal against this conviction and sentence was dismissed by the Court of Criminal Appeal. Although Plevic had always asserted his innocence, he applied in October, 2004, for a redetermination of his life sentence. Justice James, in the Supreme Court of New South Wales, set that term at 25 years, commencing in 1989, with a non-parole period of 19 years. Plevac will be eligible for release on parole from the earliest possible date of September 21, 2008.

A COLD CASE

A killer escapes detection for eight years, but then is caught out by DNA testing following another attack on a woman.

The body of Natalie Maree Henderson, 21, was found in her bed at her Sydney unit by her partner on July 10, 1990. The mother of a small daughter had been strangled by a football sock which was tied around her throat. Other stockings and socks were tied to the corners of the bed, with part of one stocking around the dead woman's left ankle. A post-mortem revealed that death had been caused by strangulation, but there was no positive evidence of sexual assault. The dead woman's car was missing, but later was found abandoned. Also, a man who ran a service station near Ms Henderson's unit told police he had seen a man with blood on his face. Police investigations led nowhere but, to preserve evidence, they placed a blood-stained pillowcase and shirt in a laboratory freezer.

Then eight years later - on March 21, 1998 - a woman who had just had a bath was attacked by a man holding a knife. He forced her into a bedroom and, as he started tying one of her arms to a bedpost with a stocking, he told her: "I have killed before you know; I'll kill again." The woman managed to wriggle free and run to a neighbour's home for help and a friend of the woman's mother, Peter John Stone, was arrested and found guilty of threatening to inflict actual bodily harm and sentenced to three years' jail.

While Stone was serving time for this offence, he was required to provide police with a sample of his DNA. This later proved to be a match with samples obtained from the pillowslip and shirt from the Ms Henderson death scene. Stone by now had been freed, but police obtained warrants and arrested him in Tasmania on January 23, 2003. When told of the reason for his arrest, he replied: "Is this a joke?" It was no joke and, in a classic cold case, Stone was asked to provide a swab for further DNA comparison. Again, it was a match. Stone, who pleaded guilty to Ms Henderson's murder, was sentenced to 21 years' jail, with a non-parole period of 15 years and nine months, making him eligible for release in 2018.

THE BODIES IN THE BUSH

Two women are reported as having gone fishing just outside Atherton, Queensland, and their bodies are discovered more than a fortnight later.

On the morning of July 26, 1991, Alan Leahy walked into the Atherton police station to report that his wife Julie-Anne, 26, was missing. He told them that she and her friend Vicki Arnold, 28, had made a late decision the previous night to go fishing at the nearby Tinaroo Dam, even though it was close to freezing that night. When police discovered that a rifle

Arnold recently had bought also was missing, they launched a massive police and emergency services search for the women.

Fifteen days later, trail-bike riders discovered a white four-wheel drive in a secluded clearing at Cheery Tree Creek, in the opposite direction to the Tinaroo Dam. Inside, they found the decomposing remains of the two missing women. Leahy's body was found in the driving seat with two bullet wounds in the side of her head. She also had other wounds as it appeared she had been struck on the head with a rock. Arnold had been shot three times, one fired at close range to the head from underneath her chin. Significantly, the weapon found in Arnold's hand was a cut-down .22 rifle altered to negate automatic reload; it could only be manually cocked before each shot.

An inquest returned a verdict of murder/suicide and the theory went that, for some unknown reason, Arnold launched an attack on Leahy and shot and wounded her through the cheek. She then bashed her with a rock, slashed her throat with a knife and finally killed her with the shot to the head. It also was theorised that she then turned the gun on herself. The case attracted enormous attention and controversy in Queensland, with many refusing to believe the murder-suicide theory. Yet, over two police investigations, a ministerial inquiry and two inquests, the mystery remains.

THE SHOPPING MALL MASSACRE

Mentally disturbed Wade Frankum goes berserk with a knife and rifle at a Sydney shopping mall and kills seven people before committing suicide.

To all intents and purposes, 33-year-old taxi driver Wade Frankum was a solid citizen who got on well with most people, even if he was something of a loner. He'd had a troubled life as his father had died and his mother had committed suicide by gassing herself. He spent most of his time reading or watching television at home and no one suspected he one day would be involved in one of the most horrific killing sprees in Australian criminal history.

Frankum on August 17, 1991, walked out of his home armed with a self-loading assault rifle and a machete packed in a bag and went to the North Strathfield rail station and bought a ticket to nearby Strathfield. From there, he walked to the busy Strathfield Plaza shopping centre and sat down in the Coffee Pot café and ordered one coffee after another. In fact, he was there for more than 90 minutes when, at around 3,30pm, he asked for the bill.

Suddenly, Frankum produced the machete and started stabbing 15-year-old Bo Armstrong, sitting in the next booth, in the back. The girl started screaming and, with other customers, horrified, Frankum continued his frenzied attack, finally leaving the knife in the innocent teenager's back. However, he was just starting his rampage of death and, after mortally wounding Armstrong, produced the semi-automatic rifle and started firing.

The mad gunman at first turned his attention to a family group sitting near him and other customers dived for cover as shots were fired. Frankum appeared to shoot only at those who were trying to flee the scene but, as he himself withdrew, he was confronted by a woman in a car. Catherine Noyce became the gunman's seventh, and final victim, with another six people wounded. Shot, she later died in hospital. Meanwhile, police were desperate to apprehend Frankum, who had made his way to the car park. They found him dead, the gunman taking his own life.

THE BACKPACKER MURDERS

The name Ivan Milat will go down in infamy as one of Australia's worst killers. Milat is convicted of murdering backpackers around the Belanglo State Forest, New South Wales.

Australians recoil with horror at the very mention of Ivan Milat's name and with good reason. He will forever be remembered as one of the nation's worst mass murderers, with seven known victims. The word 'known' has special significance as there are many who believe the number of victims could be well into double figures. Yet Milat, the

Backpacker Murderer, could have been apprehended much earlier in his bloodthirsty spree around the Belanglo State Forest area south of Sydney.

It probably will never be known when Milat turned to murder, but his first known victims were British backpackers Caroline Clarke and Joanne Walters. Both 22 years of age, their bodies were discovered in the Belanglo State Forest on September 19, 1992, five months after being reported missing after leaving Sydney for Melbourne. Both women had been stabbed, but Clarke also had been shot numerous times in the head. In fact, forensic examination revealed that Clarke had been shot from different angles, suggesting she had been used as target practice. Indeed, the wounds of both young women were horrific, with Walters slashed to the neck, chest and head with a large hunting knife. Clarke also had been stabbed. NSW police were horrified but, despite a number of clues, were unable to determine a suspect.

Then, just three weeks after the bodies of Clarke and Walters were discovered, English tourist Paul Onions accepted the offer of a lift by a man driving a silver four-wheel vehicle. The young Englishman was on the Hume Highway when approached and was on his way to work at the fruit orchards in Mildura. The four-wheel driver, who had a large, bushy moustache and introduced himself as 'Bill', slowed down just outside Mittagong and then pulled over to remove some item. 'Bill' by now had started to act aggressively, so the concerned Onions got out of the vehicle on the pretence of stretching his legs.

However, 'Bill' barked at him to get back into the car. Onions obliged, but then had a black revolver pointed at his head. Terrified, Onions immediately jumped out of the vehicle and ran down the road. A shot was fired while the

Englishman tried to flag down a passing car. 'Bill' eventually caught up with Onions and grabbed him, only for the young man to again break free. Onions waved down a car carrying two women and five children, jumped into the vehicle, locked the door and told the woman behind the wheel to drive off as the man who had been attacking him had a gun. The driver, Mrs Joanne Berry, dropped Onions off at the Bowral police station where an officer took down details. Then, incredibly, Onions was given directions to the railway station.

He caught a train back to Sydney and stayed in Australia another six months, his near escape never far from his mind, although seemingly far from the minds of Bowral police. Back in England two years later, Onions read in a newspaper about bodies being found in the Belanglo State Forest. Perturbed, he went to his local police station and then was advised to contact the Australian Embassy. Onions eventually reached the task force investigating the Backpacker Murders.

Police by now were dealing with the appalling fact that seven bodies had been discovered and, despite every effort, they seemed no closer to solving the murders. They accumulated files on dozens of suspects, including Milat. He once had owned a silver four-wheel vehicle, had a bushy moustache and sometimes was known as 'Bill'. Police decided to have a closer look at Milat's background, especially after learning that he had a long criminal record and had once been charged with rape after picking up two girl hitchhikers along the Hume Highway in New South Wales. The two girls alleged that Milat had threatened to kill them, but he was found not guilty. However, his profile both alarmed and appalled the police investigating the Backpacker Murders.

Finally, police read Onions' claim that he had been threatened when hitchhiking along the Hume Highway. His description was too much of a coincidence so, after being flown to Australia, Onions was asked to pick out his attacker from photographs of a dozen other suspects. He picked out Milat without hesitation. This was just the break the police needed, so they raided Milat's home at Eaglevale, near Liverpool. Significantly, the house was close to the Hume Highway, the road to death for so many.

Milat was arrested on May 22, 1994, and when police searched his home they had no doubt they finally had nabbed the Backpacker Murderer. The evidence they gathered was overwhelming and, for example, they found the .22 rifle that had been used to kill Caroline Clarke, as well as the dead woman's camera. Milat was charged with the murder of seven backpackers and the attempted murder of Onions.

His trial started in March, 1996, and lasted more than three months. Jurors heard from more than 100 prosecution witnesses and had to deal with more than 300 exhibits and photographs, many of them gruesome in the extreme. Justice David Hunt in his summary said: 'It is sufficient here to record that each of his (Milat's) victims was attacked savagely and cruelly, with force which was unusual and vastly more than was necessary to cause death, and for some form of gratification. 'Each of two of the victims was shot a number of times in the head.'

A third was decapitated in circumstances which establish that she (German backpacker Anja Habschied) would have been alive at the time. The stab wounds to each of the other three would have caused paralysis, two of them having their spinal cords completely severed. The multiple stab wounds to three of the seven victims would have been likely to have penetrated their hearts. There are signs that two of them were strangled. All but one appear to have been sexually interfered with before or after death. The jury deliberated for three days before returning on July 27, 1996, for their verdict of guilty on all charges.

Milat was sentenced to life imprisonment on the seven counts of murder and to seven years' jail on the charge of attempted murder. Then, in 1998, the NSW Court of Criminal Appeal rejected a Milat appeal and declared that he was to spend the rest of his life behind bars. However, several questions remain, with many police convinced that Milat did not act alone in at least some of his murders. Also, were there other victims of the Backpacker Murderer? It is doubtful whether these mysteries will ever be solved.

THE WOMAN-HATING KILLER

A drifter goes on a seven-week frenzied killing spree in Melbourne's south-east bayside suburbs and is jailed for life.

Triple murderer Paul Charles Denyer added insult to injury for Victorians in 2004 when he announced that he wanted to change his sex to become a woman and was seeking details on government policy. Earlier, Denyer had been refused permission to wear make-up at the Barwon prison, where he was serving a life sentence, with a minimum of 30 years.

Yet Denyer, when asked to explain why he killed three women in Melbourne's bayside suburbs in 1993, had replied: 'I just hate them'. When pressed by a police interviewer as to whether he hated his particular victims or women in general, Denyer said chillingly 'general'. Denyer had gone on a murder frenzy over seven weeks from June to July, 1993, stabbing and slashing three women, with another just managing to escape with her life at the hands of the monster.

Denyer was born in 1972 in Sydney, but moved to Melbourne with his family when he was just nine years of age. A lazy, indolent boy, he had few interests and, on leaving school, drifted from job to job with long periods of unemployment. However, he struck up a relationship with a girl named Sharon Johnson and moved in with her at her Frankston flat in 1992.

Then, on June 12, 1993, Denyer struck for the first time, killing 18-year-old student Elizabeth Stevens, whose body was found in Lloyd Park, Langwarrin. Her throat had been cut, she had been stabbed several times in the chest and her torso slashed. Significantly, however, she had not been sexually assaulted.

Police launched a massive hunt for the killer but, less than four weeks later, on July 8, their attention turned to two attacks, one in which the victim survived and the other not so fortunate. The first attack occurred after bank clerk Roszsa Toth stepped from a train at Seaford. Dragged into bushes by a man she believed was carrying a gun, she eventually managed to fight off her assailant and then called police.

However, that very night another woman was attacked, with fatal consequences. Young mother Debbie Fream, 22, had driven to a store in Seaford to buy some milk but never returned home. Her body was found four days later in a paddock at Carrum. She had been stabbed 24 times but, again, there had been no sexual assault. Then, 12 days later (on July 30), the killer struck in broad daylight after carefully planning his third murder. Denyer, after cutting wire along a fence at a reserve, waited for a victim to drag through the gap and into bushes.

Schoolgirl Natalie Russell, just 17, was Denyer's third victim. She was riding her bike home from school when the monster struck and her body later was found in bushland. She had been stabbed and her throat cut. However, police soon were onto their man as they discovered a piece of skin on the neck of the dead girl. Also, a policeman had taken down the registration number of a yellow motor vehicle sighted near the bike track earlier in the day.

Police soon discovered that the car was registered to Denyer. Police called at the flat where he lived with Johnson, but Denyer was not home. Police told Johnson that they merely were making 'routine inquiries' and asked if her partner could call them when he returned home. Johnson called them two hours later and police returned to the flat, where they noticed Denyer had cuts on his hand. He explained these had been caused by trying to fix a motor fan, but the police knew they had their man. Denyer was taken to the Frankston police station where he confessed after intitially pleading his innocence.

After asking about what DNA tests would prove, he blurted out: 'OK, I killed all three of them.' In his statement, Denyer said of killing his first victim, Stevens, that he followed her and then grabbed her from behind before marching her into Lloyd Park. He then said he reached a particular area and then started strangling her. The statement said: 'She passed out after a while. You know, the oxygen got cut off to her head and she just stopped breathing.' Denyer then stabbed her repeatedly and admitted 'I stuck my foot over her neck to finish her off'. Asked why he had killed the teenage student, Denyer callously replied: 'I just wanted … just wanted to kill. Just wanted to take a life because I felt my life had been taken many times.' Denyer admitted attacking Toth and said he was 'gunna drag her in the park and kill her'.

When Toth escaped, Denyer went in search of another victim and saw Fream get out of a car outside a milk bar. He then let himself into the back of the car and waited for his intended victim to return. He said in his statement: 'I startled her … and she kept going into the wall of the milk bar, which caused a dent in the bonnet. I told her to, you know, shut up, or I'd blow her head off and all that shit.' Debbie Fream drove herself to her death and, after Denyer told her to stop the car, pulled out a length of cord and started strangling her. Then, just as she was passing out, he stabbed her repeatedly before dragging her body into bushes and then covering it with branches.

When police asked why he had killed the young mother, who had given birth to a son less than a fortnight earlier, Denyer said: 'Same reason I killed Elizabeth Stevens. I just wanted to.' Of the killing of schoolgirl Russell, Denyer said in his statement that he grabbed her from behind and held a knife to her throat. Russell, obviously fearing for her life, offered Denyer sex in exchange for letting her go, but he kept telling her to 'shut up'. In the most appalling part of his statement, he said: 'I cut a small cut (in her throat) at first and then she was bleeding. And then I stuck my fingers into her throat … and grabbed her cords and twisted them.'

When police asked him why he did this, he replied: 'Stop her from breathing … so she sort of started to faint and then, when she was weak, a bit weaker, I grabbed the opportunity of throwing her head back and one big large cut which sort of cut almost her whole head off. And then she slowly died.' But, to make sure his victim was dead, the callous killer kicked the body before slashing Russell's face. Denyer pleaded guilty to the murders of Stevens, Fream and Russell and the attempted murder of Toth.

His trial opened at the Supreme Court of Victoria before Justice Frank Vincent on December 15, 1993. Just five days later, Justice Vincent sentenced Denyer to three terms of life imprisonment with no fixed non-parole period. Denyer appealed to the Full Court of the Supreme Court against the severity of the sentence and subsequently was granted a 30-year non-parole period. This outraged the victims' families and, of course, there was further outrage a decade later when the woman-hating killer declared he wanted to become a woman.

KILLED IN JAIL

Prisoner Ahamid Ibrahim feels he is humiliated in a fight with another inmate at a correction centre and later stabs him to death.

It appeared to be just another day at the Cessnock Correctional Centre, New South Wales, on May 1, 1994. Two inmates, Ahamid Ibrahim and Clarence English had just completed kitchen duties in preparation for lunch and were playing cards when Ibrahim, who had been jailed for armed robbery, suggested English was a "screw lover". English reacted by punching Ibrahim in the face and knocking him to the ground before kicking him in the back. Ibrahim, who lost a tooth during the attack, appeared upset but worked with his attacker during the serving of lunch. He then went back to his cell and produced a knife he had sharpened into a dagger. Ibraham then went into English's cell and stabbed him with the knife, which had a 10 centimetre blade. English had sustained five separate wounds and died of blood loss before he could be taken to hospital.

Ibrahim hid the knife under the seat of a toilet bowl in his cell and denied killing English, insisting another prisoner was the attacker. Ibraham was charged with murder and in a written application at his trial referred to being attacked as a severe beating in which he was kicked while on the ground. Ibrahim was sentenced to a cumulative jail sentence of 23 years, with an 18-year minimum.

DEATH OF A STANDOVER MAN

A pimp and standover man is shot dead after wounding another man in a drugs robbery.

Stuart Pink was known in the seaside Melbourne suburb of St Kilda as a pimp and standover man who mingled with drug dealers. On March 3, 1995, he attacked a man named Tom Juricic, who had to be treated for a cut hand. Pink had stolen heroin and cash from Juricic and, eight days later, Juricic and associate Mende Georgiev saw Pink, prompting Georgiev to return home "to get something". That "something" was a gun and Georgiev then returned to where he had spotted Pink, near Fitzroy Street, St Kilda. When Georgiev returned home at about 10.30pm, he told girlfriend Joanne Guziak that he had "got him". Pink had been shot dead and Georgiev even returned to the scene of the killing to make sure Pink really was dead. Georgiev also said he disposed of the gun somewhere in the western suburb of Sydenham.

Justice Hampel, in the Supreme Court of Victoria, told the jury it had to be satisfied beyond reasonable doubt of Georgiev's confession to his girlfriend. He also pointed out that there was other evidence and although Georgiev's counsel challenged Guziak's evidence, Georgiev did not give evidence at his trial. In sentencing Georgiev to a term of 20 years, with a fixed 16-year period, the judge said: "It (the murder) can be seen as nothing but a premeditated revenge execution style killing in the context of the heroin trade ... the sentence must reflect the tragedy which you caused and the very serious crime you committed."

THE SWIMMER WHO DROWNED

A Tattslotto agent is drowned near Bendigo after his wife arranges to pay a hitman $40,000 to kill him.

When Tattslotto agent Ian Freeman drowned at the Cairn Curran Reservoir, near Bendigo, in November, 1996, his adult children reacted with disbelief. Son Paul and daughter Claire kept asking themselves how their father could have drowned in water less than a metre deep. After all, he was a strong swimmer and a proficient and experienced windsurfer.

An autopsy at the Bendigo Hospital revealed that Freeman indeed had drowned and that seemed the end of the matter, despite problems Paul and Claire immediately had with their stepmother. Sue Freeman had arranged for her husband's body to be cremated, without even discussing it with her stepchildren. Then, to compound problems, Sue Freeman told Paul and Claire that there would be a small private funeral with only a handful of guests. This horrified Paul and Claire, who eventually discovered their father's most recent will, made three months before his death. This will named them as his beneficiaries and they eventually had their own way, with a well-attended funeral service. Sue Freeman was furious, but there was nothing she could do about it.

Then, the day after Freeman's funeral, a woman contacted Bendigo police with the amazing claim that Sue Freeman had been asking local identities whether they could have her husband killed. The woman even gave police a name — Ian Richard Brown — and said he knew something about Freeman's death.

Police launched an immediate investigation, but were partly stymied by Freeman's cremation the previous day and had to rely on the original pathology report that death was caused by asphyxia, or drowning. To make matters worse, there were no photographs of Freeman's body at the hospital as the mortuary camera had been sent away for repairs. However, police did have a photograph of Freeman's Mitsubishi Colt car hanging over a ledge above shallow water and another photograph of the body immediately after it was discovered on the morning of November 29.

These photographs, in conjunction with the telephone call they had received, finally made police extremely suspicious that a murder had been committed. Police therefore contacted Brown, who told them Sue Freeman once had told him she wanted her husband killed. She even asked if he knew anyone who would murder her husband. She wanted rid of him because, she told Brown, he no longer showed interest in her and, besides, she suspected him of giving Paul and Claire Tattslotto 'scratchy' tickets.

Brown told police he then came into contact with Greek motor mechanic Emmanuel Chatzidimitriou, who was known as Max Chatz, and told him about Sue Freeman's determination to have her husband killed. Chatz was interested, for a $10,000 down-payment and another $40,000 on completion of the job. Chatz and Sue Freeman met to discuss 'business' and, on the night of November 28, he launched his murderous plan.

Ian Freeman, who also worked at the Adult, Community and Further Education Regional Council, left this job at close of business and arrived at the Tattslotto agency to relieve his wife just before 7pm. Freeman, according to security records, left the shop at 9.39pm and was not seen alive again. Chatz, it later was argued in court, abducted Freeman at gunpoint and forced him to drive his Mitsubishi to the reservoir. Chatz then tied his victim's hands behind his back, pushed him into the back of the car and drove it into the water. It also was claimed in court that Chatz told a prisoner while on remand that he pulled Freeman out of the car and then held his head under water until he was dead. Freeman's hands then were untied and the body floated on top of the water. Meanwhile, police had to prove their case and their whistle-blower was a self-confessed drug addict — hardly an auspicious start to their case in proving murder.

Police therefore interviewed Brown and after he gave them details of the Freeman-Chatz pay-for-murder arrangement, launched an under-cover operation. Brown subsequently had several meetings with Sue Freeman, all taped. Finally, Brown met up with Chatz and, despite the motor mechanic frisking him, Brown managed to hide a bugging device.

Police arrested Chatz and four days later, Sue Freeman and her solicitor went to the police. Neither Chatz nor Sue Freeman made any admissions, but police were able to build a strong case, especially as they found money in a drawer at Chatz's home. However, Chatz insisted that, in fact, Brown had killed Ian Freeman. Eventually, Chatz and Freeman went to trial separately for murder, Chatz in Bendigo and Freeman in Melbourne. Both were found guilty of murder.

Freeman, at her plea hearing, was portrayed as a hard-working woman whose husband had been violent towards her. However, Justice Hempel said: 'This is not a case of a desperate, trapped woman or a case of highly emotionally charged circumstances in which some people react and kill ... This is a case of a plan to kill, when each of you had ample time to realise and reconsider what you were about to do.' Chatz and Freeman each were sentenced to 22 years' jail, with a minimum parole period of 17 years.

DUMPED IN THE BUSH

A Sydney man suffocates his wife and two children, dumps their bodies in the bush and flees to Korea.

Sung Eun Park arrived in Australia from Korea as a boy, married Chinese-born Qian Qin and had two children with her, son Andrew and daughter Amy. However, there were problems with the marriage as Park was a chronic gambler and also entered a relationship with another woman, 19-year-old Korean So Yung Hwang (known as Demi). Park, 26, left his family home in the Sydney suburb of Eastwood in July, 1996, to live with Hwang in a flat at Ashfield. However, Mrs Park did not know of this relationship for several months and eventually went to the Ashfield flat to confront Hwang.

The two women quarrelled so fiercely that police had to be called, upsetting Park, who was only too aware that his girlfriend had extended her visa. To make matters worse, Park received a letter from the Child Support Agency on October 17, 1996, stating that although he did not earn enough to be responsible for the support of his family, this could change in the future.

Park went to the Eastwood flat and killed his wife and then his children. He bound their hands and feet with rope and stockings and placed plastic bags over each victim's head, thereby suffocating them. Park then rang Hwang to tell her he had sorted out the domestic problem and that they now could travel to Korea. Then, two nights later, he drove Hwang to a beach and suggested they suicide together. Even more significantly, he looked at the stars and told his girlfriend that his children were up there, "peacefully".

Park went back to the Eastwood flat a few days later and placed the bodies of his wife and two children in large suitcases and dumped the bodies in the bush at the Watagan State Forest near Cessnock. He told Hwang his wife and children had moved to Queensland and, meanwhile, travelled with his girlfriend to Korea on October 29 after he got wind that the police were investigating the disappearance of his family. His family already had been dead almost a fortnight then, but their bodies were not discovered until fire fighters back-burning in the Cessnock area made a truly gruesome discover.

After police had completed their investigations, Park eventually was arrested in Korea in March, 1998, and extradited to Australia. He was sentenced to an overall term of 26 years' jail, with a non-parole period of 19 and a half years.

'COLLECT THE BODY'

A man with a history of violence shoots his lover dead and tells her husband to "collect the body".

Colleen Edith Sharpe, 53 years of age, seemed happily married and lived a quiet life with her husband at Katoomba, New South Wales, Then, late in 1995, she started having an affair with 66-year-old Arthur Edward Whitmore. After Mrs Sharpe and Whitmore went separately to Brisbane and met up with each other there, she returned, and told her husband of the affair. She also informed him that she was leaving him and, indeed, already was packing her clothes,

However, Mrs Sharpe contacted her husband the next day to say she wanted to return home. A few minutes later, Whitmore rang him to say Mrs Sharpe had changed her mind. The following morning, Whitmore rang Sharpe to say he had shot Colleen Sharpe and that he could "collect the body". When arrested, Whitmore told police he had killed Colleen

Sharpe because she had demanded money for sex and that she had assaulted him. However, Whitmore had a history of violence, with a conviction for inflicting grievous bodily harm on his then wife in 1968. Whitmore was found guilty of murder and sentenced to 25 years' jail, with a minimum term of 15 years.

THE U-TURN TO DEATH

A young man runs down several pedestrians and kills one of them after he is taunted about his driving.

When Brian Morgan Hall went fishing with a friend on December 15, 1996, he would not have known the pleasant Sunday afternoon would lead to a night of tragedy, a charge of murder and a long jail sentence. Hall, 22, arrived at Birkenhead Point, New South Wales, after their fishing trip and started drinking at the local tavern in Roseby Street. They left there at closing time at 10pm and headed for their car in the multi-level car park next door. Then, when Hall drove over a low barrier separating the car park from the footpath, he was subjected to taunts from several on-lookers.

Hall, upset over some of the comments, replied with an outburst of his own and was invited to get out of his car by a man named Mark Webber. Hall took up the invitation, but Webber got the better of him before they were separated. Although Hall got back into his car, Webber punched him in the face through the open window. Hall then drove off but, at the next intersection, did a U-turn and drove to where Webber and others were still standing. The car struck Webber and another man, Wayne Piper. People rushed to the injured men's aid and these included Webber's sister Brooke and a man named Paul Allen.

Hall, after reaching the bottom of Roseby Street, turned and drove back up the street and his car hit Brooke and Mark Webber and Allen. Although Allen was not seriously injured, Brooke Webber died of her injuries a week later in the Royal Prince Alfred Hospital. Hall was charged with murder and a number of other serious offences. A jury found Hall guilty of the murder of Brooke Webber, maliciously wounding Mark Webber with intent to do him serious bodily harm and maliciously inflicting grievous bodily harm on Wayne Piper with intent to do grievous bodily harm.

In a record of interview with police hours after the incidents which led to Brooke Webber's death, Hall was asked why he did a U-turn and he replied: "I suppose it was out of anger just 'cause I had the shit kicked out of me and I just wanted to get them back, I suppose." Hall, whose blood alcohol level at the time was 0.170, appeared to have several gaps of memory in relation to the incidents. However, Justice Hidden said it was a "wonder" how "a young man of his character could have embarked upon such a dreadful criminal enterprise". He sentenced Hall to 19 and a half years' jail for the murder of Brooke Webber, with a minimum of 14 years and six months. On the charges of maliciously inflicting grievous bodily harm with intent to do grievous bodily harm, the judge sentenced Hall to concurrent fixed terms of 10 years. Hall will not be eligible for release on parole until late 2013.

THE BODY IN THE ACID

A husband kills his wife in Melbourne, drives her body to Sydney and tries to eradicate all trace of her by placing the body in a drum of acid.

Tony Kellisar arrived in Australia from Iran in 1990 and, three years later, met Svetlana Podgoyetsky. They eventually moved in together and, despite their stormy relationship, married in April, 1996. The marriage did nothing to cement the relationship and, if anything, they bickered more and more. So much so, in fact, that they separated in September, 1997. That could have been a simple end to yet another failed marriage, except that Kellisar heard that under Australian law, all property would be shared on divorce. It appears that Kellisar then decided on a course of action that would see his wife killed and her body disposed of in the most horrific circumstances imaginable.

Kellisar was able to put his murderous plan into action when he learned his wife would leave Sydney to attend a travel agents' conference in Melbourne. Ms Podgoyetsky was staying at the Crown Casino and Kellisar told her initially that he would be joining her in Melbourne. This, it seems, was so he could be sure she would not share a double room with another conference member. However, Kellisar later told her he would not be going to Melbourne and she subsequently decided she would have a quiet night watching a video on the night of Saturday, November 15, 1997.

Meanwhile, Kellisar hired a Budget car fast enough for him to drive to Melbourne within seven or eight hours so that no one would notice he was missing from Sydney. He spent the Saturday at work and started driving to Melbourne at 6pm, sometimes exceeding 190 kilometres an hour to make good time. Then, as soon as he arrived at the Crown Casino, he called his wife from a public telephone to tell her he was in Melbourne after all and could she meet him outside the casino. His wife agreed to this meeting and unwittingly walked to her death.

No one knows for sure what happened after the couple met, but Kellisar said they drove to Queensbridge Street, near the Crown Casino, and started arguing. He claimed his wife launched an unwarranted attack and that he acted in self defence, without intending to hurt her. Regardless, Ms Podgoyetsky was killed and Kellisar put her body into the back of the hired car and drove back to Sydney as fast as he could.

However, he ran into problems, especially when he was pulled over for speeding by a New South Wales police officer at Yass. Kellisar, with his wife's body in the back of the vehicle, had to produce his driver's licence and knew then that the police would know he had left Sydney and that any alibi no longer would stand scrutiny. He also realised that there would be video footage of him through security cameras outside the Crown Casino. He therefore knew he had to act with even greater haste and he put the final part of his plan into action. Once back at his workplace, Metropolitan Radio Repairs, he put his wife's body in a wheeled plastic rubbish bin and filled it with hydrochloric acid he had ordered a week earlier.

Police, alerted to Ms Podgoyetsky's disappearance, soon became suspicious of Kellisar, who had left a trail of clues, apart from the video footage. The police eventually tracked down the hire car and found that it had been cleaned of stains at the Polaris Car Spa. Finally, police found what was left of his wife's body – two legs protruding from the drum of acid, part of the lower left arm and hand and some organs.

Kellisar was charged with murder and although he pleaded guilty to manslaughter, this was rejected and after a 22-day trial a jury found him guilty of murder. Justice Vincent told him: "Your conduct constitutes a particularly serious example of a very grave crime. It was committed after careful deliberation and involved a considerable measure of cynicism and deceit. I wonder what thoughts passed through your mind in the course of more than seven hours which were occupied in your journey to Melbourne. You were highly unlikely to have been troubled by conscience or remorse as there is, in my assessment, nothing which even remotely suggests that you experienced any such emotions at any later stage. Even on your own and rejected versions of events, your major pre-occupations following the death of your wife concerned your own situation. Your treatment of the body … belies the presence of any sense of respect for her or regret for what had occurred."

The judge sentenced Kellisar to 22 years' jail, with a non-parole period of 18 years. He appealed against the sentence, but this appeal was dismissed.

THE BOWLING PIN KILLING

A young man in Sydney kills a virtual stranger by hitting him over the head with a bowling pin and stabbing him and then mutilates the body.

Christopher Andrew Robinson and a friend, Andrew Newman had been drinking before they went to the Central Railway station, Sydney, on the night of December 27, 1997. Police arrested Newman for drinking at the station and was locked up for three hours and, when he eventually returned to where Robinson and girl-friend Summer Morris were living, Robinson walked in carrying a bowling pin wrapped in a plastic bag. More ominously, the bag also contained a knife which appeared to be stained with blood.

Robinson then told Newman of an incredible story, of how he met a man "where the coaches go" and agreed to go back to the man's home. There, he hit him over the head "a couple of times" with the bowling pin he found on the floor. Robinson then told Newman: "He dropped to the floor and was gasping for air. I got the knife and gave him a good going over. It took him a while to die. I cut him down the stomach. There was heaps of blood and it stank." Adding that he thought "killing was liberating", Robinson told Newman he would kill him if he went to the police.

Police found the body of Trevor John Parkin at his unit in Glebe on December 29 and Robinson was charged with his murder. Parkin indeed had been hit over the head with a heavy object and had had his chest cavity sliced open. Even more gruesome was the fact that the man's left testicle had been removed and was found in the kitchen sink. Parkin's hands had been tied with an electrical cord and the pathologist who performed the post-mortem indicated that the mutilation of Parkin's body had occurred after death.

Parkin had convictions for sexual assaults, but Robinson said he had no knowledge of his victim being a paedophile and that the only reason he went to Parkin's unit was that sometimes when he needed money for heroin he would pose as a male prostitute. Regardless, Robinson's attack on Parkin was brutal in the extreme and Summer Morris, who had started dating Robinson about 10 months before the killing, told of incidents in which her boyfriend showed a sadistic nature. In one, he set a cat's tail alight while he held a plastic bag over the animal's head.

In another incident, Summer Morris said: "I caught a cat and was patting it. Me and Chris got into a fight but I can't recall what it was about. Chris grabbed the cat and was looking at it. He then got a knife out of his pocket; I think it was a flick pocket knife and started cutting the cat's ears off; he cut its tail off and then he cut the cat's toes off. The cat was still alive and then he cut it straight down the stomach. I could tell that it was a mother cat and was breast feeding. My mother breeds cats and I know a lot about them. When he cut the stomach open he just started pulling its stomach contents out. I was in shock from the time he first started cutting up the cat and was frozen scared."

Robinson pleaded guilty to Parkin's murder and Justice Adams said: "I have, with some reluctance, come to the conclusion that the murder of Mr Parkin was deliberate and unprovoked. The blows to the head were extremely violent. The offender intended to kill, not merely to disable. The mutilation of the body must have extended over a considerable period of time and required a great deal of physical effort. The offender told a friend 'do you know how strong those tubes and things inside you are? I do not know how doctors operate; they must have some really sharp knives. Do you know how long it takes to cut all those organs and those tubes that connect everything together? I couldn't believe it, man'."

The judge added: "I consider that the offender did not mutilate Mr Parkin's body in order to kill him, although this must have occurred if he were not already dead, but primarily because doing so satisfied some deep-seated need or provided an unimaginable pleasure." He sentenced Robinson to 45 years' jail, with a non-parole period of 35 years. This means Robinson, 17 and a half at the time of the murder, will not be eligible for release until 2034.

DEATH IS NO JOKE

A New Zealander is offended by racist jokes and stabs an Aboriginal to death after a drinking session on the banks of the Murray River.

A number of people were drinking on the southern banks of the Murray River, near Tocumwal, at the fortieth birthday party of a man named Greg Baldwin when Aboriginal Wayne Jackson and others started telling racist jokes. Jackson even told a story against his own race and this offended New Zealander Glen Ian Ford. Jackson, knowing Ford was a Kiwi, then told a joke offensive to New Zealanders. As a result, Ford tried to pick a fight with Jackson, but the Aboriginal and some friends decided to leave the camp site where the party was held on December 14, 1987.

Ford followed them, still wanting a fight, and when he caught up with Jackson, who was lagging behind his friends, said he would stab the Aboriginal – not in the back, but in the chest. Jackson threw a can of beer at Ford, who then grabbed hold of the man he considered had been offensive and stabbed him three times, with one wound penetrating the heart. Jackson was rushed to hospital, but died as a result of his wounds.

Ford, meanwhile, left the camp, took off the blood-stained T-shirt he was wearing and washed himself in the river. He also went back to the camp and kicked dirt over the blood left by Jackson's wounds. Ford then tried to drive away, but was arrested by police and charged with murder.

Justice Barr, in the Supreme Court of New South Wales, said: "I think that the only explanation of the offender's extraordinary conduct which led to the killing of the deceased is a combination of the ingrained desire to control others and the disinhibiting effects of the alcohol he consumed. There is no evidence of precisely how much he had had to drink, but I think it must have been a significant amount." Ford, who had convictions for offences of violence, was sentenced to 16 years' jail, with a fixed non-parole period of 12 years.

THE DEADLY DELUSION

A former apprentice jockey, under a delusion that his mother is conspiring to rob him of an inheritance, shoots her in the head.

Solomon Bannon was a promising apprentice jockey under the tutelage of his stepfather Michael Bannon in Melbourne. However, the youngster had weight problems and then developed a mental disorder in his late teens. He lost touch with reality and was bordering on schizophrenia when he convinced himself that his parents were dead and that his mother Raewyn and Michael Bannon were conspiring to rob him of a multi-million dollar inheritance. This preyed on the young man's mind and, while he was living in Brisbane, he came into possession of a .22 rifle.

He returned to Melbourne on May 9, 1997, and was so broke that his mother had to pay the taxi-driver who had taken him to her house. However, she would not let him sleep there and Bannon therefore got some rest in a car parked in the garage before he unlocked the back door of the house at Five Ways. He waited until his stepfather went to the stables and then demanded that his mother tell him all about the supposed inheritance. Then, when she called out to her husband, her son shot her in the head, killing her almost instantly.

Bannon at first blamed his stepfather for her death, but later claimed the shooting was an accident. Bannon was charged with murder but Justice Vincent, in the Supreme Court of Victoria, told him "there can be little doubt that you were suffering from a severe mental disorder at the time at which you caused your mother's death". The judge, who said Bannon required treatment for his mental illness, ordered the 23-year-old to be admitted to and detained in an approved Mental Health Service for 11 years, with a fixed non-parole period of seven years.

A DRUNKEN RAGE

A man bashes his de facto wife so savagely in a drunken rage near the Victorian town of Ruffy that her head injuries are similar to those suffered in motor accidents.

Ian Edward Hoare and de facto wife Sally Anne Lorraine Hansen spent much of November 20, 1997, drinking and undoubtedly were under the influence of alcohol. On their way back home to a property known as *Ardroy*, Hansen went into the Longwood Hotel to buy some beer. However, she returned soon after to ask someone to call the police because Hoare had become abusive. Hoare, in return, threatened violence with anyone who interfered with him and/or Hansen.

Hoare started attacking Hansen on the 15 kilometre trip back to the property and Hansen even went to a neighbour's house to get help. However, there was no one home and Hoare became increasingly violent. The ferocity of his onslaught was incredible as Hansen's entire scalp was bruised, along with other serious injuries. In fact, Hansen's brain injuries were so severe that it was noted that they usually occurred in motor vehicle accidents.

Justice Vincent, in the Supreme Court of Victoria, said: "Miss Hansen sustained a subdural haemorrhage and damage deep in the brain which involved the tearing of the linkages between the two hemispheres. Professor Cordner, whom it must be borne in mind is an extremely experienced and highly qualified forensic pathologist, had not encountered an injury of this last type that was not associated with skull fracture and a motor vehicle accident."

The judge told Hoare: "It is evident that you attacked the deceased, unleashing drunken uncontrolled rage. Although you did not intend to kill your victim, the jury has, understandably, found that you intended to inflict really serious physical injury upon her." He sentenced Hoare to 16 years' imprisonment, with a fixed non-parole period of 12 years.

KILLED OVER MANGOES

A man is knifed to death after apprehending a teenager who had been stealing mangoes from a back garden.

Following the breakdown of his marriage, David Laxalle went to live with his mother at Berala, New South Wales. On the night of February 23, 1997, Laxalle saw a group of teenagers stealing mangoes from a tree in his mother's back garden. He pursued and caught one of the four teenagers and became involved in a fight with 18-year-old Choi Kia Tang.

Tang admitted that he punched and kicked Laxalle, but indicated that he also was punched. As the two fought, Laxalle was stabbed seven times to the body and left arm. He staggered inside his mother's house and although she called for immediate help, her son died in hospital the following morning.

Tang, who arrived in Australia from Cambodia with his mother and siblings after his father had been killed in the Pol Pot regime, was found guilty of Laxalle's murder and Justice Hidden told Tang the public had an abhorrence of young men carrying knives and sentenced him to a total of 15 years' jail.

DEATH OF A FATHER

A troubled young man kills his father with blows from a heavy metal pipe at the family home in suburban Sydney.

William Peter Victorson's life, by his own admission, was "a complete mess" after his mother died in November, 1995. Victorson was devoted to his mother, but also should have been grateful to his father who bailed him out after losses in the futures market. Victorson wallowed so heavily in a combination of Valium, marijuana and alcohol that his father limited supplies of money to his son.

On November 1, 1997, while his father was out with a lady friend, Victorson's thoughts turned to murder. After drinking heavily and using drugs, Victorson, 24, thought he heard voices in his head suggesting he should kill his father. Then, when his father returned to the family home in the suburb of Eastwood, he struck him with a heavy metal pipe as he entered the back door. There were repeated blows and a post-mortem later revealed that the dead man had suffered massive head injuries, extensive fractures of the skull and the destruction of brain tissue.

Victorson removed money and credit cards from his father's pockets, washed his blood-stained clothes and went to the Darling Harbour Casino, throwing the credit cards into the water. Then, when he returned home at 5am, he dialled 000 and later told police that because he had owed a considerable amount of money for drugs, dealers had killed his father in a case of mistaken identity. However, Victorson eventually pleaded guilty to murder and was sentenced to a total of 18 years' jail, eventually being eligible for release in 2015.

THE VIOLENT HUSBAND

A violent husband goes berserk in the Albury suburb of Springdale Heights, killing his wife and seriously wounding a step-daughter.

Dale Wesley Barry had a stormy relationship with his wife Sharon after marrying on September 19, 1992. In fact, he was found guilty of assaulting her just months before their wedding and even assaulted her on their wedding night. Sharon Lee-Anne Barry had two children, a boy and a girl, from other relationships and then, in February, 1995, they had son Jaimyn together.

However, the violence continued and, after Barry struck his wife on the jaw in November, 1996, she took out an apprehended violence order, which later was extended. Despite this, husband and wife got back together, until they separated again in October, 1997. Then, two months later, Mrs Barry told her husband he no longer would have access to the children. Finally, on the night of December 8, 1997, Barry made his way to the family home after a drinking session at the Boomerang Hotel, Lavington. He had keys to the house, which he entered at around 2am and became embroiled in an argument with his estranged wife.

Tara Barry, just 12 years of age, saw and heard them arguing before returning to her own bedroom. While standing at the doorway facing the hall, Barry headed in her direction and stabbed her in the upper abdomen, the knife penetrating several centimetres into the right lobe of her liver. He then forced Tara and his wife to the kitchen and stabbed Mrs Barry at least four times, three of these thrusts into her right breast, penetrating a major vessel in her lungs.

Tara managed to make her way back to her bedroom and waited there until her step-father had left the house. She then went to the bedroom of her six-year-old brother Benjamin and asked him to get the help of a neighbour. However, that neighbour found Mrs Barry already dead in a pool of blood. Tara survived her stabbing, but only through the expertise of surgeons and her 39-year-old stepfather was charged with murder and maliciously wounding the 12-year-old girl.

Barry, who had previous convictions for crimes of violence, was sentenced to 18 years' imprisonment for the murder of his wife and 12 years for maliciously wounding his step-daughter. He will not be eligible for parole until 2021.

DEATH OF A CALL GIRL

An Albury call girl is strangled to death in a motel room in Wangaratta by a young man who has just been released from jail.

Soon after Graeme Leslie Green, 23 years of age, had been released from Beechworth Prison on August 28, 1998, he caught a bus to Wangaratta and booked himself into the Gateway Motel. After serving a two-month sentence for theft and related offences, Green had a few drinks in the motel cocktail bar, won more than $200 on pokies and made several telephone calls for the services of a call girl. That girl was

24-year-old Tracey Holmes, the mother of a three-year-old son, and she arrived at Green's motel room at 8.40pm, along with an escort agency driver, who also acted as her security.

Then, when Ms Holmes had been in Green's motel room for about 20 minutes, she telephoned the agency to say that the original booking was to be extended from one hour to two hours. However, when Ms Holmes did not meet her driver at 10.40pm, he and the motel manager went to Green's room, where they found Ms Holmes' naked body on the floor. She had been strangled to death. Green had fled through a window, taking his and some of his victim's belongings. After another drinking and gambling session, he was arrested by police at 5.30am. In a record of interview with police, Green said he sat on Ms Holmes' stomach and grabbed her by the front of the neck and choked her to death.

Green was tried at Wangaratta, but this trial could not be completed. He then was convicted of murder at a second trial, but this was set aside in the Court of Appeal and Green therefore faced a third trial, in which he again was found guilty.

Justice Osborn, before handing down his sentence, told Green: "The killing of Ms Holmes was totally unjustified ... the circumstances of the killing and our conduct thereafter were particularly callous. After an initial confrontation you prevented your victim from escaping and you deliberately strangled her with your bare hands until she was dead ... more, significantly, perhaps, you did not seek help for her as you might have done at the time of or after fleeing the motel." He sentenced Green to 18 years' imprisonment, with a minimum term of 14 years.

THE HEAD IN THE SINK

New South Wales police are horrified when, two weeks apart, they find the mutilated bodies of two middle-aged men.

When New South Wales police went to a townhouse in Albion Park on June 14, 1998, they could hardly believe the scene of utter horror. They had had reports that a mutilated body had been found in the flat, but could not possibly have been prepared for what they encountered in this house of horrors.

David John O'Hearn, 59, had been the victim of one of the most vicious, most sickening attacks in Australian criminal history. Among other gross wounds, he had been decapitated and his head found in the kitchen sink. The left hand had been severed and there were deep wounds to the abdomen. On medical examination, it was revealed that there were five intersecting and parallel cut wounds to the lower chest and the wounding of the abdomen showed the shaft of a hammer had been rammed up the anus. The dead man's penis had been mutilated and parts of his intestine were found on a breakfast bar. Naturally, police had never seen anything like it.

Police also found a number of knives and implements used to mutilate the body and these included a saw, four knives, a razor blade and a corkscrew. The word Satan had been written in blood on a mirror and the severed hand was resting just above that word, with a pentagram (a star-shaped figure with five points, often used in the occult) also written in blood.

The post mortem revealed that mutilation of O'Hearn's body had taken place after trauma blows to the head had caused death. There were numerous injuries to the head and, in fact, the left eyeball had been punctured by a sharp object and there were gross lacerations to the brain. It was estimated that there had been at least 10 to 12 blows to the head, delivered with extreme force.

Police were still recovering from the shock of the O'Hearn death when another body was discovered two weeks later, on June 27. This time the victim was 68-year-old Francis Neville Arkell, a former mayor of Wollongong. His mutilated body was found in a granny flat adjoining his weatherboard house and, once again, the scene was sickening. The body, dressed in tracksuit pants and a white singlet, was on its back with legs outstretched. The head had been bashed in and three tie pins had been pushed through various places, one in the left cheek, one in the corner of the left eye and another in the right eyelid. Arkell also had an electrical cord around his neck and some timber embedded in his neck; it also was obvious he had been bashed with a heavy glass ash-tray. The post mortem revealed that there were no less than 34 head injuries, with numerous deep lacerations and fractured teeth. The hyoid bone (in the neck region) was broken and the left jugular was punctured.

Then, three months after the discovery of Arkell's body, a 19-year-old walked into the Wollongong police station and admitted to killing both Arkell and O'Hearn. Mark Mala Valera told police his surrender "seemed the right thing to do". He told them he went to O'Hearn's home because he felt he "could kill someone". After O'Hearn admitted him to the townhouse, Valera struck him over the head with a decanter. He also described to police how he mutilated the body.

Valera said he killed Arkell – "a very, very horrible man" – after he went to the former mayor's home and "pretended to be gay" and attacked him a couple of minutes after being admitted to the home. Valera said he did not like Arkell because of "all the nasty things he has done to kids – read about him". He admitted to strangling him, with a cord and kicked him in the face. However, when on trial, Valera said he had no intention of killing either man and pleaded not guilty to murder but guilty to manslaughter, pleas rejected by the Crown.

During Valera's trial, the court was told he had been sexually abused by his father from a young age. However, after Valera had been found guilty of murder, Justice Studdert said: "There are, in my opinion, features of these crimes of very great heinousness ... David O'Hearn was subjected to a most savage attack, and I am satisfied beyond reasonable doubt that the prisoner acted in such attack with intent to kill and that it was a random and utterly senseless killing. The way in which the prisoner mutilated the body of his victim showed his utter contempt for his victim and so too did his use of the severed hand and the writings on the wall and on the mirror. Indeed, this first crime exuded evil of the prisoner's making. Francis Arkell was likewise subjected to a most brutal attack, and again I am satisfied beyond reasonable doubt that the prisoner conducted the attack with intent to kill. The prisoner sought to explain, and indeed to justify, his attack upon an adverse judgement he had formed of the second victim. Once again he demonstrated his utter contempt for his victim after inflicting the savage injuries which inevitably would have led to death by inserting into the head of the body three tie pins he found." The judge added that there were no mitigating circumstances and sentenced Valera to two terms of life imprisonment, with no non-parole period.

THE PARENT KILLER

A man is convicted twice of the murder of his parents at their home in the Melbourne suburb of Altona North.

When Guiseppe Russo was convicted the second time for the murder of parents Gaetano and Maria Russo, he kept protesting his innocence and insisted that DNA eventually would clear him. Russo's parents were bashed to death with a walking stick at their Altona North home on April 18, 1998. Their injuries were severe, with Russo's father being beaten with 18 blows, while Mrs Russo was unrecognisable after her head was pounded on concrete steps.

Russo insisted after his second trial that DNA found on the walking stick would prove his innocence, yet expert testimony at this trial stated that the evidence would have been left on the stick by a cough or a sneeze by an unidentified person. The jury had taken two days to find Russo guilty of murder, more than two years after he was found guilty at an earlier trial. That verdict, at a trial conducted by Justice Redlich, was overturned on appeal on legal grounds, but it really was little more than a stay of fate as, at the second trial,

Justice Bell imposed the same sentence of 28 years' imprisonment, with a 23-year non-parole period.

Justice Bell told him: "The nature and the gravity of the crimes are of the most serious kind and deserve the strongest denunciation. You and other people must be deterred from committing such crimes in the future. The most precious human right your parents possessed was the right to life itself. Respect for the sanctity of human life, especially for the lives of those who have given *us* life, is our most fundamental moral and legal obligation."

The near penniless Russo was an only child and the sole beneficiary of his parents' $200,000 estate. His parents doted on him and he repaid their devotion with death. Justice Bell told him: "You were retrenched and then dissipated your own modest savings. Under pressure of money, you called on your parents' generosity, as you had done so often in the past. When they refused, you exploded into a murderous rage and bashed them to death."

THE BODY IN THE BATH

A former boarder attacks and strangles a woman in Narre Warren, on the outskirts of Melbourne, and places her body in a bath.

Craig John Whittle had boarded for a couple of weeks at the home of Judith Fowler in Narre Warren and visited her on the night of December 2, 1998, along with two other men. It was a social visit but, during the night, Fowler offended Whittle by pointing out to one of his friends that he had taken a can of beer which did not belong to him. Whittle, 35, felt Fowler, in her 30s, had "dobbed" on him and, after leaving the house with his friends, returned and confronted Fowler.

He punched her several times in the face before she went from the kitchen to the bathroom, where he ordered her to undress. Whittle punched her again, causing several injuries, and then strangled her with his hands. He then took her to the bathroom, placed her in a bath and filled it up with water. Whittle cleaned up as best he could and left the house.

The body of Judith Fowler went undiscovered for five days and although Whittle at first denied any knowledge of what had happened to the woman, he finally admitted that he had killed her. In sentencing Whittle to 17 years' jail, with a minimum term of 13 years, Justice Teague told him: "I weigh in your favour that the murder of Judith Fowler was not premeditated. You did not, at the time you first went to her house or when you went back to her house, intend to kill her. Your plan on returning only was to remonstrate. As events developed, your intention changed. It is of great concern that your relatively spontaneous reaction to circumstances was so terrifying and so brutal."

THE CAMPUS KILLING

A disgruntled employee arms himself with a gun and goes on a rampage at Melbourne's La Trobe University.

On the morning of August 3, 1999, Jonathon Brett Horrocks left Chisolm College on the campus of Melbourne's La Trobe University with mayhem and murder in mind. Horrocks armed himself with a .38 calibre revolver and 45 rounds of ammunition and headed for the Eagle Bar, on the lower level of the university's Union Building.

On his desk at Chisolm College, Horrocks left a note which read: "I'm not crazy. I tried every legal way possible to find justice for being wronged. This is a warning to employers, politicians and corrupt men of authority. The little guy is getting tired of being used and shat upon with no avenues for fair play." There also was a quotation from Shakespeare: "Cry havoc and let slip the dogs of war."

Horrocks, 38, was intent on killing three people he believed had cost him a reduction in his work hours as a part-time barman at the Eagle bar. They were Leonardo Capraro, Sally Mitchell and Kevin Coates, and Horrocks chose his hour carefully as the bar did not open until noon. He therefore knew he could confront the three intended victims with relative ease. However, he knew that if he got involved in a mass shooting, he most likely would have to sacrifice his own life. With this mind-set, Horrocks entered the bar where Ms Mitchell was making herself a cup of hot chocolate. He said "hi Sally" and, when she turned, he fired the handgun at her, hitting her a glancing blow to the chest.

The gunman then walked to Capraro's office and fired five shots at the bar manager, hitting him four times and killing him. Horrocks then started reloading the gun but, in the meantime, Ms Mitchell had scampered for help and people were starting to lock themselves in their offices. A man named Michael Torney, who had an office on the second floor, was trying to lock a door to protect other personnel when confronted by Horrocks. A shot was fired unintentionally, but no one was hit and Torney struggled with Horrocks to get the gun. Then, when other staff went to Torney's help, the gunman was overpowered and held until police arrived.

Horrocks pleaded guilty to the murder of Capraro, the attempted murder of Ms Mitchell and of endangering the life of Torney, and Justice Vincent told him before passing sentence: "It cannot be forgotten that you staged, what you declared and intended to be, an act against specific individuals and, symbolically, against the wider community. This court, representing a community which has experienced other such incidents over recent years, must through the sentences it imposes upon those who act in this fashion, express societal denunciation and make it perfectly clear that conduct of this kind will not be tolerated. Those who act in the fashion that you have done must anticipate that, as a matter of just retribution, if committed, very substantial penalties will be imposed."

Meanwhile, a note by Horrocks handed to the judge by his counsel read: "Your Honour, I stand here as your suppliant. I know I have done a terrible, terrible thing and I caused great sorrow and pain to the family of the victim. Please believe me that I am very remorseful for any crime and find it difficult to come to terms with. Every day I think of what I have done and still cannot believe what drove me to it. My plea to you, Your Honour, is for leniency despite the degree of culpability of my crime and it is my heartfelt wish to one day be allowed to go back to my small home town and look after my ageing mother and at the same time help the community in any way I can. My life is in your hands."

Justice Vincent sentenced Horrocks to life imprisonment, with a fixed non-parole period of 23 years.

'PSYCHO AND SCHITZ'

A teenaged admits to "going psycho and schitz" in attacking a former employee with a jack handle and throwing a car battery at his victim.

Mohamed Heblos, who arrived with his family from Lebanon when he was two years of age, was employed as a tyre fitter at Sam's Tyres, in the inner northern Melbourne suburb of Brunswick. In 1998, Heblos stole $3500 from his employer, Samuel Borenstein, but was caught out and was asked to return the money. Despite this, Borenstein continued to employ the teenager – until Heblos slashed a number of tyres. Then, when Heblos was in debt in early 1999, he formulated a plane to rob Borenstein. On February 23, 1999, he watched the Sam's Tyres premises from a bus shelter and then entered the premises between 7 and 8pm. Heblos hid in a storeroom before confronting his former employer. He hit Borenstein eight times over the head with a jack handle and threw a car battery at him, inflicting terrible head injuries. Heblos then ran away with $9000 and buried the cash in several locations around Sydenham.

Interviewed by police four days later, Heblos gave a false alibi but later, in a long recorded interview, admitted he was responsible for Borenstein's death. Heblos, 18 at the time of the killing, pleaded guilty to manslaughter at his trial in April, 2000, but was found guilty of murder. Mr Justice Hempel then told him: "In light of the number and nature of the blows inflicted which caused death, and your admissions to the police, it is, I think, not surprising that you were convicted of murder." However, the judge added: "Despite your behaviour after killing Mr Borenstein, I think that your admissions in the record of interview overall show that you intended to co-operate with the police ... your behaviour and efforts in custody now over a year also help me to conclude that, at your age and with your supportive family, you have reasonable prospects of rehabilitation." He then sentenced Heblos to 15 years' jail, with a fixed period of 10 years.

THE MUTILATING MONSTER

Short and podgy, Peter Dupas earns himself infamy as one of Australia's worst killers and serial sex offenders.

Peter Norris Dupas was just 15 years of age when he first came to the attention of the Victoria Police. Dressed in his school uniform, he visited a neighbour and asked to borrow a knife. He then started slashing her before breaking down in tears and then explaining to police that he did not know what he was doing. Dupas was put on probation but, despite being given psychiatric treatment, he was found guilty of rape in 1973 and sentenced to nine years' jail. However, he was released after five years, only to almost immediately re-offend and was sentenced to a further five years' jail.

Although a report in his file noted that Dupas was a 'disturbed, immature and dangerous man' he was freed again in 1985. Then, just a month later, he raped a 21-year-old woman at a Rye beach. This time he was jailed for 12 years, with a 10-year minimum. Released in 1992, he held a woman at knifepoint in a toilet block at Lake Eppalock and was sentenced to a further two years and nine months in jail.

A serial sexual offender, he was convicted in 2000 of the murder of 28-year-old psychotherapist Nicole Patterson, whose mutilated body was found at her Northcote home on April 19, 1999. Both Miss Patterson's breasts had been removed, but never found. She had been stabbed 27 times Dupas was sentenced to life imprisonment, with no possibility of parole for this murder, but then faced another charge of murder, of 40-year-old prostitute Margaret Maher, whose mutilated body was found by fossickers in long grass at Somerton on October 3, 1997. Significantly, her left breast had been removed and stuffed into her mouth.

Police believed that the body of Maher, who had plied her trade along the Hume Highway just north of Melbourne, had been dumped after her death elsewhere. A black glove was found near the body and evidence was given at Dupas' trial for the murder of Maher that it could be linked to him. Forensic scientist Dr Henry Roberts told the Victorian Supreme Court there was strong evidence that DNA taken from the woolen glove came from Dupas and at least one other other person. He also said that a DNA test revealed that the glove was more than 450,000 times more likely to have come from Dupas and another person than from two other randomly selected Caucasian people in the state of Victoria.

Dr Roberts added in the trial before Justice Stephen Kaye: 'In my opinion it (the test) provides very strong evidence the

DNA came from Dupas and at least one other unknown person.' Dupas, 52, pleaded not guilty, but the jury took less than a day to announce its verdict. As the guilty verdict was announced, a relative of Dupas' other victim, Nicole Patterson, shouted 'yeah'. Dupas, however, described his trial as a 'kangaroo court'.

Meanwhile, police said they would review at least two other unsolved cases in which they believe Dupas was involved, one being the murder of 25-year-old Mersina Halvagis, who was killed in the Fawkner Cemetery in November, 1997, when she was visiting her grandmother's grave. Halvagis, a quiet, reserved young woman who was very close to her family, was stabbed to death.

Police also believe Dupas could be connected to the death of 95-year-old Kathleen Downes in a Brunswick nursing home in December, 1997. Mrs Downes was stabbed to death and, significantly, the murders of Maher, Halvagis and Downes all occurred in Melbourne's northern suburbs, where Dupas lived (in Pascoe Vale) over just three months. Dupas, short, bespectacled and podgy, was sentenced to a second term of life imprisonment. Australians therefore can be thankful the Mutilating Monster will never be released.

KILLED FOR HIS KINDNESS

A gentle, generous man is killed by a "chancer" who believes his victim's house is a good target for a burglary.

Samuel Macumber, fast approaching his 60s, was known for his kindness, generosity and unsuspecting nature. He lived in the south-east Melbourne suburb of Clayton and was always willing to help anyone in need. A man named Stephen Morison borrowed from him and told a friend, Lorenzo Favata, that Macumber did not always keep an eye on his cash or possessions. He introduced Favata to Macumber on March 26, 1999, and the 31-year-old Favata returned two nights later with overalls, an old pair of boots, gloves, a balaclava and a small crowbar.

He brazenly knocked on Macumber's front door and, when the middle-aged man opened the door, Favata demanded to know where he kept his money. Macumber then made the fatal mistake of telling the burglar he recognised his voice. Favata hit him with the crowbar and stabbed him before searching for cash. After stealing several thousands of dollars, Favata drove off in a stolen car. He later abandoned the car and left the boots, gloves, balaclava and crowbar at a local tip.

When questioned by police, Favata said he had been in bed with his wife at the time of the killing and she supported the claim. However, in a police "sting" two years later, Favata admitted in a recorded account that he had killed Macumber.

Justice Teague, in sentencing Favata to 21 years' jail (with a minimum of 16 years), said: "You acted totally out of self-interest. You went to his (Macumber's) home with a premeditated plan to commit a very serious crime. You intended to rob him because you wanted his money. You preyed on his vulnerability. Although you had not planned to kill him, you were quick to do so when you saw a risk of your being caught out … once you made the decision to kill him, you did so with particular savagery."

'DON'T DO IT MY HEART'

A Turkish migrant drives to his girlfriend's house in a Melbourne suburb and, after taking a gun from his car, shoots her twice.

Mustafa Acikoglu migrated to Australia from Turkey in 1992 with his wife, but found it difficult to settle in Australia. He worked as a fruit picker near the northern Victorian town of Shepparton, but separated from his wife. He met Adelet Demir at about this time and they made plans to move away together as Acikoglu knew she was having marital problems.

Acikoglu and Demir moved into a house in the northern Melbourne suburb of Reservoir, but the relationship lasted just a few months. However, Acikoglu drove Demir's children to school and did much of her shopping while they were estranged, even though the relationship was fragile. Acikoglu disapproved of Demir smoking marijuana and said she was trying to humiliate him.

Finally, on August 31, 1999, 39-year-old Acikoglu telephoned Demir to ask about picking up her children. As there was no reply, he went to the house and an argument developed. Acikoglu again accused Demir of trying to belittle him and then left the house to go his car. He collected a gun from the glove box, returned to the house and accused Demir of trying to make him "a man without honour". He then fired a shot into her chest, prompting Demir to say in Turkish: "Don't do it, my heart. Don't do it." About 30 seconds later, he shot her a second time, this time at very close range to the head. Acikoglu fled the scene, disposing of the gun and ammunition as he drove to Shepparton, where he wanted to see his children before he was arrested.

After pleading guilty to murder, Justice Bongiorno said: "For sentencing purposes, I characterise this murder as one carried out with a degree of anger and with only such premeditation as is necessarily implied in your deliberate retrieval of your hand gun from the motor vehicle parked in the street, which necessitated your leaving the scene of your argument with the deceased, going to the car and returning. It is thus distinguished, if only to a minor degree, from a cold blooded execution. After obtaining the gun your actions in shooting the deceased twice in the presence of her four-year-old son and in the circumstances where, after the first shot she pleaded for her life, are horrendous indeed." He sentenced Acikoglu to 18 years' jail, with a minimum of 14 years.

KILLED OVER A DEBT

A Melbourne man is bashed to death with a car's anti-theft lock after he asks his attacker to repay money taken in a bank loan.

When George Rakos was experiencing financial difficulties, he approached workmate Darren McArdle to help him get a bank loan. Rakos' credit rating was poor, so they devised a plan in which they would tell a bank Rakos was planning to buy McArdle's car and a bank cheque therefore would be made out to McArdle. Rakos handed McArdle a bank cheque for $7000 and the money should have remained in the bank. However, McArdle withdrew the money and gambled it away on poker machines.

After the two had worked a night shift finishing on the morning of September 14, 1999, Rakos asked McArdle if he could have some of the money. Arrangements therefore were made for McArdle to make a withdrawal when the bank opened and he left his workmate watching television at Rakos' Ferntree Gully home. McArdle went to drive off, but noticed a car steering lock in the car. He picked up the lock, took it into Rakos' home and struck his workmate to the head five times.

McArdle cleaned up after the killing, left the home and threw the lock away. However, he was always the chief suspect and, after being arrested, pleaded guilty to Rakos' murder. Justice Teague, in the Supreme Court of Victoria, noted that although McArdle had a serious gambling problem, he had worked hard and kept out of trouble with the law. The killing was described as "inexplicably out of character" and the judge noted a "high level of remorse". He sentenced McArdle, 38 years of age, to 17 years' imprisonment, with a non-parole period of 12 years.

A 'FANTASY' GONE WRONG

A man kills his de facto wife and two sons after he is affected by enacting one of his wife's sexual fantasies.

Sandor Cikos appeared to leave a normal life with de facto wife Allison Penrose and their two sons, four-year-old Jake and 18-month-old Travis at their home in West Dapto, New South Wales. Then, on December 6, 1999, Cikos, 39 years of age, returned home from his work as a fitter and turner to find his wife and sons dead. He immediately notified police, who reported that Penrose had two wounds to the left rear of her head. All three had plastic bags placed over their heads and the house had been ransacked, with jewellery missing.

However, police were suspicious from the start as there was no obvious point of entry for a burglary and Penrose's missing jewellery was found later in Cikos' lunch box. Finally, fibres taken from Penrose's body matched shorts worn by Cikos, while fingernail clippings taken from her body matched her husband's DNA profile. Cikos, who had been born in Yugoslavia near the Hungarian border and had migrated to

Australia with his family as a four-year-old, was charged with murder and pleaded guilty.

Cikos had been profoundly affected by events of February, 1999, after Penrose had suggested to a friend that she had a fantasy of watching her husband have sex with another woman. Penrose then invited her friend home and, after initiating sex with her husband, told her friend that it was her turn. She then watched as Cikos turned her fantasy to reality. However, Penrose then turned on her husband and her friend, arguing he should not have given in to her fantasy. She even assaulted Cikos and slashed his elbow with a knife, the wound requiring eight stitches.

Police took out an Apprehended Domestic Violence Order against Penrose on Cikos' behalf, but Cikos later said his wife threatened to kill him if he did not kill her friend. She even gave him a deadline, of February, 2000, Cikos said. Of course, there was no proof of this and Cikos admitted he had thought of killing his wife for some time. He said he got a piece of pipe on that fateful day of December 6 and hit Penrose over the head with it before choking her. He said he then placed a pillow over her face before choking his two sons to death. Cikos also said that although he placed plastic bags over the heads of all three, they did not suffocate, but were choked. He also said the only reason he could give for killing his sons was that he thought they could not bear the pain of knowing that their father had killed their mother.

Justice Dunford said: "However unreasonable the conduct and reaction of his wife to the situation which, as I am satisfied, she initiated, he was under no immediate physical threat and he had plenty of opportunities to seek advice and pursue other options. Three people, two of them his own innocent children, have been killed without any justification and the law must take its course." Although the judge noted that Cikos had shown remorse for what he had done, he was sentenced to 21 years on each count, the sentences to be served concurrently and with a fixed no-parole period of 15 and a half years. Cikos will not be eligible for release until the middle of 2015.

THE VALENTINE KILLING

When a Melbourne man is told his wife is planning to leave him, he attacks her with an iron bar and makes out that there has been an intruder in the family home.

When Andrew Stephen Doherty and his wife Vivienne were experiencing marriage difficulties in 2000, she approached a minister of the Church of Christ, in the eastern Melbourne suburb of Mitcham, to ask him to convince her husband the marriage was over. The minister passed on the message to Doherty, whose engineering business was struggling, but there did not appear to be an immediate reaction.

Then, on February 14 (St Valentine's Day), 2000, Mrs Doherty, took her two young sons (she also had 21-year-old twin sons from a previous marriage) to school and stayed talking to other mothers before returning to the family home at Donvale. She then was attacked in the home, suffering severe head injuries caused by blows from an iron bar. An autopsy revealed that she had taken seven blows to the head, some fracturing her skull. The house had been "turned over", with cupboards and drawers open, as if an intruder had entered the house.

Doherty, meanwhile had prepared documents to help him account for his movements on the morning of the murder. However, he was charged with his wife's murder and Justice Bongiorno told him that his attempt to create an alibi had suggested "a degree of premeditation". The judge also described the killing of Mrs Doherty, 46, as "horrendous". He told Doherty: "Whilst no amount of punishment can rectify the wicked wrong which you have committed, the community demands that your sentence reflect the punishment for that wickedness." He sentenced Doherty to 21 years' jail, with a minimum term of 16 years.

SET ALIGHT

A Victorian man is so upset about domestic issues that he lures his de facto wife to a caravan and sets her alight.

Although Claude Monks had been living with his de facto wife Viola Klein at the Victorian town of Kyabram for a number of years, he became increasingly disenchanted with the relationship. The couple had a son, seven-year-old Grant, while Monks had an adult son, and Klein a son, Ashleigh. Monks complained that Klein did not feed Grant well enough and also told her he believed his step-son treated Grant roughly.

Monks, 58 years of age, eventually assaulted Ashleigh on February, 21, 2000, and Mrs Klein, 48, obtained an intervention order against her de facto husband. Monks therefore left the family home and went to live elsewhere in the fruit town of Kyabram. It was then that Monks started describing Klein to friends as "a slut". He also intimated that he was going to kill her with one friend telling him: "You're mad, that's rubbish. You'll go to jail for that."

Then, on September 27, 2000, Monks asked Klein and Grant to help him to clean up a caravan. They agreed but, when they got to Monks' house, he told Grant to stay in the lounge room. After about 10 minutes, little Grant heard screaming, just before Monks ran through the back door with superficial burns to the face, hands and the left leg. Monks had set the caravan alight with petrol and a cigarette lighter.

Mrs Klein took the full fury of the fire and was engulfed by flames, with burns to all parts of her body except the right foot. She screamed: "Help me, please, help me. I'm burning. God's punishing me. I don't want to die. I've got to live for my kids." She eventually lapsed into unconsciousness and was rushed to Kyabram Hospital, where she died of her burns. Monks, who was treated for his burns, said at the hospital that Klein had been in the caravan when a can of petrol had been knocked over while he had lit a cigarette and there then was an explosion.

However, a jury found Monks guilty of murder and Justice Coldrey, in the Supreme Court of Victoria, told him that his insistence that Klein's death was an accident "deprives you of the benefit of any remorse". He said: "On any reasonable view of the evidence, the offence was premeditated. It involved not only the dispersion of petrol throughout the caravan but the luring of Mrs Klein to come to your house and to enter the van. Having caused her to be engulfed by flames, you left her there to suffer in agony until, perhaps mercifully, the depth of her burns destroyed the nerve endings beneath the skin." He sentenced Monks to 20 years' imprisonment, with a minimum period of 15 years.

BASHED AND BURIED

A truck driver bashes his wife to death and buries her body in the bush after she tells him she no longer loves him.

Raymond John Prior had been married for 12 years before he and his wife separated over his reliance on drugs, particularly heroin. He went to live in the New South Wales town of Lismore, while his wife remained at the family home in Tenterfield. During this separation, the wife decided she wanted a relationship with someone who was not a drug-user and started seeing a Queensland truck driver, Colin Booth. Prior, who also was a truck driver, confronted Booth but resorted only to slashing his love rival's truck tyres. Then, when Prior visited Tenterfield in late August, 2000, his wife allowed him to sleep in a caravan at the back of her home.

Early in the morning of August 24, Prior went into the house to use the toilet and then confronted his wife. She told him she did not love him any more and he attacked her with considerable fury. The woman suffered severe facial injuries and, more than likely, also was strangled. Prior wrapped the body in a blue tarpaulin and bound it with electrical tape before driving it into bushland 17 kilometres away and burying it in a shallow grave. When Prior's wife failed to turn up for work, police became suspicious and questioned Prior. Finally, a friend advised him to turn himself in and, after making a statement, Prior was arrested.

At Prior's trial in the Supreme Court of New South Wales at Grafton, Justice Michael Grove said after Prior had been found guilty of murder: "My conclusion is that the genesis of the prisoner's offence was his uncontrolled rage at being discarded by his wife for her new lover. I am, however, persuaded that the probability is that the prisoner is genuinely remorseful for what he has done, and in this regard I have paid careful attention to letters which he has written and the candour with which he has expressed his remorse." He then sentenced Prior to a prison tem of 16 years, with a non-parole period of 12 years.

THE UNWANTED PREGNANCY

A young man who already is making child support payments kills a pregnant women in Melbourne.

Daniel Vance Mizon, a science graduate from Monash University, met Lucille Rosalie May through the Save Albert Park movement in protest against the Australian Grand Prix being held in that part of Melbourne. That was in 1995 and they had an on-off relationship for several years, even though Mizon at one stage left Miss May to live with a another woman.

Then, in March, 2000, May, 40, visited Mizon, 41 at the time, at work to tell him she was pregnant and that he was the father. Several months later, on September 9, Mizon visited his first wife and was told that she was concerned about child maintenance payments for their son. Next day, he visited his mother and she told him she had spoken to May and that she had told her of the pregnancy. Enraged, Mizon headed to May's home in the bayside suburb of Highett and killed her.

May's mother and sister rang her the following day and, when there was no response, paid her a visit. The front door was locked, but they used a key to gain entry to the house and found May's body in a pool of blood on the rear living room floor. There also was blood in the kitchen and bathroom and a post mortem later revealed that the woman, seven months pregnant, had been stabbed in the neck and that there had been an attempt to strangle her.

Police interviewed Mizon, but he at first denied any knowledge of May's death and, in a second interview, said he went to May's back door, found it open and discovered her body on the living room floor. However, a jury found Mizon guilty of murder and Justice Bongiorno said the likely motive was the financial and social inconvenience to Mizon of May's pregnancy.

The judge, in sentencing Mizon to 21 years' imprisonment, with a minimum of 17 years, said: "The most significant aggravating factor so far as sentencing in this case is concerned is the fact that at the time you killed her, Lucy May was pregnant. She was accordingly extremely vulnerable. From time immemorial, society has regarded pregnant women with particular solicitude. That this is so is beyond argument. It needs no elaboration. I regard Lucy May's pregnancy as a significant aggravating factor in this case."

THE BODY IN THE BOOT

Police find a badly decomposed body in the boot of a motor car left in an inner Sydney suburb.

Married couple Patrick and Mary Joiner went to the wedding of Mrs Joiner's cousin at the Greek Orthodox Church in Redfern, an inner Sydney suburb, on October 8, 2000, even though they were having counselling over marital problems. They went for a drink at the Brighton RSL before the wedding reception and had another argument. Mrs Joiner stormed out and was not seen alive again.

Patrick Joiner later claimed he caught up with his wife and the couple drove south from Sydney, only for the argument to flare again. He said he accidentally struck Mary to the side of the face and, after she screamed, punched her. However, he claimed, she then had spasms and fell to the ground. Joiner said he was unable to revive her and put her in the boot of the car he was driving, a VW Golf. He also claimed he ran out of petrol and had to call the NRMA for assistance before driving to Redfern and then walking to the church where the wedding had taken place earlier in the day before returning home.

Mrs Joiner was reported as missing and Joiner even went on national television with pleas for his wife to return or let authorities know where she could be located. Indeed, he played the upset husband for what it was worth before police on October 26 opened the boot of the VW Golf left in Redfern. Inside, they found the badly decomposed body of Mrs Joiner, who had been severely assaulted. A post mortem revealed she had a deep laceration to her upper lip, extensive bruising around her jaw, a cut above the right eye and severe tears to the scalp as if she had been kicked or hit with a heavy object like a rock.

However, Joiner was the major suspect when police not only learned of his violent behaviour towards his wife, but also that he had called the NRMA for assistance when the VW Golf found in Redfern earlier had run out of fuel. Then, amazingly, Joiner suggested his wife might have died as a result of an epileptic fit or blackout. He was found guilty of murder and sentenced to 18 years' jail, with a non-parole period of 13 years and six months.

'I JUST KILLED MY MISSUS'

A taxi-driver walks into a Tasmanian police station and announces: "I have just killed my fucking missus."

Taxi-driver Desmond John Waddington, 46, had been drinking beer and watching football on television at his New Town, Tasmania, flat on September 15, 2001, and was in good spirits as he prepared a meal for himself and 52-year-old de facto wife Diane Ellen Mudge. However, Mudge started making telephone calls and this upset Waddington, who often complained about her telephone calls, especially at meal times.

During Mudge's telephone conversation with friend Georgina Males, Waddington was heard to yell: "Get off that fucking phone. I've been putting up with it for the last 10 years. I'm sick to death of the fucking phone." Males rang back, but Waddington shouted "fuck off" down the line to her and hung up. Males, concerned for her friend, went around to see her friend, but Waddington refused her entry to the flat. He then headed off to a hotel but, after just one drink, went to the Liverpool police station and said: "I've just killed my fucking missus."

Waddington had held a pillow over Mudge's face and smothered her for about three or four minutes until she died. He pleaded guilty to a count of murder and was sentenced to 17 years' jail, with a fixed non-parole period of 12 years. However, on appeal, the none-parole period was reduced to 10 years.

DEATH AT THE ABORTION CLINIC

A loner plans a massacre at a Melbourne abortion clinic and shoots dead a security guard.

Peter James Knight, 47, was something of a loner, a recluse who at one stage lived in a humpy in a forest in New South Wales. In 2000, he became interested in the anti-abortion movement and attended rallies and protests. The following year he moved to Melbourne and took more than a passing interest in the Fertility Control Clinic in Wellington Parade, East Melbourne. Finally, on July 16, 2001, Knight put a murderous plan into action.

He went to the clinic at about 10.20am, holding two bags, one of which contained a well-concealed rifle. Knight was intent on mayhem and entered the reception area by the main door. However, his plan of a massacre ran into trouble almost immediately as security guard Steven Rogers walked in from a different door. Near the end of his shift, Rogers moved towards Knight, who told him he had a gun. Knight then pointed the rifle at the security guard and pulled the trigger. Rogers fell mortally wounded to the floor and, after Knight reloaded the rifle, he pointed it at the stomach of a pregnant woman. The woman's male friend, Sandro De Maria, grabbed the gun to wrest it from Knight and it went off, firing a shot into the ceiling. However, Knight eventually was overpowered and arrested.

At his trial in Melbourne, Justice Teague told Knight: "The murder of Steven Rogers was a very serious crime. It is to be treated more seriously because of the context in which you carried out the murder. You were a loner on a personal crusade when you went to the clinic. Your crusade was to effect social change. Steven Rogers was just doing his duty. He got in the way of your crusade. He was one of those who was characterised by you as being in 'the abortion racket'."

He also said: "In July, 2001, you were able to put together a collection of items that had the potential to result in the death of dozens of people who were going about their normal lives in the East Melbourne clinic. You engaged in detailed planning and preparation. Your planning included having noted the usual timing of the departure from the clinic of Steven Rogers. Your entry to the clinic was at a time shortly after he would have been expected to have departed … You have not shown any remorse, in the sense of showing any sincere repentance or regret that Steven Rogers was killed. The closest you have come to that has been to argue that his death was just bad luck." Justice Teague then sentenced Knight to life imprisonment, with a non-parole period of 23 years.

THE GRIEVING SON

A young man goes on a spending spree after killing his parents and sister and blames their death on Asians.

To all intents and purposes, Sef Gonzales was the epitome of a heartbroken young man dealing with a tragedy of monumental proportions. The fresh-faced Gonzales gave an emotional eulogy at the funeral of his parents and sister in singing pop hit 'One Sweet Day' made famous by Mariah Carey and Boys II Men. It went:

> Sorry I never told you
> All I wanted to say
> Now it's too late to hold you
> 'Cause you've flown away, so far away …
> And I know you're shining down from me from heaven
> Like so many friends I have lost along the way.
> And I know eventually well be together –
> One Sweet Day

Gonzales was the ultimate hypocrite because he had killed parents Teddy and Mary-Loiva and 18-year-old sister Clodine at the family's home in the quiet north-west Sydney suburb of North Ryde on July 10, 2001. The Gonzales family had migrated to Australia from the Philippines after an earthquake had destroyed a hotel the family had built. Sef, just 10 years of age, was trapped by debris on a staircase, but father Ted pulled him to safety.

Despite having his life saved by his father, Sef resented the strict discipline imposed on him and, besides, there was the question of $1 million he would inherit if his parents died. The 21-year-old Sef Gonzales therefore tried to poison his family with seeds he had bought on the internet. His mother was admitted to hospital, but recovered, so Sef waited just two weeks before setting in motion another plan.

This time he stabbed his family to death and blamed it on a mystery intruder. Sef Gonzales even painted the words 'f… off Asians' on a kitchen wall to divert attention from himself. Police were suspicious from the start, but Gonzales appeared to have the perfect alibi as he told police he was having dinner with friends at the time his family had been slaughtered. Gonzales after making out that he had found the bodies of his three family members, called police and told them: 'Somebody shot my parents, I think. They're all bleeding; they're on the floor.'

Police: 'What suburb are you in?'

Gonzales: 'They're not breathing. What do I do?'

Police: 'What suburb are you in?'

Gonzales: 'North Ryde?'

Police at a press conference later said: 'Young Sef and his family have cooperated with the investigators at this stage, and we're satisfied with the explanation so far.' Then, when the dinner alibi turned out to be a lie, Gonzales said he was having sex at a brothel at the time and had made up the story about having dinner because his mother would have been horrified at the thought of him going to a brothel.

Police then broke through his tissue of lies bit by bit, starting with disproving Gonzales' claim that he had been to the brothel. It turned out that the particular prostitute Gonzales referred to was not at the brothel at the time he suggested. Police dogs were unable to pick up the scent of any intruder and traces of the paint used to daub the wall were found on one of Gonzales' jumpers. Also, he claimed to have hugged members of his family after he had found their bodies, but no trace of these signs of affection could be found on his clothes.

Meanwhile, Gonzales visited his father's accountant just three days after the family tragedy and then paid deposits on luxury motor vehicles. He moved into an apartment, sold his parents' car and generally lived it up. Gonzales was charged with three counts of murder 11 months after the slayings and he eventually pleaded not guilty before a six-week trial in the Supreme Court of NSW.

Crown prosecutor Mark Tedeschi told the jury: 'Feeling his life unravel, Sef set in motion a plan to murder his parents and his sister.' The court was told that when police seized Gonzales' computer they found reference to internet sites such as 'How to Kill' and 'White Man Killer'.

The jury took just four and a half hours to find Gonzales guilty and, as the decision was announced, his aunt, Annia Paraan, broke down and muttered 'thank you'. She said later: 'I think justice has been done, but it would have been easier to accept if it were another person. It's just so hard to accept.'

A FAMILY ROW

A grief-stricken Melbourne woman kills her mother's de facto husband during a row soon after her mother's death.

Julie Calway was close to her mother, even though she did not get on with her mother's de facto, Michael Pitts. Calway's mother was seriously ill in mid-2001 and moved in to help look after her at her home in the western Melbourne suburb of Newport. Calway and Pitts had a row on August, 2001, when she complained that he was smoking in her mother's room; he reacted by punching Calway in the face. Calway's mother died a couple of months later and Calway was upset by Pitts' behaviour as Calway, a sister and an aunt went through the dead woman's belongings.

On October 19, Calway drove from her East Malvern flat to Newport and was involved in a fight with Pitts. She suffered several bruises, but Pitts died from severe head injuries, a post-mortem revealing 16 linear lacerations to the scalp and a fractured skull. Calway was tried for murder and, at her trial, Justice Teague said "the indications are that it (the killing) was done with a brick or rock or garden form that happened to be on hand". In sentencing Calway, Justice Teague told Calway: "There is not sufficient basis for a finding that the killing of the deceased was premeditated. I sentence you, therefore, on the basis that it was not." Calway was sentenced to 15 years' imprisonment, with a non-parole period of 10 years.

KILLING FOR PLEASURE

A teenager watching a movie early one morning goes berserk and slashes his girlfriend and her mother to death in truly horrific circumstances.

When teenager Melissa Joy Maahs elected to move in with her boyfriend Lloyd Maurice Crosbie, she had no idea that she and her mother soon would be the victims of a truly sadistic and brutal killer. The teenage couple originally lived with 18-year-old Crosbie's father in the Victorian town of Morwell, but later moved to another house in Morwell with 19-year-old Melissa's mother Kaye Lucy Maahs, 54, in April, 2001.

Just a few months later, at around 3am on August 18, Crosbie was watching a movie in bed while his girlfriend slept in the double bed next to him. For some reason, Crosbie wore a scabbard containing a skinning knife with a curved blade. Some time during the movie, Crosbie removed the knife from the scabbard and, using his right hand, stabbed Melissa three times in the head. The wounds were not fatal and Melissa woke and screamed. This prompted Crosbie to hold her by the back of the head while he slashed at her throat. Melissa somehow managed to get into a sitting position, but Crosbie kept attacking her, cutting his own hand in the process.

Mrs Maahs, hearing her daughter's screams, left her own bedroom and was confronted by the knife-wielding Crosbie, who stabbed her to the throat and upper back. Mrs Maahs fell to the floor while he slashed and cut at her. She screamed: "Melissa, call an ambulance. I think I am dying."

Crosbie then turned back to his girlfriend and stabbed her again and again in the throat and body. He then paused before he returned to Mrs Maahs, pushing the knife into her throat and then pulling it sideways. Believing Mrs Maahs was still alive, he then struck her several times across the head with a ceramic ornament before going getting an iron from the laundry and smashing her again over the head.

Crosbie made the scene look like a burglary went wrong but, before he left, he committed more ghastly acts. He rubbed his girlfriend's anus and vagina and his penis with lubricant and then had sex while looking at pornographic magazines placed on Melissa's back. He ejaculated twice and then removed his clothing to take a shower. Crosbie then caught a cab to the Morwell station and caught a train to Melbourne before moving on to his father's house at Wangaratta, in northern Victoria.

While on the run, he made calls to fantasy sex lines with Melissa's mobile telephone before throwing it into a creek. Police apprehended Crosbie on August 20 and, at the Wangaratta police station, he made admissions about killing Melissa Maahs and her mother.

He pleaded guilty to two charges of murder and the prosecution argued that he had killed for the "sheer pleasure of killing". Justice Kellam, in the Supreme Court of Victoria, told him: " There is not a scintilla of evidence to suggest that either of your victims had given you any cause or provocation or reason for anger which could in any way explain your murderous behaviour towards them. The depravity with which you treated the body of your victim Melissa after her death is not only an aggravating factor but it demonstrates a total lack of remorse by you at that time."

He added: "The two murders to which you pleaded guilty before me were particularly callous and brutal. Your victims must have suffered painful and terrifying deaths. The only explanation for your behaviour is that the killings took place in a context of sadism involving sexual excitement linked to the murderous acts to which you subjected your victims. There is the aggravating circumstance of your defilement of the body of Melissa. Furthermore, it must be remembered that not one but two decent members of our community have lost their lives at your hands." Justice Kellam sentenced Crosbie to life imprisonment, with a minimum 30 years.

DEATH OF AN INFANT

A Geelong man, unable to stand the "grizzling" of his girlfriend's two-year-old son, loses his temper and kills the little boy.

From all accounts, two-year-old Lewis Blackley was a happy little two-year-old and his mother Daisy De Los Reyes was a good and attentive mother. However, Ms De Los Reyes had the misfortune to take up with a man named Haemon Gill. The relationship had existed for about three months to November 11, 2001, when Ms De Los Reyes was preparing an evening meal at her Norlane home in the suburb of Geelong, with Lewis yelling and screaming. Lewis ate his dinner in a high-chair, but started crying again.

Ms De Los Reyes and Gill had been drinking and smoking marijuana and, after little Lewis had cried himself to sleep, his mother went to bed. She found her son cold and blue in the face the next morning, despite a blanket being placed over him; the boy was dead. When Ms De Los Reyes was told a week later that her son had died of head injuries, she attributed it to Lewis banging his head.

However, Gill later admitted that Lewis' death was his fault and stated that he had bit him on the lip and then tried to conceal this by punching the affected area. The boy's post-mortem revealed that the fatal injuries could not have been caused by head banging and, in an interview with police, Gill said: "I intended to let him (Lewis) know who was boss 'cos he's a little shit. He was demanding, he was terribly demanding - demand, demand, demand. Just cry, sook, try and get his own way and usually Daisy would give up and give him his own way."

Justice Coldrey told Gill: "The jury were satisfied that at the time you inflicted the fatal blow or blows you did so with the intention of causing him really serious bodily harm." The judge added that although he did not think the killing was premeditated, Gill "refused to fully accept responsibility for Lewis' death" and that his "state of mind falls well short of genuine remorse". He sentenced Gill, 30, to imprisonment for 19 years, with a fixed period of 14 years.

GUILTY, BUT NO BODY

Jeffrey Kevin Mitchell is found guilty of the stabbing murder of Andrew Preston, even though Preston's body has never been found.

Jeffrey Kevin Mitchell, 47, had been in a relationship with Leanne Brown for a number of years and had two sons, aged 11 and nine, when a younger rival, 23-year-old Andrew Preston came along. Preston struck up a relationship with Brown and the couple moved to a caravan park at Lilydale, on the outskirts of Melbourne. Then, on April 29, 2002, Mitchell and Brown's brother Gavin went to the caravan park and accompanied Preston to a four-wheel drive vehicle. Preston was never seen again but, after about a year, Gavin Brown started co-operating with police and searches were made for Preston's body. These searches proved unsuccessful and police believed this was because of roadworks in the area several months earlier.

Then, shortly before Mitchell's arrest, he made admissions to Leanne Brown in conversations taped by the police. At Mitchell's trial in February, 2005, Gavin Brown said he and Mitchell had driven Preston to a remote location near the timber township of Powelltown, where Mitchell stabbed and killed the young man. Mitchell, who was worried about the possibility of losing custody of his sons, and Brown then pushed the body into the bush. Mitchell, who pleaded not guilty, said he only took Preston away to "warn him off". However, the jury was not convinced and Mitchell was found guilty of murder. Judge Whelan told him: "The offence of which you have been found guilty is clearly a most grave and serious one. Andrew Preston was a drug user, and the evidence in your trial suggested that he encouraged drug use in your partner, Leanne Brown. I accept, as your counsel submitted in your plea, that the circumstances of the relationship between Leanne Brown and Andrew Preston were such as to make any father concerned. That matter, however, does not detract from the gravity or the seriousness of the offence of which you have been found guilty and for which you are responsible.

The judge added: "On any view of the facts, Andrew Preston went through a terrifying ordeal prior to his death. He was forcibly taken at night from the caravan and driven to an isolated spot. I have no doubt that he was terrified before he was murdered by you." He sentenced Mitchell to 18 years' imprisonment, with a non-parole period of 14 years. Gavin

Brown, who had successfully applied for a separate trial and pleaded guilty, gave an undertaking to give evidence against Mitchell. He was given a suspended sentence.

THE HOTEL SHOOTING

A man is shot dead and another seriously wounded following a minor altercation at a Sydney hotel.

Vietnamese migrant Phuoc Giau Nguyen and two friends were at the Pavillion Hotel, in George St, Sydney, in the early hours of February 2, 2002, when they came across two other men, Khanh Thanh Nguyen and Tri Binh Tran. All these men were on the second floor of the hotel, in a dance bar, when someone flicked a cigarette butt at Tran, sparking an argument. Khanh Thanh Nguyen and Tran left to go downstairs to a gaming room, with Phuoc Giau Nguyen and his friends following them. When an argument broke out, Phuoc Giau Nguyen produced a handgun from his clothing and shot Khahn Thanh Nguyen twice, in the stomach and the lower back, before firing three shots into Tran, hitting him in the right shoulder, left hip and left thigh. The gunman fled from the scene as the mortally wounded Khanh Thanh Nguyen also pulled a handgun from his clothing and asked one of his friends to "get him back". This gun was dumped in a toilet bowl and later recovered by police. However, the gun used by Phuoc Giau Nguyen was never recovered.

An arrest was made almost two months later, on March 20, but the accused man declined to be interviewed and then did not give evidence at his trial. The 24-year-old Phuoc Giau Nguyen, who had migrated to Australia with his mother and four siblings after completing his primary schooling in Vietnam, was sentenced to 12 years' jail for the wounding shooting of Tran and 20 years for killing Khahn Thanh Nguyen, with a non-parole period of 14 and a half years. The aggregate sentence imposed by Mr Justice Hidden was 22 years, with a non-parole period of 16 and a half years. Phuoc Giau Nguyen will be eligible for parole in 2018.

DEATH OF AN ANGEL

A father slams his 10-week-old daughter against a wall following a domestic row in suburban Melbourne.

Brent David Quarry, 32, lived with partner Sonia Elizabeth Tate and their 10-week-old daughter Sharni Montaana Quarry in a ground-floor flat in the southern Melbourne suburb of Moorabbin. At around 3pm on August 7, 2002, Quarry started drinking port from a two-litre cask and, at the same time, was taking anti-depression pills. By 10pm he had started quarrelling with Tate and, after striking her in the face hard enough to make her nose bleed, she ran upstairs to a neighbour's flat. Quarry followed her but neighbour Laura Lidker told him Tate would return in half an hour. Quarry went back downstairs but returned to the Lidker flat when Tate did not turn up after half an hour. This time he had a knife in one pocket and a claw hammer in another. He also had baby Sharni and, after striking Tate again, went back to his own flat and started smashing furniture.

Police and an ambulance were called and, while Tate was taken to hospital, a police dog squad arrived. This was about 11.10pm and police could hear Sharni crying. They therefore knocked on Quarry's front door, but he told them he had a gun and would kill anyone who tried to get into his flat. Police, worried about the safety of little Sharni, repeatedly asked Quarry to leave the baby at the door. However, they then heard a loud bang against the front wooden door, followed by other loud thumps. Tragically, Quarry then told them: "That was the baby and I hit it against the wall. It's gone; its head's stuffed; it's too late."

Quarry at that stage was cradling the baby with one hand, with a knife in the other. The baby, dressed in a jumpsuit, appeared to be motionless as Quarry told police: "She's going to go with me. She's my little angel and I'm going to take her to heaven. I won't let that bitch get her. I'll take her with me." Police tried to talk Quarry into handing over the baby and giving himself up, but he replied: "I'm going to be carried out of here in a body bag. A big one and you're going to need a little one for her … she's fucked. She's almost there, almost gone. She's breathing only every few minutes." Quarry eventually let go of the baby, with little Sharni falling about a metre to the floor. He picked her up and said: "She's fucked."

Discussions between Quarry and the police continued until 2.30 in the morning when members of the Special Operations Group entered the flat. Quarry was sitting on a chair in the kitchen with the baby in his arms. Quarry slashed a police officer across the face before being restrained. He then said he had killed his daughter by throwing her against the wall four or five times. An autopsy revealed the baby had died of extensive head injuries, with five fractures of the skull. Dr David Ranson said that by the time Quarry had dropped Sharni to the floor, the baby "already was suffering from a very significant head injury which in all probability was a fatal injury which was proceeding inevitably to death".

In a record if interview, Quarry said he was angry with Tate for leaving him and at the police being called. He said he had been drinking port and taking pills and, when asked why he did not hand the baby over to police, he said he was frightened they would take the baby away. He also described Sharni as a "beautiful baby" and "the best thing that ever happened to me." Quarry, who pleaded guilty to the murder of his baby daughter, was sentenced to life imprisonment, with a none-parole period of 24 years.

THE SCALES OF JUSTICE

A Melbourne man is murdered over the disappearance of electronic scales used for weighing cannabis.

Matthew Charles Rendle had a set of small electronic scales, which he kept at his unit in the Melbourne suburb of

Ashwood. On July 25, 2002, he and four others – Craig Bohn, Andrew Johnson, Wayne Jewell and Adrian Kilner – smoked cannabis. Rendle used the scales to weigh the cannabis, but realised the next day that his scales were missing. In fact, he was so angry over the disappearance of the scales that he told another friend that there was only one way to deal with whoever had taken them. He then showed his friend a set of knife blades and, selecting the largest of them, said: "This is going to do the job. This is the only thing that is going to fix it."

Rendle, 38 years of age, then started making phone calls in an effort to find out who had taken the scales and finally convinced himself that Wayne Jewell had them. He therefore went to Jewell's house where the door was answered by Jewell's mother. She said her son was not home and Rendle then produced the knife and told her "I don't carry this for nothing". Mrs Jewell called the police but, in the meantime, Andrew Johnson told Rendle that it was Craig Bohn who had stolen the scales, along with Rendle's anti-epilepsy medication.

Rendle went to Bohn's unit in Ashwood and waited for him to return home. He then confronted Bohn and slashed his friend across the face. Bohn admitted he had taken the scales, but no longer had them. Rendle reacted viciously and killed Bohn with three stab wounds to the abdomen. There also were stab wounds to the leg and a post-mortem revealed that one of the stabs to Bohn's abdomen had perforated the bowel.

At his trial, Rendle pleaded guilty and Justice Kellam told him: "That a person should lose his life over such a relatively insignificant matter is disturbing indeed. It is apparent that for many hours prior to your attack upon the deceased man you had ruminated over the theft of the scales ... Clearly you were prepared to use the knife if necessary. The incident which led to the death of the deceased cannot in such circumstances be said to be a spontaneous eruption of emotion. You had an opportunity to consider the possible consequence of your actions, but you continued with your chosen course of conduct to obtain recovery of the scales, if necessary by the use of violence." The judge sentenced Rendle to 14 years' jail, with a minimum term of 11 years.

THE JEALOUS HUSBAND

A jealous husband repeatedly stabs his wife in a frenzied attack after she had made a false confession of infidelity.

Vasily and Tina Karageorges, from the northern Melbourne suburb of Diamond Creek, had been happily married for 29 years and, to all intents and purposes, were a devoted couple. However, Vasily Karageorges, 53, was prone to fits of jealousy and, on March 8, 2003, accused his wife of being unfaithful after finding bruises on her legs. Tina, 47, eventually felt overwhelmed by his obsession and made a false confession to affairs. Her husband, in a red mist of rage, went berserk. He stabbed his wife 27 times and, after killing her blacked out and, when he woke, found his wife on the ground with a knife in her stomach; he then dialled 000.

After a jury had found Karageorges guilty, Victorian Supreme Court Justice Stephen Kaye sentenced him to 18 years' jail, with a minimum parole term of 14 years. He told Karageorges: "You stabbed to death your faithful wife of almost 30 years, and you did so with repeated brutal and merciless blows from a sharp knife. The violence which you inflicted on the woman you loved so much was of considerable magnitude. Whatever your feelings of anger, indeed, rage, they provided no excuse or justification for you inflicting violence on her, let alone repeatedly stabbing her as she desperately fought to protect herself." The judge said there was "unanimous and overwhelming" evidence that Karageorges' wife had been a "loving, faithful and devoted wife and mother".

THE VIOLENT HUSBAND

Battered wife Thao Thi Tran escapes a custodial sentence despite being found guilty of the manslaughter of her violent husband.

Mother of three Thao Thi Tran endured beatings by her husband Chung Manh Tran, but boiled over with rage after his final attack, on November 4, 2003 — Melbourne Cup day. Mr Chung's attack was so violent that neighbours had to restrain him. However, what upset Tran most was that her husband had smashed a sacred Buddhist shrine she kept in memory of her late mother. Tran rang her husband, who was at a neighbour's home, and asked him to return. She then stabbed him five times, including one wound to the heart.

Tran insisted she had acted in self defence and, in April, 2005, a Victorian Supreme Court jury acquitted her of murder although it convicted her of manslaughter. However, Justice Stephen Kaye imposed a suspended three-year sentence, which meant Tran walked free. Justice Kaye said Tran had been the subject of a "brutal and cruel beating" and told her: "By its verdict, the jury accepted that an ordinary person might, in the same circumstances, have reacted in the same manner in which you did." He said he had taken into account several mitigating circumstances, especially the care of Tran's three children, aged nine, seven and six. Justice Kaye said: "It would be an affront to common sense and human decency for a sentencing judge to ignore such a factor."

THE WHEELIE BIN MURDER

Belgian national Youssef Tecle Imnetu is found guilty of killing Shoukat Ali Mohamed and dumping the body in a wheelie bin outside an apartment in Sydney.

Belgian Youssef Tecle Imentu found himself involved in murder when he helped flatmate Basheeruddin Mohamed, known as "Ben" eradicate a $20,000 debt. "Ben" allegedly owed Mohamed $20,000 he had borrowed for a bridging visa. But, in the inner Sydney suburb of Redfern on June 29, 2003, the pair force-fed Mohamed heroin and hit him over the head with a baseball bat before strangling him. They then dumped his body in a wheelie bin and left itself outside an apartment block. Closed circuit television showed "Ben" and Imnetu return from a sports store with a sleeping bag and a baseball bat on the day of the murder. On the same footage, the couple is shown several hours later pushing a wheelie bin, with Mohamed's feet protruding from it. They pushed the bin through the apartment block and into the street.

Although Supreme Court Acting Justice Peter Newman said he accepted that "Ben" had been the ringleader in the crime said: "What is not clear from the evidence is who it was who administered the heroin to the deceased, struck him with a baseball bat and who it was that strangled him. However, I have no doubt that they were committed by the prisoner and 'Ben' acting in concert." He sentenced Imentu to jail for a minimum of 20 years and a maximum of 26 years. "Ben" had been deported for being in breach of his student visa before his involvement in the murder was known and his whereabouts were unknown when this edition went to press.

THE WIFE-SLASHER

Estranged husband Joseph Vella tricks his way into the family home and bludgeons his wife Ruth before slashing her throat.

On December 29, 2003, former insurance manager Joseph Vella waited outside the family home in the Perth suburb of Kallaroo. Then, when Mrs Vella's boyfriend Alan Susta left the house, he gained admission on the pretext of talking to his wife about possible custody arrangements for the couple's four sons. However, Vella then hit his wife four times over the head with a baseball bat and then slashed her throat from ear to ear with a hunting knife. He had bought the bat and the knife from a sports store just a few days before the murderous attack, which was witnessed by the Vellas' six-year-old son.

The West Australian Supreme Court had been told that Mrs Vella had taken out a restraining order against her husband following a previous attack in which she was left with broken ribs and a punctured lung. In sentencing Vella to life imprisonment, Judge Ralph Simmonds said the murder was one of the worst he had come across and added that the fact that the six-year-old son had witnessed the crime was a serious aggravating factor. However, Vella insisted that he did not know his son was watching the attack on the boy's mother. Detective Senior Constable Brian Hill said outside the court after the sentencing of Vella: "I have only done a number of these (murder cases) and it certainly is the most horrific of the ones I have witnessed".

THE 'VICIOUS CRIMINAL'

A judge describes a killer as a "cold, callous, vicious criminal" after a Sydney chemist is shot to death.

Mild-mannered pharmacist Emad Youssef, 38, was shot dead outside his shop in the Sydney suburb of Canley Vale on August 1, 2003, and robbed of his day's takings. Police later arrested a 33-year-old man and his 14-year-old nephew. The man, who could not be named at the trial for the murder of Youssef for reasons relating to the identity of his nephew, was referred to as "Dudley Hill". The killing of Youssef, shot through the chest, was part of a three-month crime spree by "Hill" who was already serving a 40-year sentence for a gang-rape when found guilty of murder. The spree included another gang-rape and numerous armed robberies.

Youssef's widow, in a victim impact statement submitted to the Supreme Court of New South Wales, said: "I am constantly depressed and have been taking medication. My life has been destroyed by Emad's pointless death." "Hill", who had been in trouble with the law from the time he was ten years of age, told the court that when he was released from jail in 2002 he had tried to "go straight", but went back to a drugs habit when his girlfriend accused him of an assault and had been using the drugs ice and heroin during his crime spree. He also claimed he did now know whether he or Youusef had pulled the gun's trigger as "once he (Youssef) saw the gun he grabbed it". He added: "We were just struggling when the gun went off."

Sentencing "Hill" to life imprisonment, Justice James Wood said the killer "presents a very serious ongoing danger to the community" before adding: "His psychological profile shows very little hope of him being rehabilitated." The judge said that although the murder on his own would have have deserved a life sentence, the overall "criminality" of Hill's crime spree, including gang rape and armed robberies, meant the community needed to be protected.

DEATH OF AN ANTIQUES COLLECTOR

A wealthy antiques collector is bashed to death with a figurine in his Melbourne apartment.

Alan Barker was a retired businessman who lived alone in his apartment in the inner Melbourne suburb of South Yarra. A keen antiques collector, he had run a precision instruments business and had even introduced speed cameras and radar guns to Australia. As a widower, he employed a housekeeper and, on March 7, 2003, when Mary Scott went about her daily duties, Barker told her he had had a surprise telephone call from his 66-year-old cousin, Bernard Saw. Ms Scott left Barker at about midday and when she called him that night there was no reply. She then went to the apartment the next morning, at around 11.30, and found the security door to the apartment ajar. Inside, she discovered Barker's body, just inside the door. He had been smashed over the head with a French figurine which usually was on a table just inside the doorway. There was blood everywhere and it was obvious there had been a theft.

An autopsy revealed that Barker had 28 injuries to the head and neck, with multiple fractures to the head and face. He had been hit to the back, front and left side of the head, with other injuries to both arms. Security footage showed Barker's cousin Saw, carrying a suitcase, walking towards the apartment at 2.30pm and leaving five hours later. Also, Saw's DNA was found on a door handle near the lift, on the lift button and on a wall inside Barker's apartment. After killing his cousin, Saw spent several hours collecting antiques and a Pro Hart painting. When police arrested him on March 10, 2003, his suitcase was packed with many of his cousin's antiques, with a collective value of $21,000.

Justice Redlich told Saw: "I am satisfied that at the time you killed Mr Barker you were showing little insight or judgment as to your conduct. You were not reasoning in a sound manner. You went to Mr Barker's apartment with the intention to steal. That is not in dispute. Usually a thief or rover who wishes to avoid detection will seek to conceal his identity from the victim and anyone else who might place them at the crime scene. You had made an appointment to see Mr Barker and informed the building supervisor of your intention to visit the deceased." The judge added that he accepted Saw did not visit Barker with the intention of killing him. It was, the court was told, "a crazy scheme to get money". Saw, who pleaded guilty was sentenced to fourteen and a half years' jail, with a fixed ten and a half years period.

THE SOCIETY MURDERS

In one of Melbourne's most notorious murder cases, a young man kills his mother and step-father and buries their bodies in the bush.

Although Melbourne newspapers, particularly the *Herald Sun*, tagged the slaying of Margaret Wales-King and husband Paul King 'The Society Murders', it was a misleading label and, in fact, had nothing to do with cocktail parties, opening nights or even champagne. Rather, it earned this slightly misleading tag because Mrs Wales-King was a wealthy woman who was worth more than $5 million and drove a Mercedes Benz. Also, the slain couple lived in the expensive and leafy eastern Melbourne suburb of Armadale.

Yet Mrs Wales-King and her second husband led quiet, exemplary lives. Indeed, Paul King had had two strokes and their daily lives were far from boisterous or glamorous. Family events took precedence as they settled into their golden years. It was at one of these family gatherings that they were killed by Mrs Wales-King's youngest son, Matthew. To all intents and purposes, it was just a normal family dinner, with Matthew and his wife Maritza as hosts at their townhouse in Glen Iris.

The evening meal was a simple affair — a first course of vegetable soup and a main course of risotto. However, there was a special ingredient, provided by Matthew Wales. He had crushed powerful painkiller and blood pressure tablets to make his guests feel drowsy.

Then, as they left the townhouse, he bludgeoned his mother and stepfather to death with a piece of pine. It was alleged at his trial that Wales first hit his mother over the back of the head and then struck his stepfather. Supreme Court Justice Coldrey told Wales: 'You followed them out the front door. Paul King was walking in front of your mother. You switched off the veranda downlight, picked up a length of wood and, wielding it with both hands, you struck your mother on the back of the neck. She was immediately rendered unconscious and fell forward onto the paved concrete surface. You then struck Paul King on the back of the neck because you knew it would be quick. Your purpose was to break their necks and your intention was to kill each of them.'

The motive? Dissatisfaction over what Wales perceived to be her dominance in financial matters and the proposed sale of a Surfers Paradise unit. Mrs Wales-King, who owned her Armadale home, the Mercedes Benz, antiques and jewellery, and also had substantial superannuation and shareholdings, also had made a will — with her five children (Sally, Damian, Emma, Prudence and Matthew) and husband Paul getting one-sixth each on her death. Paul King was the elegant Margaret Wales-King's second husband.

Born in 1933, Margaret Lord, had married airline pilot Brian Wales and bore him five children before moving in with

King. Matthew Wales, born in 1968, and his mother long had had rows over financial matters and it all came to a head in the lead-up to that fatal dinner on April 4.

However, it all went pear-shaped for Wales as soon as he wielded that one-metre length of pine. He might have planned the killings, but his movements from there were clumsy at best. Although the Chile-born Maritza Wales had no involvement whatsoever in the deaths of her in-laws, she saw her husband drag the bodies across the front lawn and cover them with their two-year-old son Dominik's deflated plastic pool.

That seemed to be the extent of Wales' planning and the disposal of the bodies was both ad hoc and poorly enacted, starting with the disposal of his mother's Mercedes. Wales drove the car to the seaside suburb of Middle Park, locked it and then caught a taxi. To help cover his tracks, he dropped the car keys down a drain. But what to do with the bodies? First, he used sheets to cover his victims' faces, so he could not see their seemingly accusing expressions, placed the pool cover back over the bodies and generally made everything look like a pile of rubbish ready for removal.

On the Friday after the killings, Wales put his body disposal plan into action, starting with the rental of a motor trailer. He hitched the trailer to the back of his own vehicle and drove home. There, he wrapped each of the bodies in a doona and then bought a mattock and ordered mulch for his garden. The following morning he loaded the doona-wrapped bodies into the trailer and headed through Melbourne's outer eastern suburbs towards the picturesque mountain resort of Marysville. Wales drove on to a track more than 20 kilometres past Marysville and started his gruesome task of burying the bodies. He dug a grave no more than a metre deep about 20 metres away from the track, and placed his mother's body face down and his step-father's body on top. Wales then drove back to Melbourne, more hopeful than convinced the secret grave would never be discovered.

Wales, in fact, was so concerned that he returned to the grave the following Monday and not only bought and then placed rocks on the site, but added soil and the newly-delivered mulch. It was a desperate but futile attempt to prevent the grave being detected. Then, on the way back home, he pulled into a car wash and thoroughly cleaned the trailer before returning it to the hire company. Meanwhile, other family members had tried to contact Mrs Wales-King and were becoming increasingly concerned. Wales' sister Emma on April 8 reported to police that Mrs Wales-King and her husband were missing.

The disappearance of the wealthy couple made the television news and, within the hour, Mrs Wales-King's missing Mercedes was found where Matthew Wales had left it. The mystery deepened, but police already were suspicious of Wales, especially after they noticed a distinct odour of cleaning fluid at his Glen Iris home. Also, they found traces of blood on the garage floor. The bodies finally were discovered on April 29, almost four weeks after the killings. Bush rangers had noticed that a vehicle had been driven in a protected area and that there was a mysterious mound — the hastily-dug grave.

Police that night recovered the bodies and an autopsy revealed that both the dead had been asphyxiated and that Mrs Wales-King had suffered facial injuries. Police recovered the trailer used in the disposal of the bodies, but no charges were laid by May 8 when Wales wept at a private funeral service in Toorak, at the church where his mother had worshipped.

The public memorial service was held the following day and Wales offered prayers on behalf of the mourners. Finally, on Sunday, May 11, Wales was arrested and taken for interview by the Homicide Squad in St Kilda Road. Wales soon after confessed to the killings and was charged with murder. Wife Maritza, meanwhile, was charged with attempting to pervert the course of justice by making a false statement. Wales was sentenced to 30 years' jail, with a minimum of 24 years. Wife Maritza was handed a two-year, wholly-suspended sentence.

DEATH OF A TEENAGER

A man shoots his de facto wife's son dead at Wodonga, Victoria, after suspecting him of having drugs.

Shaun Francis Finnigan, 17, lived with his mother Gillian and her de facto husband Boriss Vjestica in the northern Victorian town of Wodonga. However, the teenager apparently was in fear of Vjestica, especially after rejecting a bricklaying job arranged for him in Melbourne.

On the morning of October 15, 2003, Finnigan and some of his friends were working on a motor vehicle in the driveway of the family home when Vjestica pulled up in his car.

Finnigan and Vjestica walked towards each other and, after words had been exchanged, Finnigan was shot in the chest with a crude pistol made from a sawn-off .22 rifle. Vjestica had pulled the gun from the waist band of his trousers after Finnigan apparently had called him "a big man".

However, Vjestica said at his trial that he had gone into Finnigan's room that morning "to see if there was something there that shouldn't be". He was referring to drugs and said he had found some foil with powder in it and a gun. Vjestica also claimed he decided to confront Finnigan about the gun, put it in his waist-band and, during the confrontation, the gun discharged accidentally. Vjestica drove away without waiting to see how seriously Finnigan had been wounded.

Although the boy did not immediately fall to ground, he later died of the gunshot wound. However, a jury found Vjestica guilty of murder and Justice Bongiorno in the Supreme Court of Victoria told him: "It (the jury) found that the discharge of the gun was a deliberate act on your part with the intention of either killing Shaun Finnigan or at least inflicting really serious injury upon him." He sentenced Vjestica to 21 years' jail, with a minimum of 17 years before being eligible for parole.

THE UMBRELLA KILLING

A man meets up with a prostitute, takes her back to his home and kills her with blows to the head from the shaft of a rolled-up umbrella.

Bricklayer Novica Jakimov left his rented house in the western Melbourne suburb of Westmeadows on the night of August 18, 2003, and met up with sex worker Kelly Hodge, either in St Kilda or at the Crown casino. The slightly-built Hodge went back to Jakimov's house and, some time early next morning, was viciously attacked. She was hit many times over the head with the shaft of a rolled-up umbrella and suffered a fractured skull. Hodge also suffered a serious wound to the vagina and the bleeding from this wound, combined with the fractured skull caused her death.

Although Jakimov later declared that Hodge initially had attacked him, he tied her hands together with her bra, wrapped her body in a sheet and blanket and drove to Beveridge, where he dumped the body. A jury at Jakimov's trial also was told that he cleaned his home, burned or disposed of Hodge's clothing – but made one big mistake. He failed to dispose of Hodge's mobile telephone and police used it to track him down.

Although Jakimov had no previous convictions for violence, Justice Teague said: "I have noted that some matters of which you spoke to the police suggest a capacity on occasions for anger and violence." However, the judge said he was prepared to accept "some degree of remorse" and sentenced Jakimov to 19 years' jail, with a fixed non-parole period of 14 years.

'I JUST SNAPPED'

A Melbourne man with a history of drug abuse "snaps" and stabs a woman with whom he has had a sexual relationship.

Marc Andrew Rookledge, 39, had had a sexual relationship with Rosehanie Marilyn Holmes for several years before he contacted her on August 19, 2003, and later visited her at her flat in the bayside Melbourne suburb of Hampton East. Rookledge and Holmes bought liquor together, while Holmes bought a carton of cigarettes. Some time during the night, Rookledge suggested he swap the cigarettes for amphetamines. Then, when he returned from the nearby suburb of St Kilda, they both used the drugs intravenously and watched television before Holmes went to bed.

Rookledge went to lie beside her and in his own word, "snapped" while thinking about his life. He hit Holmes over the head with a heavy object and then stabbed her repeatedly, inflicting 17 wounds. In an attempt to cover his crime, Rookledge ransacked the flat to make it look as if there had been a burglary and stole credit cards. Holmes' body was not discovered for six days but police almost immediately wanted to talk to Rookledge and arranged to meet him.

At the Homicide Squad office, Rookledge said: "You don't have to look any further. I'm the one you're looking for ... I just snapped." Rookledge pleaded guilty to Holmes' murder and Justice Smith told him: "The offence was extremely serious and specific and general deterrence must be reflected in the sentence to be imposed. I am satisfied, however, that his long standing abuse of drugs was a factor in the commission of the offence and to a limited extent reduces the level of moral culpability." He sentenced Rookledge to 17 years' imprisonment, with a non-parole period of 12 years.

THE AGGRESSIVE NEIGHBOUR

A 70-year-old man said to be an "aggressively friendly" neighbour repeatedly stabs a woman who lived across the street from him in Melbourne.

Peter John Howard was a 70-year-old recluse who lived in the eastern Melbourne suburb of Boronia. Described as an "aggressively friendly" neighbour, he sometimes was in dispute with those who lived near him. For example, he had told Olive Martha Maas, who lived opposite him that he did not like cars parked outside his house and she, in turn, told friends to comply with this wish.

Some time in the middle of 2001, a house in the street was vandalised and another neighbour asked Ms Maas if she would keep an eye on it. Howard therefore seemed to take a close interest whenever Ms Maas and the property owner, who also was Howard's landlady, met in the street. Then, in the early hours of June 12, 2002, Howard put a murderous plan into operation.

He prepared a long carving knife as a murder weapon by wrapping the handle in the sleeve of a rubber glove and securing this with a black tape. He then broke into Ms Maas' home through a laundry window and confronted his victim, dressed in her nightgown. Screams were heard from the Maas house some time just after 5am and there was considerable banging and shouting for 30 seconds, then silence. Ms Maas' body was not discovered for a week, but she had been the subject of a vicious attack and a knife was protruding from her left side. She had been stabbed up to 57 times, with one wound penetrating the right eye and entering her skull. Ms Maas, 59 years of age, also had cut wounds on her hands, indicating she had fought her attacker.

Howard, who had a criminal record for armed robbery and kidnapping, was arrested, charged with murder and was found guilty. Justice Williams, in the Supreme Court of Victoria, told him: "Your crime involved planning and preparation. You made an apparently unprovoked brutal attack on a woman living alone, in what should have been the safety of her own home, in the early hours of the morning." The Judge, in noting Howard did not appear to show any remorse, said that, despite the offender's age, the sentence had to reflect the need for community protection. He sentenced Howard to 20 years' jail, with a minimum term of 15 years.

KNIFED FOR NO REASON

A 17-year-old is stabbed to death on the south bank of the Yarra River in a vicious and unprovoked attack.

Hani Ghaleb Jaber was walking with two friends, Hassain Hussain and Alexandra Berry, on the south bank of Melbourne's Yarra River towards the Crown Casino on the night of September 24, 2003, when they were approached by another group. The initial contact between the two groups seemed amiable but, when Hussain was asked if he wanted to have a knife fight, Jaber suggested he and his friends continue their walk.

The three friends, to avoid further confrontation, walked across a footbridge, but were followed by the other three, Bollus Angelo Athuai, William Angok and Birag Kuat. Athuai approached Jaber and started wrestling him. Although much taller and stronger than Jaber, Athuai was unable to restrain the young man he had attacked and pulled out a knife.

Athaui stabbed the 17-year-old Jaber, who fell to the ground wounded. Athaui then lent over his victim and stabbed him three more times before leaving the scene. Incredibly, Athaui smiled as he turned to look at what he had done. Jaber had three wounds to the left side of his face and had two stab wounds to the upper part of his back, with one of these gashes piercing the aorta. Another stab wound had penetrated Jaber's heart.

Justice Kaye, at the 17-year-old Athuai's trial, told him: "Your attack on the deceased man was particularly cowardly.

You had a superior advantage in height and reach. Both you and Angok were larger and stronger than the deceased man. You used a weapon. Your victim was unarmed. You used that weapon with the maximum of surprise and ferocity, depriving your victim of an opportunity al all to defend himself. It is not surprising that the pathologist did not find one single defensive wound on the body of the deceased man. He did not get any opportunity to raise his hands in self-defence, let alone strike out at you …

" … Your brazen and totally unjustified attack on the deceased man and his two companions going about their lawful business was utterly unacceptable. Your use of a knife was a contravention of a basic standard and value of our society. You took the life of an innocent and decent young man. Your conduct violated the most fundamental norm of civilised behaviour."

Athuai was born in Sudan but he and his family were forced to flee because of civil war and arrived in Australia in 1997. The family originally lived in Queensland and moved to Melbourne in 2003. At the time of the stabbing, Athuai already was on bail on two charges of occasioning actual bodily harm and, a month later, was arrested again and charged with armed robbery, with an allegation that he had used a knife.

In sentencing Athuai to 22 years' imprisonment, with a minimum period of 17 years, Justice Kaye said: "The murder by you of Hani Jaber was committed in circumstances which were particularly callous. You demeanour during the killing, the defenceless nature of the victim, the savagery of the blows inflicted by you, and the entire lack of reason for you to attack him cause me to have some reservations in evaluating your prospects of rehabilitation."

THE SON WHO 'SNAPPED'

A middle-aged Melbourne man loses his temper after his mother chastises him for drinking and strangles her with a tie.

Robert Isles Hewitt, 53, looked after his 87-year-old mother Ivy Jean Hewitt at their home in the bayside Melbourne suburb of Hampton. Hewitt led a relatively lonely life but there was no doubt he was a loving and dutiful son – until one evening after he had been drinking at a football match.

On April 27, 2003, Hewitt walked down to the local shopping centre and bought himself some beer before going to watch his local football team, Sandringham. He watched the senior team play and, after drinking the contents of his six-pack, also consumed another 10 pots of beer. Then, when he returned home, his mother told him off for drinking so much and asked him why he made a fool of himself.

Hewitt went to his own room and "snapped". He grabbed a tie from a cupboard, went back into the kitchen where his mother was standing at a sink and tried to strangle her. Ivy Hewitt fell to the floor, her son then stomping on her upper body and neck. A post-mortem revealed that Mrs Hewitt suffered injuries to the neck, chest and head and that she died as a result of the force used in her son stomping on her.

Hewitt then rang a relative to tell her not to visit his mother the following day as she was ill. He then drove to a hotel and drank more beer before returning home at around

4am, with his mother dead on the kitchen floor. She remained there for a week, until Hewitt presented himself at the local police station and confessed to killing his mother. Hewitt pleaded guilty and Justice Kellam noted that there was "full, frank and open honesty" about the killing. The judge sentenced Hewitt to 13 years' jail, with a minimum of 10 years.

THE SPEAR-GUN MONSTER

Depressed husband John Sharpe, feeling he is trapped in a loveless marriage, kills his pregnant wife Anna Kemp with a shot from a spear-gun and, four days later, kills his 20-month-old daughter Gracie with a spear-gun shot to the head.

Melbourne television viewers were saddened in May, 2004, as a tearful John Myles Sharpe begged for his missing wife Anna and daughter Gracie to return home. Sharpe had claimed Anna had left him for another man and had taken Gracie with her. However, police had their doubts and kept a watch on the moody and socially-inept Sharpe, and eventually arrested him on June 22. During an 11-hour interview, he eventually confessed to two horrific killings. Sharpe, feeling that his wife was controlling his life, shot her dead with the spear-gun on March 23 and buried her body in a shallow grave at their Mornington home on Melbourne's outer south-east.

Then, five days later, he turned the spear-gun on little Gracie's head to help him maintain his story about the 41-year-old Anna leaving him for another man. The 38-year-old Sharpe then dug up his wife's body, dismembered it with a chainsaw and dumped it and Gracie's at a tip. The Victorian community was horrified and there were no tears for Sharpe when, after pleading guilty to two counts of murder, Justice Bernard Bongiorno sentenced him to life imprisonment, with a parole period of no less than 33 years.

The judge said the murders were barbaric and unspeakably horrific. He said: "Killing your wife was an act of desperation." Describing Gracie as "a defenceless child", Justice Bongiorno added: "Whatever your motive for killing Anna might have been, in Gracie's case it was simply so that your first crime would not be discovered." Sharpe will not be released until after he turns 70.

KILLED OVER A BREATH TEST

A police officer is killed after what at first was just another roadside traffic interception for a breath test.

Senior Constable Tony Clarke was on patrol near Launching Place along Victoria's Warburton Highway on the night of April 24, 2005, when he pulled over a car driven by 27-year-old Mark Bailey, a man with a history of mental illness. It seems Clarke wanted to test Bailey for alcohol consumption and there was a struggle. Bailey threw the breath-testing unit away and then somehow managed to get hold of the police officer's service revolver from its holster and fired a shot as Clarke tried to take cover.

Bailey then confronted Clarke and forced him to lie on the ground, where the policeman was shot execution-style to the back of the head. Bailey then rang his mother to tell her of what he had done, then drove off and shot himself dead. The killing of Senior Constable Clarke sparked outrage among the police community, especially as he had left behind a widow and a six-year-old son.

THE REVENGE KILLING

A man in Morwell, Victoria, fires a shotgun into the abdomen of a man he believed had bashed him two years earler.

In June, 2003, David Neil Pyke was bashed by two men outside the Gippsland town of Morwell and suffered a fractured skull and some brain damage, also losing the hearing in one ear. He believed one of his assailants was a man named Mark Logan.

Then, on May 22, 2005, Pyke drank heavily from a cask of wine and smoked marijuana before leaving his home at about 6pm armed with a shotgun and cartridges. He took a car, a Ford, belonging to a friend of his mother and drove to Logan's home. After knocking on the front door and inviting Logan outside, he fired a shot at the man he believed had attacked him two years earlier. Logan, shot in the left arm and chest, slumped to his lounge-room floor, where he was attended by his fiancé. Pyke left, got into the car, but then did a U-turn before returning to Logan's house. He then shot Logan a second time, this time at point-blank range in the abdomen, killing him.

Police caught up with Pyke several hours later and he fully co-operated in their investigation of Logan's death, even telling them he had intended to kill. Justice Teague, in the Supreme Court of Victoria, told Teague: "The sentence must recognise that your execution of Mark Logan was premeditated and cold-blooded. It was fuelled by the ingestion of alcohol and marijuana. There was planning in the preparation of the shotgun, and the stealing of the Ford. The shooting was inside a family home. The second shot was especially cold-blooded given that it was fired after you returned to the house and in the immediate presence of a loved one." Justice Teague sentenced Pyke to 27 years' jail, with a non-parole period of 22 years.

BIBLIOGRAPHY

Archibold, B., *The Bradley Case*, Horwitz, 1961

Bouda, Simon, *Crimes That Shocked Australia*, Bantam, 1991

Brennan, T.C., *The Gun Alley Tragedy*, 1922

Clegg, Eric, *Famous Australian Murders*, Akron, 1976

Ellis, John, *Diary of a Hangman*, True Crime Library, 1996

Encell, Vivien and Sharpe, Alan, *Murder*, Kingsclear Books, 1997

Fitzgerald, J.D., *Studies in Australian Crime*, Cornstalk, 1924

Green, Jonathon, *The Directory of Infamy*, Mills and Boon, 1980

Gurr, T., *Killers at Large*, Southdown Press

Gurr, T. and Cox, H., *Famous Australian Murders*, Shakespeare Head, 1957

Kelly, Vince, *The Charge Is Murder*, Rigby, 1965

Kelly, Vince, *The Shark Arm Case*, Angus and Robertson, 1975

Kidd, Paul B., *Never to Be Released*, Pan, 1993

Main, Jim, *Murder Australian Style*, Unicorn Books, 1990

Main, Jim, *Murder in the First Degree*, Margaret Gee, 1990

Main, Jim, *Australian Murders*, Bas Publishing, 2004

Mallon, Leon, *The Brown-Out Murders*, Outback Press, 1979

Opas, Phillip, *Defence Counsel*, Hill of Content

Pearl, Cyril, *Wild Men of Sydney*, W.H. Allen, 1958

Porter, Trevor J., *Executions in the Colony and State of Victoria*, The Wednesday Press, 1999

Porter, Trevor J., *Notable South Australian Crimes*, The Wednesday Press, 1999

Porter, Trevor J., *The Hempen Collar*, The Wednesday Press, 1992

Sharpe, Alan, *Crime and Punishment*, Kingsclear Books, 1997

Shears, Richard, *Highway to Nowhere*, Harper Collins, 1996

Sheppard, Julia, *Someone Else's Daughter*, Ironbark Press, 1991

Wilson, Colin, *The Giant Book of Serial Killers*, The Book Company, 1996

Wilson, Colin, *The Mammoth Book of True Crime*, Robinson, 1988

OTHER SOURCES

Advertiser, Adelaide

Age, Melbourne

Argus, Melbourne

Australasian, The

Australian, The

Courier, Brisbane

Daily Mirror, Sydney

Daily Telegraph, Sydney

Herald, Melbourne

Herald Sun, Melbourne

Hobart Town Gazette

Mercury, Hobart

News, Adelaide

Parade Magazine

Sun-News Pictorial, Melbourne

Sydney Morning Herald

Truth

West Australian

Various law reports, including those of the Supreme Court of Victoria, Supreme Court of New South Wales and the Supreme Court of Tasmania and the various courts of criminal appeal.

JIM MAIN is one of Australia's most respected journalists. He studied law at the University of Melbourne, but preferred to pursue a career as a writer. He worked on the Melbourne *Herald* before spending almost two years on Fleet Street with the *Daily Express*. On return to Australia he combined journalism with studies for his Bachelor of Arts degree (majoring in History) at La Trobe University. Chief football writer on *The Australian*  for more than a decade, he has covered Olympic and Commonwealth Games and his byline has appeared from London, Dublin, Tokyo, Los Angeles and even Panama City. The author of more than 50 books, he is a winner of the Sir William Walkley Award (Australian journalism's most prestigious award) and, while in London, a Lord Beaverbrook Award. Inducted into the Melbourne Cricket Club Media Hall of Fame in 2003, his interests are wide and varied.

OTHER BOOKS BY JIM MAIN INCLUDE:

Only the Dead (Fiction)
Murder Australian Style
Murder in the First Degree
Australian Murders
An Australian's Travel Guide to Europe
EJ – The Ted Whitten Story
Honour The Names
Fallen – The Ultimate Heroes (with David Allen)
Pants – The Darren Millane Story (with Eddie McGuire)
Whatever It Takes (with Jim Stynes)
The Encyclopedia of AFL Footballers (with Russell Holmesby)
This Football Century (with Russell Holmesby)
How To Play Cricket (with Greg Chappell)

More great books from Bas Publishing

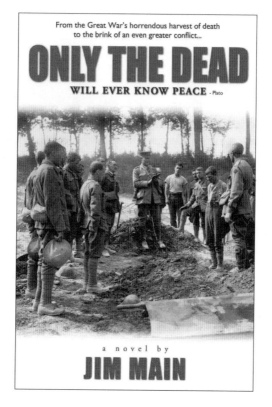

From the Great War's horrendous harvest of death
to the brink of an even greater conflict...

ONLY THE DEAD

WILL EVER KNOW PEACE - Plato

a novel by

JIM MAIN

Two Australian mates march off to war, fall in love with the same woman and make a pact. But only one survives and, many years later, in honouring the pact, becomes entangled in a deadly web of intrigue. Ted Paxman fights for his survival against forces – the British Union of Fascists and the Irish Republican Army – waging a frantic power struggle, and discovers only he can stop an event that would change the world forever. His desperate race against time takes him to England, the United States, Ireland and finally Scotland. Only The Dead is an action-packed, suspense-filled thriller spiced with romance. The ending is as surprising as it is moving. RRP $24.95

When Tom O'Toole was a poor kid in Tocumwal, a small NSW border town that was going backwards, he used to watch the Murray River fingering its way into the bigger towns. One day while wagging school, little Tommy and his mate sat by the river and suddenly Tom had that Irish knowing and in that instant he understood that one day he would be a successful businessman.

Tom, who left school without even learning the alphabet, is the founder of Australia's most successful bakery. It is bigger than the corporate breadshops, the franchises and the city bakeries, and he has done it in the little town of Beechworth, Victoria. Beechworth has a population of 3149, yet the Beechworth Bakery turnover is the equivalent of $1 from every person in the Sydney metropolitan area, every year. Can you believe it? How does he do it? This book will show you how.

It will also tell you about incredible determination and happiness, as well as sadness and madness. It is the power of positive thinking and beyond. RRP $21.95

Peppered with passion and inspiration, this is the latest edition of the Beechworth Bakery's immensely popular selection of 'secrets', featuring even more recipes and snippets of wisdom, and challenging life's recipes. RRP $24.95

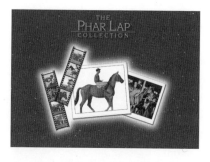

Phar Lap's hero status has endured for some 75 years and shows no sign of abating. Such was his grit that his spirit transcended racing. He was the foal from the backblocks of NZ who became champion of the world; the tall poppy who refused to be cut down; the winner who continually beat the odds.

Until now, despite how much has been written about Phar Lap, there has been one thing missing - photographs of his wins. This book remedies that situation with his story being complemented by pictures of his 37 victories which emphasise Phar Lap's power and the ease with which he won many of his races. RRP $49.95

Most encyclopedias are dry, humourless tomes. And so they should be, you may be saying. They're books from which one seeks knowledge … not the rantings of a comic writer attempting to get a few cheap laughs – no siree. An encyclopedia is to be revered as an important building block in creating our civilized world. Quite so.

But because food and the eating of it is one of the great pleasures of life … so too should the writing be relaxed, comfortable and entertaining, as well as educational. Of course one must gain knowledge from consulting such a book as this, but that shouldn't mean that it should be considered a sleeping draught either – agreed?

Then plunge into this book and enjoy! RRP $49.95